PEACE WITH THE DICTATORS?

PEACE WITH
THE DICTATORS?

by

NORMAN ANGELL

HARPER & BROTHERS PUBLISHERS
New York and London

CONTENTS

colonies—briefly since the facts are now fairly familiar—but
touches upon the misapprehension still so rife in Germany—and
England—as to the real differences between us on the Colonial
issue. He then goes on to examine whether in fact Germany and
Italy are asking the right to do what Britain has done in the
past; deals with the relationship of our Commonwealth of scattered democracies to the general method of Totalitarianism and
examines whether the cardinal principle of Totalitarianism—
that the nation must be self-sufficient both as to the materials of
welfare and the means of defence, is compatible with similar
rights for others, including the British Empire.

We must credit the Dictators with really believing their own
doctrines which so many of their apologists in Britain insist that
they do not. They will act on those beliefs. We cannot assume
that the Dictators' creeds are mere 'flourish,' for even if they
themselves did not believe them whole peoples are now being
'conditioned' by all the forces of suggestion contained in modern
instruments like a controlled universally read Press, a universally heard wireless, and universally seen cinema, to respond
violently to convictions which are never allowed to be questioned, and which are likely, therefore, to have a power of
fanaticism comparable to the fanaticism of religions like Islam
of the past engaged upon a Holy War.
This does not mean that the Dictators are monsters, or the
Germans, Italians and Japanese fundamentally different from
ourselves, or that we are fundamentally any better. Neither understanding, nor conciliation, nor permanent peace is possible if
we gloss over plain meanings, plainly declared beliefs and intentions. These manifestations are not merely capitalist manœuvres.
Behind the ponderable material claims lie deep psychic forces.
'Human nature' so often invoked by the 'practical man' includes
forces of wild fanaticism we ignore to our peril. The Russian
problem.

It is fashionable now to attribute the post-War unrest to the injustices of Versailles. But the Treaty of Versailles did not cause
the Great War, nor are the states—Japan and Italy—that have
been very potent elements of post-War disturbances victims of
that Treaty; they are among its beneficiaries. The root of our
trouble with the Totalitarians lies deeper, particularly in the fact
that if we satisfy their supreme grievance it will be at the cost of
creating a grievance just as severe elsewhere. They claim a form

of defence which in fact kills the defence of others; rights which
if granted would make it impossible for others to have similar
rights. This is not a specifically 'German' fault for we have in the
past committed it in equal degree. But if both sides persist in this
attempt to square the political circle, there will be war, whatever revisions and remedying of specific grievances be made.

It is clear that we have given up our historic Balance of Power
policy; chiefly because to maintain it would involve association
with the Soviets, though we were prepared in the past to ally
ourselves with the Czar or the Sultan. We are in consequence
prepared to grant to the Totalitarians—particularly to Germany
in Europe—a position of potential preponderance which we
fought the War to prevent. What is our substitute for the now
abandoned 'Balance'? Surrender of defence to the preponderance of just those Have-Not expansionist states whose policies,
ambitions, political creeds, constitute the gravest menace to the
'owner' of a quarter of the globe? There is a large and perhaps
growing school of thought in Britain which demands just that
thing because the alternative involves associations which are to
some more distasteful than a strategically dangerous situation for
the Empire.

'John Smith'—the plain man who by his vote will in the last resort settle the country's foreign policy speaks up. The simple
hard fact, he says, is that the John Smiths will not vote for going
to war for Czechoslovakia or any other place with a name so
hard to pronounce. Moreover, he thinks that the old Balance of
Power policy can be made to work in another way: by letting
the foreigners—particularly the Hun and the Bolshie—eat each
other up while we look on, the end being that all the combatants
will be so exhausted that Britain will easily be able to defend
herself and Empire. In any case the risks of such a policy will appear to Smith, with the memories of the Great War still with
him, less than the risks of once more mixing in the continental
mess. If law or its sanctions mean war then Smith will let law go
by the board.

The American member of the group shows that the American
John Smith has not only a more plausible but a genuinely

stronger case for Isolationism than his British counterpart. Yet it is not strong enough, because it ignores the Totalitarian technique of domination which can be applied to America as to others and which is not open war upon powerful democratic nations but their weakening by (a) fomenting internal divisions (as in, e.g., Austria, Czechoslovakia, Spain and to some degree in France); (b) exploiting their fear of Bolshevism and (c) their fear of war.

Terrorism based on these fears has been employed to prevent the democratic states from combining for mutual collective defence, the only method which would give them equality of power with the Totalitarian group and effective defence against it. Americans, like others, are unconscious of the degree to which their policy and moral standards are re-shaped in obedience to the threat of war. The ways in which the Totalitarian methods might and probably will be applied to the United States are indicated.

Looking back over the last six or seven years it is quite clear that the process of foreigners eating each other up does not lessen but increases the danger to us. The steady advance against British interests and security alike of Japan in the Far East, Italy in the Mediterranean and Germany on our Rhine frontier, are cases in point. Isolationism is a myth, a sham. Unless we are prepared to accept the Pacifist position at least in so far as occupying the position of a Norway or a Denmark, isolation is almost a contradiction in terms. For if we renounce international combinations while the other fellow adopts them, we cannot possibly keep our end up defensively. In fact we are taking sides—against the law—and by our failure to take risks for a European law or code or constitution are accelerating the coming of the European civil war, the class war, not, however, quite according to Marx.

The absence of any principle of order, rule of the road, code on the highway, must mean 'disorder,' collision. Of old, the collisions, like those between ox-carts, were relatively innocuous. But in modern conditions, on the motor-car road, for instance, collisions are infinitely more destructive. If we assume this to be broadly true, we must get a code or mutually destroy ourselves. But the Totalitarians proclaim a religious hatred of, and a holy war against any international code. What then must we do? If, for purposes of 'conciliation,' we cede bit by bit any possibility of law, we render Britain and the Empire impossible of defence. If

we are not ready to take any risk at all to sustain the law and the
Totalitarians are prepared to take very great risks to destroy it,
then plainly the law perishes, or can never be born.

some element of Pacifism has entered even—indeed particularly
—into Conservative foreign policy; and that the complete Pacifist faith animates very large numbers of our youth and our
intellectuals, and may therefore play a very important part in
the future use of our immense power, its assumptions are worth
examination.

PART III: CONCLUSIONS AND PROPOSALS

INTRODUCTION

A word or two as to the method and procedure of the Symposium which constitutes Part I of this book.

The Group includes an educated and intelligent German putting the case for his country; a similarly educated and travelled Italian putting the case for his. An Englishman in reply voices what he feels would be the 'collective view' of the other Englishmen of the circle, who thereupon supplement that reply or make qualifications, or put somewhat different views; an American indicates the way in which his country is concerned in the problem under discussion.

The discussion is directed to the specific purpose of finding whether the democracies can maintain peace with the dictatorship group without accepting a position of such inferiority of power as to render them incapable of defence, incapable of resisting Totalitarian claims if these should finally grow into demands completely inacceptable.

Each speaker is given the floor for an evening; sometimes reading a paper, sometimes speaking from notes; sometimes reading a group of separate notes, which, though not necessarily making a closely linked paper, are none the less related to the subject in hand.

The Symposium is confined to Part I.

Part II of the book is devoted to an examination of the Pacifist position; Part III to brief summaries of certain points and a final general summary and conclusion. The method involves some unavoidable repetition of points; which may not be altogether a disadvantage.

The raw material of much of these discussions has appeared in somewhat different form in *Time and Tide,* the *Daily Telegraph and Morning Post,* and the *Manchester Guardian.* I am indebted to the Editors of these papers for permission to reproduce the material in question.

PART I: A SYMPOSIUM

I

THE GERMAN SPEAKS

This statement shows that the Nazi phenomenon is not that of a 'cruel oppressor' holding down resentful subjects (the picture we commonly form of past despotisms), but of great masses of a people ardently embracing a political faith and national way of life. This exponent of the Nazi creed tries to show that Germany's ambitions are, at least in part, inspired by very much the same ideals that have gone into the building up of the British Empire; that Germany is trying to do to-day what Britain has so successfully done in the past; is applying economic and political beliefs to which many Englishmen still hold as good for Britain. He ends by declaring that Englishmen have no real fighting faith in the alternative creeds of internationalism and constitutionalism, and that if only for that reason Germany cannot trust to those creeds, build her future destiny upon them, or accept them as a substitute for her own defensive might. 'One half of your country would refuse to fight for the League, the other half for the Empire.' Britain has no faith she will fight for. She has not made up her mind whether Bolshevism or Germanism is the greater danger.

The German who entered our Circle was particularly suitable for the purpose which we hoped his entrance would achieve: to help us understand not only 'What Germany wants' but how much she wants it; what risks, that is, she is prepared to take to get it; what alternatives, if any might satisfy her and bring about appeasement.

Here was a German, educated, knowing the criticisms which had been levelled against the German régime, yet supporting it and, possessing, we had been told, an almost

3

psychic understanding of the Führer's mind and personality and feeling.

The conversation had run discursively at first on the background of the crisis of the moment, the background of Nazism, Italo-German relations, the Rome-Berlin Axis, Japan's advance in China, the Russian purges, Sanctions, Abyssinia, Anglo-American relations, the Cagoulard troubles in France, the Strikes there, Spain, non-intervention, 'piracy,' Blum, Chautemps, the collapse of the Franc, the Halifax visit, the Eden resignation. . . .

But our informal Chairman had warned the German that to-day we wanted to hear him reply to definite and special questions.

'Can we have friendship, appeasement, understanding, co-operation with Germany? Can you tell us what you really want? At what price? Can we, in a word, have peace?'

The German spoke quietly at first, but plainly with deep feeling, rising at times to passion. And broadly to this effect:

Of course you can have friendship, on terms, and there can be peace between us. It is what we have been begging for all along. And the price of peace with us ought to be clear enough to you English, a people so much of our race and blood that every homely word you use—flesh and blood, father and mother, son and daughter, man and God, and a thousand others—are German words; you, whose Royal line, whose Reformation, whose organised social services, whose physical science, educational methods, come so largely from us. What we want should to you be manifest in what we are.

What we want is first of all, of course, what every living thing wants—the conditions of self-preservation, the means which will enable us to live and grow, to expand. We want our fair share of the earth's resources; a secure physical basis of existence. You and your allies have proved to us by your behaviour during this last twenty-five years that we shall never be assured of even this mere physical basis of life, unless we are able to take it and guard it by our own strength. That strength we mean to have; and are getting.

But there is something more. We see much of the world around us in utter chaos, the victim plainly of some process or principle of degeneration, disintegration. We must either dominate that chaos and disintegration, or share it, become one of its victims. We do not intend to share it; or become one of its victims. We intend to dominate it. As between control or chaos, we choose control: it was the Roman choice, as it is now ours.

We are pushed to that role also by deep instinct, an impulse to satisfy spiritual needs as real and definite as the physical need for bread, as a woman's desire for children. We believe—and the Führer has never hidden that belief—that the German race has certain moral values, absolute virtues, peculiar to itself, inherent in its blood.[1] It is a race which by virtue of those very qualities of the blood feels an irrepressible urge, a moral hunger, to lead, to rule, to civilise. It has never yet enjoyed its right to fulfil that destiny, to take its due part in the world's government. It has not yet played its role. What we ask is power and freedom to fill that role. We now ask it with the

---

[1] Professor F. G. Parsons writes to the *Daily Telegraph*:

'As an anthropologist, I cannot agree that we share much Nordic blood with Germans. . . .

'Wherever the Nordics have conquered the great Central European Alpine race the existence of the former, in the course of centuries, has been largely bred out.

'This is because the Nordic stock is not able to compete with the physically better-equipped Alpine race in its own surroundings; for the Nordic is an expensive animal to rear, and requires more fresh air, nourishing food and freedom than the Alpine, if it is to breed at the same rate. Hence the Germany that once was a country of long-headed Nordic conquerors nas been slowly changed into one of short-headed Alpine people. . . .

'The head contains the brain, and a differently-shaped brain leads to differences in mentality and outlook on life.

'When, some twenty years ago, there were many German prisoners of war in England, Professor Le Gros Clark, of Oxford, and I were able to examine them carefully. We found that, even in Schleswig Holstein, their heads were broader and shorter than the English average.

'The English, fortunately or unfortunately have received comparatively little Alpine blood in their present country, and my contention is that we cannot claim the modern Germans as kinsmen, in spite of their belief that they are true Nordics. Nor can I think that, with brains so different, we are likely to have the same mental outlook on things or the same moral or sentimental standards.

'It is well to face facts without rancour and to realise, for instance, that what to one people may seem only a "scrap of paper" may to another be a binding contract; and we cannot make due allowance for different outlooks and interpretations if we believe that we are dealing with a people closely related to ourselves by blood, whose brains are like ours.'

sure knowledge that we shall get it; that you are powerless to prevent us, and we hope sincerely that you will not try.

What that means you can understand by looking back at your own history.

Suppose that in the time of Queen Elizabeth, or a little later, you had been asked, in the name of law and peace to regard as permanent, fixed, unalterable, the world as it then was; to recognise as fixed for all time the position occupied by Spain, Portugal, France and Holland. You were at that time not even an Island Power, for you had not yet accomplished the unification of the States within the British Isles. As compared with Spain and France and Holland, and even Portugal, you simply did not count as an Empire. Spain and Portugal claimed on quasi-divine authority the whole new world; you had no foothold there. France and Portugal were to forestall you in Asia.

If at that moment Spain, France, Portugal, Holland, had come to you talking 'peace' and order and constitutionalism, inviting you into a nascent international government constructed on the basis of the position and possessions they then held; inviting you to accept the kind of world which then existed, had solemnly adjured you to forgo all expansion, to 'renounce war as an instrument of national policy'— well, if you had cravenly accepted that invitation the Anglo-Saxon world of our day, the United States, the British Empire and its lusty young States, straddling between them the whole planet, would never have come into being. 'American' would not mean in the least what it now does; for the United States as we know it would not exist. There would be no great vital civilisation of English speech and law and tradition covering the American continent from the North Pole to the Mexican border. Because the blood of England is so largely Nordic, Germanic, and because English statesmen, anticipating the Nazi creed in this respect, 'thought with their blood' the Latin element —French, Spanish, Portuguese—gave place to something nobler, more virile, more Germanic.

It is well that it did that; that 'European Civilisation' which spread over the world and until yesterday dominated Asia should be an Anglo-Saxon, that is to say, a Nordic and Germanic rather than a Spanish, French or Portuguese culture; better an English United States than a Spanish or Portuguese one.

But just as it would have been craven for you in the name of 'law' to have accepted the old sixteenth, seventeenth or eighteenth century distribution of authority, to have accepted the Latin domination, so now for us Germans, it would be profound treason to our blood, our race, our destiny to accept the neat little patterns of Professor Wilson at Geneva as the final expression of human destiny, as the last word for the German race. We feel ourselves at a stage of our development comparable to the Elizabethan stage of your development. Do you suggest that what was humanly beneficent and noble for you should be denied to us? When one reflects upon the German's genius for organisation, discipline, valour, self-sacrifice, and then takes note of the gabbling disorder in some of the 'mongrel' nations which surround Germany; the semi-savage Balkanisation of so much of Europe, of the vast areas dominated by Mongol or Jewish gunmen envenomed by pathological hatreds, hatred particularly of our Nordic moral values; when one thinks that Portugal is regarded as being fit to possess an empire, but Germany as unfit; that there are to-day millions of Germans under the rule of these hybrid or mongrel states in Europe; that something like a million Germans—the population of your Dominion of New Zealand—live under Spanish-American or Portuguese-American rule because in the whole new world not one square yard of territory has come to the German—in the face of such facts, do you really expect us to accept Professor Wilson's World Constitution and Universal Law and all the rest of it? Are you surprised that we reject 'collective security' with its implication that it is to be security for the present order of things; do you wonder that we refuse to co-operate in the Geneva talking shop, which presumes to sit in moral judgment upon efforts like those made by Italy, efforts which would have rejoiced the hearts of your own Clive or your Drake; that the Führer protests against the notion of subjecting Germany's behaviour to the final verdict of copper-coloured gentry from Haiti or Afghanistan or Abyssinia, or San Domingo; that Von Neurath the other day made it plain that to offer Germany standardised and crystallised legal institutions so framed and administered comes near to being an insult? They are an invitation to her to deny her greatness, to renounce most of what she might be and do; an invitation to betray her posterity, to be guilty of national treason.

You have merely to judge us in the light of your own history during the last three hundred years, and of Europe's during the last twenty-five years, to see that ever since your disastrous error of

1914 you have been attempting to thwart an irresistible historical process. It is an attempt which failed utterly in 1914, as most of your writers, journalists, politicians are now admitting. For the German domination of the Continent which you fought the War to prevent, is now much nearer to accomplishment than it was before you achieved your 'victory.' The Treaty which you used your victory to impose is already moribund—dying without a single military blow being struck for its destruction. We can now give it the *coup de grâce* at any moment that we choose, and you know that you will not be able to resist. For the alliance which gave you victory and enabled you to write the Treaty, your alliance with Japan, with Russia, with Italy, with the United States is not moribund—it is dead, decomposed, buried beyond all hope of resurrection.

If you repeat the effort of 1914, try, in the altered circumstances of the post-War world, without the aid of America, or Russia, or Japan, or Italy, with much of that power against you, once more to thwart history, you will be utterly destroyed, engulfed, finished. And we should regret that. For part of your heritage would be certain to go to Asiatic and Latin folk with whom later we might have to deal.

'Yes, but—' intervenes a timid Englishman—'are we to be expected to submit to the fate of the Portuguese, the Spanish, the Dutch and the French Empires?'

Well, the French and Dutch have had to accept certain adjustments at your hands—in Canada, the Cape, India. Yet you are friends with both; and the adjustments have been made without either of the two other Empires coming to an end. We should not have to ask of you any such adjustments as France and Holland had to make with you, or indeed to surrender one square yard of what is properly yours. Of course, we should have to have our colonies back—not one or two, but *all*, to the last inch. If a gangster or a gipsy kidnapped your children, what would you think if he proposed to return half their number 'as a reasonable compromise'? You would reject it as we reject any proposal to compromise on the return of our political children. And, of course, unconditionally—no nonsense about mandates and reporting to Geneva. You have no more right to ask us to govern our territory according to your ideas than we have to ask you to govern your territory according to ours. We think that our way is just as good as yours, which, incidentally, does not seem notably successful just now in Palestine and elsewhere.

But while we shall insist upon the return of colonies, we recognise that our immediate task is in Europe itself. We must lick some sort of order into Central and South-Eastern Europe, and make our position to the East of Europe secure. We don't want to annex non-German States, but we insist (as you insisted in the case of Egypt, and certain Arab and Indian States) on the possession of such authority over them that they shall never become sources of danger or irritation to us. We might demand in the case of the Ukraine the sort of relationship which your Government occupies to the native States of India.

The need for Germany to apply that method of order is, even on purely economic grounds, infinitely greater than was your need in the eighteenth century. You fling so easily at us the accusation of 'economic nationalism.' But we are all economic nationalists these days, for the same reason that we are all Socialists. The days of *laissez faire* are over and done with for everybody, and we have come to the planned economy in lesser or greater degree. But 'planning' means economic nationalism, because it necessarily means State control of certain vital economic activities. A 'planned economy' is quite incompatible with the independent action of a great number of small States. How could you get a sufficient extent of agreement by 'free co-operation' of the Geneva kind? What real economic plan could come from a Talkfest of sixty-two nations? Our people, thirsting for virile decision, resolute action, did not end parliamentary gabble at home in order that it all might be started afresh at Geneva.

It is not from there that the real job of civilisation and order will be directed. But why should our task of order in Eastern and South-Eastern Europe, of acting as a barrier to Slav barbarism, bring us into conflict with *your* imperial task? Or are you once more going to fight Germany in order that Russia may treat us as you did in 1914, when you sided with the Slav against the Teuton. You British seem quite to have forgotten that you fought for Russian influence then. Russia championed Serbia and you took Russia's side against us. How does that policy of promoting the power and influence of Russia look now? We defeated Russia, made a treaty which would have brought a large part of Russia under Western control. You prevented us from making good that settlement; destroyed it. With what result? You had to intervene with money, munitions, expeditions, troops, in order to try and destroy the government which arose as the result of your victory over us. Do you think *now* that a Brest-Litovsk settlement would have been worse for Europe, worse for you, than the settlement which you got as the result of our defeat? Do you *now* want Russia to become the Protector of Little Nations? Do you really think *now* that it was wise to back Russian influence against German in South-Eastern Europe? *Would* it have been so disastrous from your point of view if Austria had been permitted to discipline 'gallant little Serbia' after Serbian use of crude assassination as 'an instrument of national policy'? Is not the whole policy which brought you into the Great War now revealed as a vast ineptitude? Is not that confession indeed now made almost daily, at least implicitly, by precisely those newspapers and publicists who were most ferocious in their anti-Germanism in the pre-War years?

There is no reason at all why Anglo-German power should not restore some sort of order to this distracted world. We would far rather, of course, be associated with you in that task than with certain other allies whom your refusal to co-operate with us compels us to seek. But if we are fruitfully to co-operate you must face our position, and the reason for the attitude we have taken towards Russia and towards Communism. Just think.

We are a people of seventy millions; the Russians are a people of at least twice that number, largely Asiatic, fundamentally so in their mentality in all that relates to spiritual values; inured by long centuries to a type of despotism which is essentially Tartar, Mongol, Asiatic in character, whether it calls itself Czarist or Bolshevist.

It was no mere coincidence that these barbaric millions, who lent themselves so readily to a policy adumbrated in the brain of an Asiatic, that is to say a Jewish, revolutionary, are hypnotised by a doctrine based mainly upon envy and hatred. But just as you can train dogs or seals to perform unquestioningly certain commands, so Jewish brains can train those 'conditioned millions' of Asiatic or semi-Asiatic fanatics to throw themselves in the name of the 'class war' at ancient European civilisations which earlier Mongol invasions did not quite manage to destroy, though they came near to doing it. We are nearer to this thing than you. You have not seen Russian armies on your soil. We have. But even you should be able to get some notion of what it feels like to have a hundred and fifty or two hundred millions of regimented Bolshevists at your doors, when you read the daily story of Moscow. If the masters of Russia can treat their own countrymen thus, what might not we, their enemies, expect if ever those armed hordes could break through our defences perhaps at some moment when we were taken at a disadvantage; when perhaps their doctrines, so fertile of internecine hates, had infected the less stable elements of our own people and weakened our own solidarity?

Are you surprised at the anti-Comintern Pact? Or at our surprise that you do not join it? And don't you see why we must dominate certain border States?

Of course we should prefer to be associated with you rather than to seek the aid of Japanese or Italians. But remember that you did not scruple to make those two people your allies when you deemed that it served your purpose; just as you made Czarist Russia your ally in a war to 'make the world safe for democracy.' You needed their aid, and because that was the case you could not be too particular. Remember that, when you criticise our present alliances. We live in a world in which more and more one must be either for or against and those who are not for us will find, not from any wish of ours, that they are against us. You really cannot any longer be 'above the battle' and not take sides. You refuse to face that fact.

Note what has happened in respect to Japan. When in 1931 America offered her co-operation with yourselves and the League to organise resistance to Japan, you refused. Your papers said it was unseemly to talk of coercing an old and faithful ally. You would not stand by Geneva. But neither would you take the side of Japan. You were sufficiently on her side to let down Geneva, betray China, worsen your relations with the United States, but not help Japan. Now she is your bitter enemy. She, Japan, defies you with complete impunity. Your papers talk of 'grave warnings' to Japan, of 'vigorous action' to assert your rights. And in the next column I am informed that you will have no truck with Russia and that M. Chautemps is to be asked to bring the Franco-Soviet Pact to an end. Now it ought to be evident to a child that you cannot possibly deal with Japan unless you are prepared to act with us or with Russia. But you will not do either. You will neither ally yourselves with America and the League to help China resist Japan, nor with Russia to the same end. Nor with us against Russia. Nor as an alternative to the alliance system, with Geneva. You love to sit on the fence, to compromise, you hate to be thorough and downright in your policy and in your doctrines; you like to defer decisions until the last possible minute (that characteristic may have been the real cause of the War) ; you hate to decide or commit yourselves beforehand.

When, therefore, you ask us to come into a system of law, and trust to it, we know that if once we are simple enough to do it, we should almost certainly be utterly betrayed; betrayed, of course, from the very highest motives, but betrayed. That is why we of the Third Reich have never taken the Locarno business seriously.

How can we or anybody else trust you?

You started out after the War talking Wilsonian peace, disarmament, the reign of law, and you asked us to believe in its reality. But you showed immediately that you had not made up your minds about it. You gave it a vague blessing but you were not prepared to back it, if violated. As a German, I am pleased at the final outcome; but also as a German, I am obliged to ask what your friendship is worth, whether we ought in order to get it surrender that of others in view of what your 'goodwill' towards the Weimar Republic, the League, Abyssinia, China, France, has meant to the fate of those five. You proclaimed yourself the dear friend of all. Well, the Weimar Republic is dead, the League is dying, independent Abyssinia has been slain, China murdered, and France. . . . Spain is typical. You professed non-intervention. The Italians accuse you of favouring Madrid; but the Madrid Government knows that it is precisely to your non-intervention that they will owe their defeat.

Oh, of course, you meant well. You merely wanted to be for the Covenant without being against those who would destroy it. When in the early days of the League, France asked if you would fight for the Covenant, should any nation violate it, you were simply shocked. The purpose of the League and the beautiful new world, you explained, was peace. We must not be so bloodthirsty as to talk about war in connection with it. Had you then become Pacifist, and would you disarm? No, you had not become Pacifist and you would not disarm. Your Navy was still the very greatest in the world; you would use it 'when the time came,' but you would not say what that meant. France asked you if you would defend her, should she be attacked by Germany. Again, you were shocked and grumbled that France was always talking about her security. So France said in effect: 'Well, if we cannot depend on the law, and we cannot depend on you, we must take our own measures.' And France in her efforts to weaken Germany destroyed the Weimar Republic, which *had* been bitten by the Wilsonian nonsense. If you had said to France: 'We will defend you to the last ship and man on condition that you behave decently to Germany,' you could have saved the Weimar Republic and the League. You sacrificed both in a desire 'not to take sides' as between France and Germany. You refused then that guarantee to France which you gave fifteen years later (when the damage was done and it could serve nothing but a mischievous purpose) because you regarded guarantees to France as 'further coercion of Germany' and 'taking sides.' By this fatal tendency of yours to refuse to say whether you are for a thing or against, you destroyed that Weimar Republic it was your intention to befriend. You encouraged China to trust to your League, and then, in the name of peace and impartiality and 'conciliation rather than coercion' refused the League power to protect China, refused it even when America offered to help you. Abyssinia went through the same experience when the law was violated to her destruction. You would have Sanctions, but not if Italy objected to them. Italy must not be alienated, but the law must be upheld. The result, of course, is that you did alienate Italy, and did not uphold the law. Would you uphold it for us if we were silly enough to trust to it? We do not believe it.

As a German who rejects the whole nonsense of an international society with a law and constitution at this stage of the world's development, I rejoice that your lawyer Simon pronounced as he did when he declared that he would not risk a single ship for the law. But what is disturbing is that you have also through your John Simons pronounced on a dozen occasions that law must at all costs be preserved. What precisely does this mean? We are *not* for the law; we believe it to be in the last analysis inevitably unjust to Germany, profoundly immoral. But do your pæons mean that, having established what we assume to be reliable co-operation with you, you will suddenly find that your conscience forbids you to stand with us further and in the name of the higher morality join with our enemies to destroy us? We may decide, you know, that it is safer to work with Allies less high minded perhaps but who at least know whether they are for us or against us.

That is why I do not know whether we can have peace with you or not. We have never made any secret of what we propose to do. We have proclaimed on numberless occasions that we intend to absorb into our State all those Germans at present outside it. We shall dominate the whole of continental Europe, and we shall forbid the erection anywhere of Bolshevist or near Bolshevist governments. Wherever in a European State a spontaneous movement against the gabble of parliamentarianism raises its head, we shall of course look with favour upon it. Wherever there is a movement to prevent the creation of a Communist government we shall look with favour upon that too. Legal niceties or punctilio will certainly not stand in the way of our doing what we believe to be indispensable to the definite triumph of Germanic civilisation in Europe. Sooner or later we shall have to reckon with Russia. That does not necessarily mean war. As things are going the purges may so weaken the moral and intellectual foundations of the Moscow Government that we shall be able to come to terms—the creation, for instance, of autonomous States on the European periphery of Russia which will be far more under the control of Berlin than of Moscow. It may not mean war at all, though it may mean certain aid given to internal movements within Russia itself. The same general technique will, of course, be employed in respect of France. We shall no more tolerate the triumph of Jewish Communism in France than we should in Spain, and we do not anticipate much more difficulty in the ultimate triumph of the French Franco than our present ally Italy is encountering in securing the triumph of the Spanish Franco.

My personal view is that you will accept all this—when the time comes. You will accept it because you will not take beforehand those steps necessary to prevent it. If and when the struggle comes with Czechoslovakia, the most popular cry in Great Britain will be 'No war for Czechoslovakia.'

When having settled accounts with the lesser States that might otherwise become your allies, we finally regulate things with Russia, you will then realise that the defence of France, to which your Foreign Minister has committed you, is just a comically impossible proposition. If, indeed, that question will ever arise. For our technique will certainly not be to provoke war with France, but to establish a French Franco who will be content to stop the further degradation of the French race by accepting the guidance and suggestions of the German hegemony.

In truth the issue is settled beforehand. Again and again these last few years events have shown that we (or even Japan, or Italy) can challenge you on vital points, but that you dare not challenge us; that we are prepared, on behalf of our cause, to assume burdens and take risks that you will not assume for yours. Again and again it has been shown—it is difficult to put it nicely—that we were not afraid, and that you were. We know what we want and are united in the determination to get it; you do not know what you want, and are deeply divided. When once more we raise the issue over which the World War was fought—the issue whether the Teuton or the Slav shall dominate Europe—half at least of your people will desire our victory. And if only for that sole reason our victory is assured.

It was to this division of opinion among our people particularly that the German kept returning, the fact that we have no fighting faith, no political convictions. We had not really made up our minds whether Bolshevism or Germanism was the greater danger, or against which of the two we had the greater prejudice. To some interjections he replied:

Perhaps you see now why when, a moment ago, you blamed us for leaving the League, for repudiating its code, for refusing to be bound by international 'Law,' to enter any system of international order, for demanding to be our own judge of our country's rights, I gave it as my opinion that our refusal was quite as much your fault as ours. You were shocked when I suggested that if war does come, it will be much more your fault than ours; and it may well come. And you were quite incredulous when I suggested that we should without any sort of doubt win that war: and that your Empire would be at our mercy.

In your own lack of faith, alike in your League and your Empire, is to be found the simple historical explanation of the reason why Germany has come to reject the League, the whole idea of an international order or law, of a constitution, institution corresponding in the life of nations to the institution which regulates the relation-ship of individuals within the state and give those individuals some security.

We could not accept such a plan as the basis of our security, as something to which we could entrust our rights and national inde-pendence for the quite sufficient reason that you Britons did not yourselves believe in the 'system' you were offering to us; never had any real faith in it, would never have been prepared to take any risks on its behalf. How could we trust our security to it?

I am not blaming you, or expressing resentment because person-ally, as I have said, I rejoice that the League is dead. I am merely reminding you of how your government has again and again at every crisis told us plainly how it interpreted its obligation in this matter, and reminding you because it has a bearing upon our future re-lationship.

Do you recall what the collective security plan, as expressed in the Covenant and the Locarno Treaties meant? The general idea was that if our rights were violated by Russia, or France, or Poland, or Italy, you would support us. The thing was solemnly worked out in some detail in the Locarno group of Treaties. Now 'supporting' us meant being ready to fight for us, for the League. The Locarno Treaties said so. We did not believe that you would fight for us, that is to say for the League. We believed if we were simple enough to trust to it, we should be at the mercy of anything that Russia, or France, or Poland, or Italy cared to do; any injustice they cared to perpetuate. Would you have fought for us, for your precious League, and Locarno arrangements? It is quite clear that you would not, that your government would not dream of vindicating that 'World Constitution' (to which you asked us to trust our national life) at the cost of war. A dozen incidents of the last seven or eight years proved it. It was proved most clearly perhaps when you announced that you would impose sanctions against Italy. For your govern-ment made it quite clear that nothing would induce you to go to war with Italy over the matter. So what it meant by imposing sanc-tions was that it would impose them unless Italy objected; an atti-tude on your part which from the first made Mussolini absolute master of the situation. Not a ship would you risk, your Foreign Minister proudly declared, in such a cause. Would it have been dif-ferent under the guarantees of Locarno? Most eminent publicists of yours have assured us again and again that it would not, and that if Mr. Wilson's League cannot exist without Britain fighting for it, then it can die. Do you call that believing in it? It is not the way we Nazis believe in the political principles we proclaim.

So when you ask me why we don't believe in international law and order, in an international constitution, my reply is, mainly because you don't. You who own about a quarter of the world, who are the Have's of the Universe, have infinitely more reason than we, who came too late to get even the crumbs, to welcome an institution which confirms the existing division. Yet you have never taken it seriously. Would you treat an attack upon your territory—an invasion, say, of Kenya, or Malta—as you treat attack after attack upon the Covenant!

Oh! I know, of course, that once a week some member of your government gets up and pronounces an incantation to the effect that the British Government stands by the League; fervently believes in it, as a great ideal, the hope of mankind; just as, also once a week, in a frock coat with his top hat under his seat, he professes his faith in doctrines which even his own bishops have recently announced do not mean quite what they say.

We in Germany have learned a truth which you, in view of its source, ought to know better than we do. It is contained in the warning: 'He who is not with me is against me.' Like most vital and neglected truths, it has its unpleasant aspects. We in Germany accept that.

Those of us in Germany who read the foreign Press—as I do—are struck by a curious attitude of our English critics. They call attention to certain imperfections and shortcomings of our present régime—disciplinary hardships, shall we call them. Do you suppose that we are not aware of some of those hardships? You wonder that we follow the Leader and give him our loyalty nevertheless. But the real test of loyalty is precisely there, namely, that you shall be loyal to the Leader when he is wrong. Any weakling, any time-server, can follow a Leader when he is right and leads to pleasant places. But the loyalty which cannot follow the Leader who is wrong and is leading into tight corners is not worth a tinker's curse.

We know of these faults of our régime. Yet, I am ready to die for it, to have my children die for it. And they fully expect one day to do so.

And that, after all, is the first and last proof of its superiority to yours. We are prepared to die for our political creed and faith; our system, if you will. You are no longer prepared to die for yours. Indeed you have none to die for. You have no longer any such political faith or religion, any real political convictions whatsoever.

During the War you had slogans. 'To make the world safe for democracy'; 'To end Prussian Militarism.' Well, you were victorious. *Did* your victory make the world safe for Democracy? *Circumspice!*

You were fighting 'to end Prussian Militarism.' Not Russian militarism, nor French militarism, nor Japanese militarism—Russia, France, Japan were then your allies. You were very grateful at the time for their militarism. No, only 'Prussian' militarism. Well, the War was hardly over, the Peace Treaty was not yet made, before one of your most brilliant of statesmen was calling upon Germany to range herself against the menace of Russian militarism, this time appearing as the armed doctrine of Bolshevism. You had suddenly found a certain use in German militarism and were rapidly discovering that there were other militarisms. And, of course, you were fighting 'the war to end war' to establish a new international order; peace, a League; Disarmament.

Well, you—Britain, France, the United States—won the War. Germany was completely disarmed, helpless to resist even a Ruhr invasion. Was our disarmament followed by yours? You, the Democracies, could have ended 'militarism' so far as any German resistance was concerned. But you were unable to agree among yourselves; did not really believe your anti-military doctrine. As little did you believe in your new international order. There was no opposition at the outset from us, but again the democracies made no effort to make it a reality. The chief democracy backed out completely—and to-day the thing stinks in its decomposition.

All that makes part of the reason why you have no political faith, nothing that you will fight for. The 'principles' for which you fought were just slogans, and empty, insincere, sham slogans at that. They have all failed, and you are determined never to fight for them again.

Now we Germans know what we were fighting for and that our cause has not failed. Though in our campaign the particular battle which you call the Great War may have been lost, we knew 'in our blood' that eventually we should win. We are now winning. Someone said of you English that you usually lose every battle in a campaign except the last. It is no longer true of you; and it *is* true of us.

We knew that in the Great War we were fighting to prevent the Slav domination of Europe and particularly of ourselves; to create a dam against the barbarian flood rolling towards us from the East and threatening to swamp us and our culture; we were fighting to preserve from the Moscovite savagery our German race, its heritage of order, of discipline; its right to bring discipline and order out of the surrounding chaos and anarchy of the Eastern and South-Eastern fringe which threatened us; order and stability indispensable to German security, welfare; to the due economic opportunity of Germany, the very food of future German millions.

Well, we are winning. The Slav is being pushed back and you —most of you—are delighted to see us doing it.[1] We *are* quite successfully asserting our right to unify the German race and give it its rightful place in Europe and the world. And you are quite unable to prevent us. You will be quite unable to prevent the extension of that process not only in Europe but in Asia, in Africa. If our needs should compel us to impinge in Africa or the Near East upon what has heretofore been your sphere, then we shall be quite able to do it, and you will not dream of stopping us—or rather, perhaps, it would be truer to say that you will only dream of stopping us. You will not do it. It is quite certain that you will not fight.

You said just now that your people would fight for your country, for the Empire. Well, I do not believe it.

Please do not mistake me. I am not thinking of the Oxford Resolution or similar undergraduate jokes.

I am not implying that your people are cowardly or degenerate. I take no stock at all in that sort of view. I do not doubt that you are just as courageous and virile as you ever were; with a potential strength as great as ever. But you will not use your courage or your strength to defend the interests of your country or your Empire, because you are in two minds as to what those interests are, what you

---

[1] In his book *I know these Dictators* Mr. G. Ward Price expresses the view that Germany will one day try to recover the Polish corridor, in which case the effort will be made to compensate Poland with territory to the east, that is, in the Ukraine. He says that the Germans believe that regional nationalism is stirring again in Russia and that the huge Soviet Union will, in course of time, begin to disintegrate. They hope that when that time comes the Western Powers will support Germany in rearranging the map of Europe to meet her needs.

ought to defend. Your love for your Empire is less profound than your dislike of causes which would be promoted if you defended it.

Defence does not mean, of course, merely keeping foreigners off your soil—you have not done that since the Norman conquest. It means defending things necessary for the nation's life and welfare: preserving a strategic position in which the defence of those things is feasible. If in the past you have been content to be pushed, inch by inch, from one strategic position after another, without fighting, there would have been no Empire.

To-day you will not defend that Empire because, though you are not afraid to fight, you *are* afraid of defeating the Empire's rivals. You fear that the defeat of Italy, for instance, might mean Communism in Spain. So you will accept immensely grave risks to your Mediterranean line of communication. You fear that the defeat of Japan might mean perhaps a Communist China, in any case an immense accretion to the power and influence of Russia throughout the world. So you are ready to place your Eastern Empire in danger. For two hundred years—and at the cost of two wars—you have opposed the establishment of a great Power in Spain or Morocco or in strategic positions in those territories. Yet to-day great masses of your people favour Franco, even if his victory with the aid of German and Italian allies does mean making Gibraltar worthless. You have toiled and bled for two hundred years to build up your Empire in the Far East, and to-day your conservative and imperialist opinion openly supports the action of the new Asiatic rival who does not for a moment bide his intention of challenging your position in Asia, who in so many words tells you to get out. There may be some subtle reason we cannot grasp. In any case it is not heroic; it is not the old John Bull. It is clear that you do not put the defence of your Empire first. That the very will to defend it is crossed with other purposes.

To-day, because you have no political convictions, because you actually disparage having any, boast that you will not take sides in 'rival ideologies,' are 'above the battle'; because you have no faith or principles of your own for which you are prepared to die, only doubts and confusions, you cannot, though prepared to fight, make up your mind when or for whom or against whom to fight.

So much is that true that on a round dozen occasions in the last ten years you have treated us to a spectacle never before seen in your history; British imperialists openly rejoicing at the success of challenges to and onslaughts upon the prestige and strategic security of the British Empire; challenges in the Far East, in the Near East, in Africa, in the Mediterranean, in Spain.

The real way out for you is, of course, co-operation with us; co-operation against disorder and barbarism—in other words against Communism. We have offered that to you. But no, that would mean taking sides in rival ideologies, which you won't do. One other alternative was open to you at one time: the League. The Germany of the Weimar Republic would have accepted that, if you had given any evidence that you had a fighting faith in its principles; if you had been prepared to go to war on behalf of the victim of aggression, of the collective principle that is; to side with Germany if she had been attacked by Russia or France, or France if she had been attacked by Germany. That was indeed the underlying principle of Stresemann's Locarno Treaties as I have reminded you. But you very soon made it clear that you would not dream of fighting for any such thing. Some of your most influential papers and public men said so almost daily. You had a sudden fit of extreme Pacifism. It was wicked, they explained, to turn the beautiful peaceful League into a sort of international war office. The League was for peace, not war. Admirals and Generals joined hands with Quakers and Conscientious Objectors in deprecating the sacrilege of thus 'making the League an instrument of war.' Had you really then abandoned armed defence in favour of Pacifism? Hardly. Your Navy was still four or five times the size of ours; you were about to enter upon immense rearmament. You would arm yourselves but would not help to arm the League; you would go to war if necessary for your own defence, not for the defence of the collective system, the League, your allies or associates in it.

In other words you did not believe in it; had no fighting faith in it; would not die for it. You believe in the League about as a man believes that it is naughty to use swear words. You love it as a man loves his mother-in-law.

Just think for a moment what your obvious scepticism implied. In return for our disarmament you offered us the protection of the League, that is to say the protection of the armed power of the great states composing it. So we were obliged to ask ourselves: Would the League powers really fight for us if we were attacked, fight for the 'law' under whose protection they asked us to place ourselves? And you—your papers and your public men—kept on saying that it would not, that it was not the purpose or the method of the League for anybody to fight for it, or for anything. Then why should you ask us to believe in it?

You see at the time you were making that quaint kind of offer, we were also being offered the alliance, the reciprocal assistance of great powers who *would* fight for us, would help us towards the defence of our rights, our common interests.

What would *you* do if you had to choose between two such offers? One party offers you active, that is to say, armed support in the event of aggression against you. The other, first of all asks you to surrender your means of defence, and then goes on to say that if, as the result of complying with the request thus to weaken yourself, you are attacked you must rely solely on your own power to defend yourself. Well, which of those two offers would *you* accept? You tell us that you believe in your League, your 'law,' but that you will not fight for it. We do not call that faith at all.

You have arrived at a point where one half of your people will not fight for the League, or the Collective System and the other half will not fight for the Empire. You can't therefore as a nation fight at all, or fight with a will to victory. And there can be no victory without that will. We have it. You have not.

II

THE ITALIAN ALSO

The Italian accepts the German statement as covering broadly his own case with, however, some special additions and qualifications. He reminds the German that Italy was the 'inventor' of the Fascist system, that she had made it a success before Germany adopted it; that the principle has very deep roots in Italian history and philosophy; that if the principle of race is really valid the Nordic must take into account the simple historic fact of the Roman Empire and all that the Mediterranean and its people have meant to civilisation. He gives his reason for believing that even if the Rome-Berlin co-operation is not 'eternal,' it may well last a generation or two until certain political and demographic adjustments (not to the disadvantage of Germany) have been made.

The Italian who formed part of our group was a good counterpart of the German—educated, travelled, a sincere Fascist, but necessarily aware of some of the defects of the régime. We found—curiously enough when one thinks of the phrases used about 'the hot-blooded south' and 'the cold-blooded north'—that he was less intense, less passionate, in a sense more human, with more of humour and the possibility of laughing at himself and his régime, than the German had shown.

Following the German member of the group, and speaking from notes—using sometimes excerpts from books or papers as was our custom—he spoke about as follows:

I shall be much briefer than the member of the circle who preceded me because I subscribe to very nearly everything that he has said, especially in view of the need of expanding peoples for more territory, to what he said concerning the necessary processes of 'adjustment' in the world. That adjustment has never taken place in the past by any means but war, and war indeed ensures that when it does take place it shall be in favour of the most vital, the most energetic, courageous; that, in other words, in the struggle the fittest shall survive.

But there are certain qualifications which, as an Italian, I should like to make when he dealt with blood and race. And I do not make them merely from national pride or resentment, but because a better understanding of certain of his assumptions are indispensable to that Rome-Berlin co-operation which is to play so large a place in the future which he and I foresee.

I would very gently remind him that great as may have been the role of the Germanic race, Germanic blood—well, there *are* others. There was after all the Roman Empire.

Yes, I know that our friend will prove that all the Roman Emperors were Germans, just as Jesus Christ has now been proven most conclusively by all the approved theologians of modern Germany to have been a true German. But still, the people out of which came this thing we still call Rome—first the world political empire, and then the world religious empire—must, I suggest, have left traces of their blood in those who now inhabit the Italian peninsula.

I like also at times to think of the differences between the nature of the Germanic and the Italian relationship to Britain. The Italian—well then, Roman, if you prefer—came to Britain in 55 B.C. We know what Britain became, and remained for about four hundred years as the result of the Italian's—sorry, I mean the Roman's—work. From being a mere savage island at about the North American stage of development it became a green and pleasant land, crossed by roads better than any it again possessed for nearly 2,000 years; dotted with beautiful country houses, centrally heated, having baths, libraries, gardens; with splendid cities where civilised folk lived a life more rich and cultured and secure than the Island was to know again after the Roman departure until the time of our own grandfathers. Indeed, one may hazard the statement that the peaceful and cultivated Britain of the Roman period was in most respects an infinitely better place than the Britain of those dark Satanic mills of the nineteenth century. I wonder if our German friend has visited, as I did the other day, the Roman Bath in Bath. He knows, of course, what that bath was when first built. It was not a bath in the sense of a modern municipal bath-house. It was a luxurious club, to which civilised folk would come as a place where, in this damned British climate, you could find warmth and comfort, could take your exercise, be massaged, swim in warm water, and pass half a day or for that matter a whole day in such relaxation, illumined by the intelligent conversation of people as educated as those which inhabit that city to-day. (That club, by the way, was better warmed and in many respects better appointed than any club in Pall Mall of modern times.) Moreover, it was a popular club. Anybody could go there for what would be in modern money about a penny. And if our German friend has been there I wonder whether he noticed a detail. At the favourite spot for the swimmers to jump into the swimming pool, a stone has been worn by the bare feet of the habitués some six inches deep. Think of the numbers and the generations of feet necessary to do that. Just think of the stability, the order, the civilisation maintained generation after generation which that little fact indicates. You British have conquered India—a far more civilised country I suggest than was the Britain of the pre-Christian era. Will you remain four hundred years in India and leave monuments as suggestive as this single monument of the Roman Club at Bath? I might remind you that the famous Twentieth Legion left Britain in 401 after a sojourn in the land of no less than 358 years. Probably no other army in the world has contained regiments whose regimental records went back for so long a time in continual service, nor any army a unit whose service was mainly devoted to the maintenance of peace.

However, it is with Nordic as compared with Roman influence in Britain of which I should like to speak for a moment, for the benefit of our Nordic friend.

The Nordic, the Saxon, the Jute, the Germanic, was in a sense our successor—the successor of the Romans—in these islands. *You* recall perhaps how he came—and what he did. He even established kingdoms in these islands. Oh, yes, you once had Nordic—Teutonic, Germanic—kings and chieftains here. But the Nordic contribution to your island story was not quite of the order of which I have just spoken—of great roads that lasted 2,000 years, of beautiful homes with elaborate civilised appointments where educated and civilised men gathered together in their libraries to discuss pleasantly over their wine the latest book, to criticise its style, to swop poems. No, the Germanic contribution was not quite of that order.

Our Italian member was perhaps too genial and polite to be more precise. But an English member of the group insisted at this point upon reading a few passages from the letters of Sidonius which have been quoted by Casson in his book *Progress and Catastrophe*.[1] Among the passages from Casson's book which he read are these:

'It has been said of Sidonius that "he saw the last sickness and the death of the Roman Empire of the west, and is our principal authority for some of the events which attended its extinction."[2] For he had seen the ravages of Attila and watched the wild Teutonic allies fighting for the first time side by side with Rome against the common oriental invader, these allies whose barbarism ultimately kills the empire they were then helping to save. He saw strangely uniformed German princelets strutting in the ancient cities of southern Gaul, taking over the titles, but nothing else, of Roman administrative posts. He has left us a famous description of a young Frankish prince, Sigismer, who walked in a procession:

'"In flame-red mantle, with much glint of ruddy gold, and gleam of snowy tunic, his fair hair, red cheeks and white skin according with the three hues of his equipment. The chiefs and allies who bore him company were dread of aspect, even thus on peace intent; . . . though the business in hand was wedlock, Mars was no whit less prominent in all this pomp than Venus."

'One is reminded of the descriptions in more recent letters from correspondents of the wedding of General Goering in Berlin. Germans seem to have changed little in some respects. Of our own ancestors we also get a glimpse. Saxons, probably from England itself, came his way.

'He is writing to a friend whose duty was to guard the northern shores of Gaul against Saxon pirates "the blue-eyed Saxon, lord of the seas," as he calls him:

'"My informant was very positive that you had weighed anchor and in fulfilment of those half-military, half-naval duties of yours, were coasting the western shores on the lookout for curved ships, the ships of the Saxon— to whom shipwrecks are no terror, but only so much training. His is no mere acquaintance with the perils of the sea: he knows them as he knows himself."

'In the basilicas and forums of Roman cities he now saw skin-clad Teutonic warriors strutting, inheriting the duties and dignities of the Roman officials of the earlier régime, but making duty and dignity alike a farce, and ruling *de facto* by force. But the tragedy was that those who had inherited the traditions of Rome, those who were complete products of Roman method and Roman civilisation either could not or would not do anything to stop the internal decay that provided soil for the new and barbarous growths. Fungus-like, the Burgundian and Visigoth already

[1] Hamish Hamilton, London.
[2] O. M. Dalton, *The Letters of Sidonius*, 1915, p. 11.

faintly civilised under Rome, fastened on to the ancient trunk of the falling Roman tree. In a sense they belonged to it, because they had ceased to be complete barbarians once they had come under its shade. Arriving in the Roman sphere as refugees, they soon became pupils and now were masters, tolerated solely because they afforded to the pure Roman element the only defence against those hordes of unromanised barbarians, like the Goths, who now sought to follow their more fortunate relatives into the rich fields of Roman provinces. All the time the Roman element lived in a fool's paradise. There is dramatic irony to the full in the descriptions in the letters of Sidonius of his dinner parties with his rich friends, in the accounts of their lovely country houses. Here were these people living in the shadow of events which meant their complete extermination. Whether they deliberately shut themselves up in their libraries and their dining-rooms as in the end they shut themselves up in the church, to escape the coming horrors, we shall never know. But the sickness of Rome had gone too far for them to devise any solution or to rely upon anything but their own personal gallantry, which had been proved in many a disturbance. The astonishing military feats of the Roman general Aetius against Attila had shown that the Roman spirit and genius for warfare of defence had not abated a whit from the time of Julius Caesar. But it was the gallantry of individuals on a sinking ship. Rome was dying for reasons which no one has yet analysed with certainty. The barbaric intrusions were more the consequence than the cause of her sickness. What had happened was that *standards had fallen.* Elements wholly alien to Roman rule and Roman freedom had emerged. In the letters of Sidonius we hear of censorship, of political murder disguised as accident, of bribery and corruption in high places, and even of persecution of the Jews. Sidonius himself is astonishingly liberal to Jews. In several letters he actually recommends to friends the services of Jews with the prefatory remark that "Even if the man I send to you is a Jew he is all the same a man of sterling character. . . ." One infers that the lot of the Jews was not a happy one.'

After which interval, the Italian returned to his statement as follows:

During the Fashoda crisis a Frenchman in the Chamber of Deputies, angered once more with 'perfide Albion' consoled himself thus:

'After all, what is this England? England is nothing but a French colony which has turned out badly.'

It could, of course, be far more truly said by the Italian that England was merely an old Roman colony which at the end turned out badly owing to the activities of the Nordic; that its fine and ordered civilisation was destroyed by German intrusion, as indeed, a bigger story still along those lines might be told. But that story does not concern us to-day. All that is very ancient history. I only reminded you of it as a little corrective of the somewhat sweeping generalisations of our German member.

For the moment the Roman and the German are partners, and I believe that we can do useful work together in that great task of European organisation—re-organisation in every sense it seems to us Italians—which lies before us.

The task is big enough to be shared. The cynic might perhaps put it that the booty was enough for both. And there are aspects of it which we Italians are perhaps better fitted than the German, to undertake.

I doubt, for instance, whether, with all his great qualities of order and discipline, the modern German is quite fitted for the task of dealing with—shall we say—the coloured world, with the re-organisation of Africa. I am inclined to think that the Negro and the Arab world would find the Italian a more welcome master than the German. The destiny of Italy lies certainly in the direction of expansion into Mediterranean countries, particularly on its southern shore.

There are a few things in that connection of which I want to remind you. A million Italian-born people have gone to France. That is to say, France has been a more considerable colony for Italians than any prospective German colony could for long generations be for Germans. But Italian immigration into France on such a scale as that suggests a pregnant reflection. Far more Italians have come into French territory than Frenchmen have gone to Algeria or Tunis or any African-French colony. Does it not suggest, (a) that France would do better to colonise France, to keep it French, than to make France an Italian or foreign colony; (b) that it is better for Frenchmen to colonise France than Africa; (c) that it is better for France, French France, that is, for Italians to go to Africa than to come into France; and (d) that France could well, even on grounds of patriotism, facilitate the process?[1]

[1] In this connection the author of *What Next, O Duce?* (Beatrice Baskerville [Longmans, p. 118]), writes:

'In the old days, Italians liked best to emigrate to the United States, France and such English cities as afforded a scope for the small trader and the keeper of restaurants. They showed a preference for districts and cities where they had friends or relatives. Ice-cream vendors went to Glasgow from certain districts in Italy. They knew all about local conditions from friends who had settled there before them. They made their pile and went home to buy small farms. But they fought shy of new colonies; it was less trouble to ply their trades in foreign countries. The expansion of British influence in Africa, with the exception of the Nile Valley, has been accomplished by the exertions of private individuals, of empire builders. No sooner had Italy occupied Addis Ababa than

Here are some of those 'adjustments' we spoke of that surely might take place peacefully.

I do not want to develop the subject in too much detail here for quite obvious reasons. Our circle includes a Frenchman who may later speak. But we Italians are an emigrating people to an infinitely greater extent than either the French or the German. We go, not by scattered few, but by hundreds of thousands—to the Argentine, to other countries of South America, to the United States—in such numbers that the Italian vote is a very important element in American politics. And many a town in America is virtually governed by its Italians. Would it not be more sensible that this migration should take place rather in the Mediterranean which is so deeply the home of the Italian? It will make for stability and order if African territories which are so obviously within the Italian migration influence should be brought within its political influence too—for all those reasons which the German member of the circle has elaborated so well in the case of the German task.

We know, of course, that Abyssinia will not 'pay dividends' for a long time; that a great work of pacification and organisation lies before us. But in Tunis, in Algeria, in Morocco, in other territories, the dividends are ready to be paid if more sensible political arrangements could be made.

I know I may shock your French member. But I would remind him of this: that a few generations ago France was a great American power; she was a great Indian power. She has left vestiges of her civilisation in America—very considerable in Quebec, less considerable in Louisiana. India might once have been hers. Well, both were evacuated in favour of you British. It did not mean the end of France as a factor in civilisation; it did not even mean great bitterness between you, for to-day—so you tell us—you are warm allies.

---

the Government proclaimed its intention of controlling the development of the country. Every settler was to be a member of the Fascist Co-operative State, under strict control. Thousands of enterprising young men have been refused permits to land in the ports leading to Abyssinia; many had already bought their stock of goods, or their tools. Individual initiative is smothered under the bureaucracy of State control. In this connection there is a certain amount of corruption. People anxious to visit Abyssinia can by devious means obtain permits; but few can put up the money demanded by the go-betweens, generally women, with influence in proper quarters. Between December 1936 and the middle of February it was easier to "volunteer" for Franco's army in Spain than for the constructive work in Abyssinia.'

Well, similar readjustments may have to be made. Yes, it may mean war. But you see, I think we Italians, looking back upon 2,000 years, seeing there in our very cities the remains of that vast grandeur which we carried even to these islands, know that war is part of the rhythm of life; that it is part of the process of human destiny, and we do not shirk it. We realise that it is not the end—as I sometimes think our Germanic allies seem to feel it is—but the means to an end; and that end just now is the reconstruction, or the part reconstruction of a great empire of which we will remain the centre. The process has begun. Rest quite assured that it will continue.

Oh, of course there are differences between ourselves and the Germans, and the Rome-Berlin axis will occasionally want a little greasing. But there is one thing that will keep us together; we are necessary to each other for that task of expansion which we both need, and both desire so ardently. Again, the truth can be put in rather highfalutin terms, or in more cynical terms. Rochefoucauld put it in the latter when he said the one thing which will keep two people from quarrelling is their common advantage in the exploitation of a third. We feel that the French, and yes, the British Empires— we may as well be frank—are now held by rather old, rather fat, rather lazy, somnolent hands. New blood is needed, and the work of making the most of these great territories, of doing what the old Romans did, must be undertaken by more energetic dynamic people. This fat and comfortable, this most likeable old John Bull, is no longer equal to the task.[1]

[1] At the moment that these proofs are being passed for the printer comes news from Abyssinia that the Italian conquest is by no manner of means complete. Detailed information shows that the Abyssinians have been gaining ground, particularly in the west. The province of Gojam is said to have freed itself almost entirely of Italian troops. In the south-west there have been serious revolts—at Bako, Gimma, Kafa and Gurafarda. The Italian garrisons have had to be withdrawn from the three last-named places. Even in the centre the Italians are unable to ensure order and the main road from Asmara, capital of Eritrea, to Addis Ababa has been cut several times. Many of the natives of Gojarn received Italian military training in Libya, were enlisted in the Eritrean armies that invaded Abyssinia, and have now deserted and returned to their own people. Their training makes them formidable adversaries for the Italians who gave it to them.

At the same time comes news of the signing by Britain of a new treaty of friendship with Italy by which Britain (in fact) gives formal recognition of the Italian Empire in Abyssinia. For advantages accorded, not to the Abyssinians but to us, we facilitate the Italian conquest of that ancient African State which we had undertaken to defend.

III

THE ENGLISHMAN REPLIES

The member of the group chosen to present the British reply to the German case deals briefly with such specific problems as colonies—briefly since the facts are now fairly familiar—but touches upon the misapprehension still so rife in Germany—and England—as to the real differences between us on the Colonial issue. He then goes on to examine whether in fact Germany and Italy are asking the right to do what Britain has done in the past; deals with the relationship of our Commonwealth of scattered democracies to the general method of Totalitarianism and examines whether the cardinal principle of Totalitarianism—that the nation must be self-sufficient both as to the materials of welfare and the means of defence, is compatible with similar rights for others, including the British Empire.

It was arranged that one chosen member of our group should present a general reply to the case as presented by our German and Italian members, though it was foreseen that most of the other contributions from the English side would be in the nature of replies to the case just reported. The British spokesman said in effect:

I shall address my reply particularly to the German because the essential principles of the Totalitarian case were presented by him, our Italian friend confining himself mainly to qualifications or addenda.

Let us separate two very distinct things with which you, the German, have been dealing. There is your indictment of the actual conduct of British policy, Britain's failure, while asking you to accept the

31

principle of law, to do her part in making law sufficiently a political reality to justify any nation in entrusting its security thereto.

And there is your case in justification of Germany's claim to Empire and to predominance of power in Europe, power to be exercised at her discretion without the trammels of law because, you allege, only by that form of power can she find the indispensable conditions of life, survival, self-preservation.

It is this latter point which is by far the more important; the part of your argument which most deserves our attention. The conduct of policy by the British Government this last ten or fifteen years may well have been inept, short-sighted, unwise. But what we have to ask is whether the wrong course taken by British policy is due to deep-rooted, widespread, passionate belief in utterly false principles, or rather to confusion, vacillation, timidity in the application of principles which would be perfectly workable if boldly applied. I suggest that the latter explanation of Britain's behaviour is the true one—as indeed the terms of your own statement towards the close suggest.

If the proclaimed principles and deep convictions of the British public were consistently applied, civilisation would be saved. So relatively small a thing, therefore, as a change of government or even change of Cabinet personnel might produce a very great change of conduct, for the foundations of the right policy are there. But it is far otherwise with Germany.

If the proclaimed principles of the Third Reich, the principles of *Mein Kampf*, the expressed convictions of Goering and Goebbels, are acted upon, civilisation will be destroyed. Our hope in the West is that Britain will act upon her proclaimed principles and that Germany won't; that German conduct will be better than German theories; and British conduct as good; that Britain will keep her word and Germany break hers.

That is a slender hope when we recall the mountain might of the German propaganda machine; the complete and absolute power of the Totalitarian State over the very minds and souls of its people; not alone over the printed word—books, newspapers, reviews, school primers; not only over broadcasting, films and theatres; and not only over the schools, the universities and the very nurseries, but over every form of organised religion. God Himself has been made an adjunct of the Totalitarian State, subject thereto, in that what men believe to be God's word must be approved by Mr. Hitler or Mr. Goebbels.

I only call attention to this because of its political importance. As good a judge as any of the power of the German machinery for idea-control is presumably the group of men who see it at work and command it. They have decided that the effectiveness of that machine is such that it is safe to challenge at one and the same time the power of the Catholic hierarchy, of German Lutherism and world Jewry.

Clearly, therefore, it is 'some' machine. Even though it be unequal to facing the three forces just enumerated, it will certainly be equal to planting so deeply in the mind of every German the political and economic ideas of *Mein Kampf* that it will be extremely difficult to uproot them, even if the little group who now disseminate them should want to do so. Again and again in history the demagogue has discovered that it is far easier to bamboozle than to debamboozle; and that governments become at times helpless in the presence of the public passions the governments themselves have created.

So the prospect that Germany will *not* adhere to her theory, her doctrine, her *ethos* is not bright.

Of what nature then are these theories, driven day by day, week by week, year by year into the minds of every man, woman and child in Germany, and so made the basis of a fanatical political religion?

Take the very first theory you yourself invoke, namely, that a nation of increasing population must expand territorially; that economic expansion should, must, involve political expansion. You put that in the very forefront of your case.[1]

Now your own immortal Kant has indicated how to test the workability of any principle of conduct: If others as well as ourselves apply it, what happens?

Apply that test to your principle of national self-sufficiency, material and moral, and what happens? If nations in general apply it, you get a series of mutually exclusive claims which must result in murderous chaos. For as soon as you begin to apply the principle

[1] Colonies, says Hitler in *Mein Kampf* (12th edition, p. 153), could only be useful where large numbers of Europeans could settle. More land in Europe is the practical aim (pp. 153, 735, 742), and this land is to be won from Russia and the border States (p. 742) by the sword (p. 741). No other military Power in Europe is to be permitted (p. 745), and France's power is to be destroyed (pp. 719, 775 ff). And the final aim? 'A State that insists on the cultivation of its best racial elements must one day become lord of the earth' (p. 782).

of economic self-sufficiency to any number, you discover that 'adequate territory,' self-sufficiency for one, means lack of self-sufficiency for some other. It is a cannibalistic theory of economics, incompatible with order, or with peace. One economist has suggested that it is as though one Papuan should say to another: 'It is plain that either I must eat you, or you must eat me. Let's come to a friendly agreement about it.' They won't come to a friendly agreement about it if that first economic assumption is accepted. They will fight.

Is it sound, this notion that a nation should have the material resources necessary to its life within its political control? I suggest it not only violates elementary ethics, it is arrant nonsense economically, contradicting the facts of the world about us.

Let us look at some of those facts:

First of all, it is a physical impossibility to organise a world of sixty independent States on any such basis, or anything approaching it. Even assuming that German power sweeps away the independence of a dozen or two of the sixty, it would still be impossible. Are you going to give Switzerland access to the sea and Sweden rubber-producing States in the tropics?

Secondly, even if you could get self-sufficiency to-day it would not be self-sufficiency to-morrow. Forty years ago no State would have attached much value to rubber or oil. To-day those things are all important.

Thirdly, not only is the thing physically impossible, but experience proves it to be unnecessary. The greatest of modern industries like the cotton industry of Britain in its heyday was based upon foreign raw material. (Britain did not need to conquer Louisiana or Georgia in order to use their raw cotton any more than America needs to conquer Malaya in order to get one of the vital raw materials of her great motor-car industry, created within the last thirty years.)

Fourthly, if experience proves that it is not necessary to have raw materials under political control, it proves equally that the fact of so possessing them in very great measure is no insurance against the characteristic economic difficulties of our times. The United States comes nearest of all nations to self-sufficiency, yet it has of late years passed through one economic crisis after another. Not only has that country at intervals a vast army of unemployed, but it has normally—has had for generations—armies just as vast of miserably poverty-stricken folk like its cotton croppers of the South, its dry farmers of the West, its miners of the Pennsylvanian and West Virginian coalfields. It is extremely doubtful whether much less self-sufficient States like Switzerland and Sweden can show such poverty. Britain 'owns' more empire than any nation of the world. Yet it carries heavier burdens of taxation than any nation of the world, it shows in its lower ranks a poverty far more extreme than any shown in Have-Not States like Switzerland and Norway; and it is doubtful whether, all things considered, its population as a whole lives at as high a standard of life and civilisation as does the population of the little States who have no empire at all.[1]

Indeed, the whole notion that territorial expansion—which really means the expansion of political sovereignty—is a vital need for peoples like the German and the Italian, is about ninety per cent mystification, confusion of thought, sheer misunderstanding. It is the outcome of certain political ideas, not of economic realities; its motives are political, military, in an ultimate sense, psychological.

In pre-War days Russia was an expansionist State pushing towards 'warm water'—towards Constantinople in the West and Port Arthur in the East. Having lost a great part of her territory to Poland, Lithuania, Latvia, she ceases to be an expanding State. Is this because her population declines?

So with America. When her population was less than half what it is, she was expansionist, talking of Cuban, Mexican, West Indian,

---

[1] The author of *Raw Materials, Population Pressure and War* (World Peace Foundation, New York) writes:

'It is a suggestive fact that some of the most prosperous states of the world—those, that is, which have evolved the highest standard of living and of civilisation—are among the least self-sufficient; while those abounding in natural resources, like some of the Central and South American nations, have an extremely low standard of living and an unstable civilisation. Compare the standard of living and civilisation in the Swiss Republic, one of the least self-sufficient states of the world, with the standard of certain South American republics, which have immeasurably greater resources and come very much nearer to complete self-sufficiency. Compare the standard in the Scandinavian and Baltic nations—Norway, Sweden, Denmark, Finland—with that of some of their larger and more powerful neighbours. These countries are deficient in some of the most vital of materials; their soil is in large part poor. Yet they do not feverishly build up their military power, nor make threatening demands for "outlets"—and do not seem to need them. They clamour for no "place in the sun," but they are prosperous, highly civilised and stable. They have recovered first and recovered most from the Great Depression without any question of "expanding" their frontiers, or engaging in military adventure.'

and Canadian annexations. Such aspirations were at an earlier stage of American history the stock in trade of the professional patriot; the raw material of Senatorial oratory and newspaper jingoism. Having greatly *increased* her population this 'urge' ceases. She dis-annexes the Philippines; no longer talks of Mexican or Canadian annexation; and everyone knows that all idea of expansions like those which used to excite jingoes of the Hearst type have been surrendered.

The terms we so often use in the discussion about this or that nation 'possessing' territory producing raw materials, implies a grave confusion between the political and the economic function. We talk usually as though a change in political frontiers involved a change of ownership in land or mines. It is impossible to discuss this subject with any clarity of thought if we accept at face value the words and phrases commonly employed. We must realise that much of this terminology is so inaccurate as grossly to distort our thought.

At the root of the proposal to remedy the economic difficulties of nations in the modern world by transfer of territory, there usually lies a confusion of thought due to this inaccuracy of terms. We talk of the British 'ownership' of Canada or the French 'ownership' of Algeria. But of course there is no ownership. Not a single Englishman owns a single thing in Canada by virtue of whatever may remain of the shadowy political relationship between Britain and Canada; nor a Frenchman a single thing in Algeria. We speak commonly as though when a province or colony passes from one government to another there is an actual transfer of property or material from one group of owners to another. But when Germany conquers Alsace or France takes it back there is no transfer of 'property,' since the real owners are transferred with the property. The farms, factories, houses, shops, shares, furniture, remain in the same hands after conquest that they were in before. There has been a change of political administration, of government, which may be good, bad or indifferent, worth dying for—or dying to resist—but there is not, properly speaking, a change of ownership.

When Britain entered upon what so many Englishmen regarded as an utterly unjust and unnecessary war against the Boers, foreign observers commented usually that 'Britain was tempted by the gold mines.' But not six pennyworth of mining shares were transferred as the result of the change of government which took place at the end of the War. And to-day, of course, the British Government has no sort of control over the mines, the Acts of the British House of Commons having no validity in the South African Union.

These are not academic distinctions prompted by pedantry; they go to the very root of things when we begin to discuss cures for our troubles. The difficulties in connection with raw materials and the utilisation of the world's resources for man's welfare are real and great enough in any case. It is of the utmost importance not to add to those difficulties. A problem already refractory enough must not be made altogether insoluble by complications which are gratuitous and which a little clarity of thought and care in the use of words would avoid.

So I anticipate your questions: If colonies are of such little value, why have we become such large possessors of them and why are we so hesitant about giving them up? Why not settle the matter out of hand by passing over worthless and expensive possessions to those who believe they need them, and believe they could make good use of them? Would it not be a very cheap contribution to peace?

The reply to which is first that we *are* 'giving them up,' that most of what we call the Empire has already gone; secondly, that though possession as such may be no advantage to us, possession and misuse of these territories by others may be a very distinct disadvantage; thirdly, that even if piratical methods of acquisition were in some degree feasible in the seventeenth or eighteenth century, these would certainly not work successfully in the twentieth.

Let us take these three points in order.

First by far the greater part of our Empire has already been surrendered to the only people to whom ultimately it ought to be surrendered, the people who live there. You do not realise how true that is; indeed many of our people do not. But it is amazingly true.

To understand how true, and why the thing has come about is to realise how invalid are those analogies you draw between the development of the British Empire, out of which the United States has grown, and the destiny which you propose for the Third Reich.

The really significant thing about what you call the British Empire is that it has ceased to be an empire; that Britain has been getting farther and farther away from the kind of thing which you propose, the domination, political and economic, of a number of subject States by the power of an Imperial centre, with policies directed from that centre.

Such an imperial conception is fantastically at variance with the realities of the British Commonwealth. The significant historical process of that Commonwealth for nearly a century has been a process of both economic and political de-imperialisation, not I beg you to believe, because the British suddenly became philanthropic or altruistic, but because the forces of the modern world run counter to the imperial method. Imperialism is economically out of date. Economic direction from an imperial centre was, of course, the method of the seventeenth and eighteenth centuries alike in the case of Britain, Spain, Holland and Portugal. What happened? Spain persisted along that line. She was not enriched, and her Empire came to an end. Portugal retains but vestiges. Holland followed broadly the line adopted by Britain. The loss of the American colonies at the end of the eighteenth century may have predisposed Britain to the new policy. Be that as it may, there began in the nineteenth century a surrender by Britain—in the end for the greater part of her possessions, a complete surrender—of her imperial authority, whether in the political or the economic field. It is so complete to-day that the Imperial Government has no more authority in, say, Canada, than the Canadian Government has in England or Scotland. Indeed the relationship is now so defined by Statute. The British Parliament has now no more authority in Quebec or New South Wales than it has in Ohio or Bavaria. The nations of the Commonwealth may meet in Ottawa and make bargains, economic or political, as the Scandinavian nations may meet in Oslo and do the same thing. But the nations meeting at Ottawa are as independent as the nations meeting at Oslo. Britain can no more command at Ottawa than she could command at Brussels or Washington. And if you say that that is only true of the Dominions, I would point out that it is very nearly as true of India, and will before long be quite as true; and that much of what is now the dependent Empire is steadily making its way towards Dominion status.

It is true that of recent years there has been deviation from this line, a tendency to return to the older eighteenth-century conception of empire. But so far as what remains of the Empire, the non-self-governing territory is concerned, Britain would still, given reciprocity, without any sort of doubt be prepared to stand for the policy of the

Colonial Open Door, equality of right, international guarantees. That is the civilised, hopeful, progressive line. And you ask us, by virtue of the conditions you attach to the return of the colonies, to abandon it and acquiesce in a general reversion to the competing economic imperialism of the older type.

Let us be clear as to this issue. We (and by 'we' I mean the progressively minded in England who want agreement with you on a basis of real equality of right) say to you: Neither we nor you shall 'own' colonies as imperial territory at all. There shall be either self-government as in Canada, or the Philippines, and to-morrow in India, or an international regimen in which the whole world shall be economically equal. That you will not have. You insist that your sovereignty shall be completely unqualified by international obligation, or any sort of subscription or allegiance to an international authority.

If we retained the colonies for the purpose of closing them against you, your case would be a strong one. But we retain them only so long as that is necessary in order that you should not close them against us. Prove to us that you are prepared to accept internationalisation, and they shall be yours as much as they are ours. You are certainly entitled to say to us: 'If your line is equality of opportunity it should apply not merely to ex-German colonies but to all British colonies.' But you do not stand for the open door all round in colonies. You demand the right to close your colonies against us in return for our right to close ours against you.

You are entitled to say that our professions of economic equality are a sham, to ask for guarantees; and in so doing you would have the whole-hearted support of all that element in Britain which is pro-League as well as of that element which until a few years since was blamed as unpatriotically pro-German and is now blamed as anti-German. But you do not ask for the surrender by Britain of her right to impose preferential tariffs, and exclusions in the non-self-governing empire; you ask to have the right to impose such tariffs and exclusions in an empire of your own—an empire, that is to say, from which we should be excluded, not admitted freely as we offer to admit you freely to ours. You do not ask for guarantees of economic internationalism, of real equality of economic right. You ask for the abandonment of efforts towards economic internationalism, and the substitution for them of an effort to establish the world in its contact with colonial territory, on a basis of economic nationalism.[1] You ask us, not to go forward, farther away from the economic competitions which have done so much to produce war in the past, but to go back to old and still worse conditions which would make war inevitable.

Meanwhile, as an illustration of the point I would drive home, note this. If economic nationalism or imperial self-sufficiency is to be the future basis, then naturally we are going to keep all the colonies we can. For we shall need them. For something like ninety per cent of that overseas trade upon which we are so vitally dependent is with territories, foreign or Dominion, to which we are unable to dictate in a fiscal sense. If that ninety per cent of our trade is to become more and more difficult owing to ever-increasing nationalist barriers, then

[1] The Reichstag speech of the German Chancellor of February 20th, 1938, is a franker expression of the German foreign policy outlined in his *Mein Kampf* than any speech of Herr Hitler since he assumed power. The statement on Colonies is given in *Der Angriff* of February 21st as follows:

'Our economic position (Herr Hitler said) is a difficult one, not because National-Socialism is at the helm, but because 140 people must live on a square kilometre; because we are not in possession of those great, natural resources enjoyed by other people; because, above all, we have a scarcity of fertile soil.

'If Great Britain should suddenly dissolve to-day and England become dependent solely on her own territory, then the people there would perhaps have more understanding of the seriousness of the economic tasks which confront us. If a nation which commands no gold reserves and no foreign exchange—not because National-Socialism reigns, but because the Parliamentary democratic State was exploited for fifteen years by a world hungry after loot—if, in other words, a nation which must feed 140 people to the square kilometre and has no colonial rounding-off, if a nation which lacks numerous raw materials and is not willing to live an illusory life through credits, reduces the number of its unemployed in five years to nil and improves its standard of living, then all those should remain silent who, in spite of great economic advantages, scarcely succeed in solving their own unemployment problems.

'No matter what we may achieve by increasing the German production, all this cannot remove the impossible nature of the space allotted to Germany.

'The claim for German colonial possessions will, therefore, be voiced from year to year with increasing vigour, possessions which Germany did not take away from other countries and which to-day are virtually of no value to these Powers but appear indispensable for our own people.

'I should like to turn here against the hope that such claims can be averted by granting credits. We do not want credits, but a foundation to live which enables us to secure national existence by our own industriousness. Above all, we do not wish for naïve assurances that we shall be permitted to buy what we need. We regret such statements once and for all; they are regarded in our country as nothing but sheer mockery.

'There exists no recipe in world economics which can offer a full substitute for the possibility of an intensive economic system within a territory having the same currency.'

we shall have to cling like leeches to every square yard of that ten per cent of our trade which is 'imperial' in any true sense, resting, that is, upon preferences or monopolies imposed by an imperial centre, hoping that it may be developed as a counterpoise to the exclusions we should be facing elsewhere.

I repeat therefore that to transfer colonies to you on the understanding that you have the right to impose such exclusions and monopolies as you saw fit, reverting to the older type of colonial empire, would not be a contribution to peace, or even appeasement, but a reversal of the tendency towards international co-operation and equality of right by splitting the existing imperialisms into still more imperialisms, a decisive step backwards, intensifying all the evils which have made for war in the past; not a step forward towards a workable economic internationalism.

I come to a somewhat wider aspect of your case.

You draw certain parallels between the Pan-Germanism of to-day and British overseas expansion in the seventeenth and eighteenth centuries. I suggest that your analogy involves a grave misconception of the nature and role of the British Empire to-day, and a misapprehension almost as complete of what really happened at earlier stages of the Empire's growth. And even if the picture you draw of Britain's past were true—which it is not—it is completely fallacious to assume that because a given method worked in the infancy of our society it would work at a later stage.

Society, after all, is a living and growing thing. Because at seven years of age or thereabouts a child sheds its teeth and grows others, we should not argue that people ought every seven years to have new teeth, and that failing their appearance existing teeth should be extracted to enable the new ones to grow. It is the nature of the argument you have employed, even assuming your picture of the past to be mainly a true one.

The implication or suggestion throughout is that because a particular political method was, or may have been, followed in the sixteenth century in one set of conditions, therefore the same methods can justifiably and as practical statesmanship be followed in the twentieth century in an entirely different set of conditions. Such a suggestion does indeed ignore reality.

I have shown that in fact the British Empire is being brought to an end, de-imperialised, resolved into a commonwealth of independent States. Yet the British are supposed to be the most successful empire builders of history, commercially the most astute, with the keenest eye to profit. And that is what has happened. Do you suppose it would have happened if the eighteenth century method of imposing economic rule from an imperial centre for the benefit of that centre had been workable? I suggest it is neither necessary nor feasible nor justifiable to attempt in the twentieth century in this field what may have been done in the past. And even if it were, the whole purpose of politics is so to improve our society that we may get rid of old evils like those of piratical imperialism; to replace bad methods by better. This must be done unless we are for ever to cling to the faults of childhood—and make an adult civilisation possible.

But in fact you do not in the least propose to follow the methods by which the British Empire and the United States grew up. You propose something which in its most vital elements is the very opposite of that method. You have outlined a programme. You propose to impose your power upon lesser States, to direct their fiscal policies from an imperial centre; to bring their economic activities within the sphere of your centralised planning; to secure unity of policy by the method of Prussia in the old German Confederation; to establish therein the dominance of one particular racial group; to discourage parliamentary institutions, or democratic discussion, or any public spirit based upon anything but unquestioning acceptance of the major States dictation. (It is extremely doubtful indeed, whether, given the conditions at the centre, you could afford to tolerate in any satellite State the existence of sanctuaries or refuges from the repressions— Lutheran, Catholic or Jewish—which you have already initiated.)

But all this is in every particular in the flattest contradiction with the policy and the methods by which for the greater part the Anglo-Saxon world has been built up.

When you cite the piracies of the Drakes, Raleighs, Frobishers, Hawkinses or even Clives, as the type of effort which laid the foundation of the British Empire and the Anglo-Saxon New World, you miss, if I may say so, the heart and essence of it all. You seem to read history through the Boy's Book of Brave Adventure.

Portugal and Spain had that type of pirate adventurer too, in plenty, and of bigger stature. But they did not give the world a United States or a British Commonwealth. I don't disparage what

Drake and his fellow-pirates did, but even their generation was too wise to believe that power, action, the energy of dynamic individuals, could be made the alternative to self government and parliamentary rule for an expanding people. What the founders of the British Empire did was to make power won by the Drakes the instrument by which self government, parliamentary government, could be extended. When the Colony of Jamestown, established purely by individual settlers, had reached about a thousand souls in 1619, a governor was sent out from the Home Government. What were his instructions? They were to avoid all attempts at martial law and to summon an assembly in which the elected representatives of the people should make 'such laws as might by them be thought good and profitable.' That is how the new Anglo-Saxon nations were founded. Do you propose to imitate the method? You disparage and deride it as gabble and absurdity.

I would remind you of this: the tiny Jamestown Colony, even when it numbered a thousand or so persons, insisted upon the reestablishment of their Assembly when the King threatened it, and also the royal dissolution of the company which had backed it. That kind of process—which was broadly the process of all the American colonies a century and a half before the War of Independence—was not 'establishing an empire,' it was establishing a series of democracies which repudiated empire.

Let me read what Adams, in his *Epic of America*, says of the beginnings of the United States. Here it is:

'The Virginians had been granted the right to make their own local laws by the King himself, but these northern settlers had come without charter or written right. The novel situation of being free from all laws whatever faced the pilgrims even before they landed from the *Mayflower*, and there were some unruly members in the mixed company. There was no one set over them to govern them. Some government was needful. It was clear that they must therefore govern themselves; and, impelled by the simple logic of their situation, they drew up a compact which all signed, agreeing that they would "submit to such government and governors as they should by common consent agree to make and choose." Simple as were both the logic and the document, the decision was peculiarly English, and in time to come was to be characteristically American also. Those who signed had no intention of creating a "democracy" or of changing any government in the world. They simply avoided the possible dangers of anarchy or an iron dictator by agreeing to abide by the expressed *common* will. Simple as it was, no group of men other than English at that period would have chosen the same solution; and it was the solution which was to occur over and over again in a thousand situations in the later history of the country.'

From the outset those colonial territories accepted very little control from the Home Government, and in a relatively short period refused to accept any at all. It is to this element of self government that we must look as explaining not only the United States, but the nations of the Commonwealth. After the experience with the thirteen American colonies Britain accepted it as a basic principle of what we call the Empire, that the new communities should rapidly cut themselves loose from Home control, should, if they liked, adopt political or fiscal principles which were not at all those of the mother-country. Thus for half a century we had highly Protectionist British Dominions imposing stiff tariffs against a Free Trade Britain. Far from Britain planning economically from London, and organising the Empire as an economic unit, it was the very thing Britain had learned she must never attempt to do. Even India, though not yet at Dominion status, possesses and exercises pretty ruthlessly in some cases her right to erect tariffs against Britain, to the very serious detriment of certain British industries. So with Ireland. So with the Boer territories which, conquered by the sword, were given their independence, had their country truly returned to them, within a decade.

Britain 'imposes' nothing on these Dominions—neither tariffs, nor laws, nor forms of government, nor acquiescence in political principles; nor culture, nor language, nor religion. There may be a French theocracy in Quebec, a Hindu or Mohammedan State in the Indies, an Erse-speaking republic in Ireland, Dutch speech and law in the Transvaal, and tariffs and economic policies hostile to Britain everywhere.

When, therefore, you say you propose to do what Britain has done, do you in fact propose to do those things, that sort of thing, to do anything like it? You propose to do the exact contrary. And in following the contrary line I would submit certain comparisons for your consideration.

You yourself have implied that as between the quality of life and government in Latin and English America there lies a whole world of difference, and have expressed strong preference for the Anglo-Saxon achievement.

Well, please note how that difference is related to this 'parliamentary gabble' and 'democratic disorder' which you disparage.

On the morrow of Independence there were in what is now the United States thirteen separate governments—parliamentary and democratic governments. For purposes of security and peaceful development they had to federate or amalgamate in some way. Think of it. Thirteen separate talking shops, thirteen States run by 'gabbling parliamentarians,' States often animated by strong local prejudices. They were faced by the supremely difficult task of federation. That task was to be achieved by co-operation or not at all. There was no one State amongst them so much more powerful than the rest that it could impose federation on the others. It was impossible to apply the method which Prussia has applied within the German congeries of States. There had been no totalitarian discipline; no management of the mind of the people by a dictator; no governmental authority anywhere over political or religious or economic doctrine. There was a military leader with most limited powers, in many spheres with none. To get things done even for the carrying on of war he had to argue and argue and argue. It was a situation which any Fascist or Nazi of to-day would have described as Bedlam itself; a situation, he would have said, impossible of remedy save by the totalitarian methods of dictatorship. But the whole instinct and training of the people of those States was bitterly opposed to any such method. Wherever such methods appeared they were resented. People everywhere had a deep, ineradicable, belief in the political doctrine which you disparage so strongly and are out to destroy.

They applied that doctrine you deride, and the result was the greatest federation, the most powerful nation, the most successful society, so far as welfare is concerned, even when all the defects and failures have been counted, that the history of the world has ever known. When every allowance has been made, that statement remains true.

Very often the diversity of which I have spoken works very badly; its practical results are sometimes exceedingly mischievous. But it expresses, and develops a spirit—the Greek spirit if you like—without which there can be no free government, no free civilisation. It is at once the spirit of independence and the spirit of compromise and tolerance, the spirit which says:

'I don't agree with you, but I'm not infallible, so I shall not force you to accept my view, and you, of course, will not force me to accept yours.

But as we both have to use the same road we must agree both to go to the left or both to go to the right. I'll accept majority decision even if it goes against me until such time as I can persuade the majority I'm right.'

That process of persuasion, the 'parliamentary gabble' that you hold in such contempt, even for the superior Nordic German, is tiresome enough, patience trying enough, heaven knows, (the views of the man who is stupid enough to disagree with you are naturally 'gabble'), but it is the price we pay for the development of political judgment. Without it you get, finally, the incredible things in Moscow to which you have referred. This thing of judgment—social gumption as I once heard it described—can only come by practice. Authoritarian learning won't give it; science won't give it. A good billiard player employs the science of dynamics; but no man could play billiards merely by knowing the science of dynamics, and some of the best billiard players have never heard of it. The American farmers and country gentlemen who laid the foundations of the United States had few books on political science, but they had had much political discussion; their judgment had been formed by 'practice.'

No such practice had entered into the formation of the Spanish American Republics, and we find there a history very different from that of the United States.

Let us turn to that very different history of the Spanish colonies south of the Mexican border—fewer in number, and, to that extent, with a less difficult task. Like the English colonies, they had a common language, a common cultural background, and, in addition as an element of unity, an immensely powerful Church exercising its authority unquestioningly throughout the whole. But the training of those colonies had been in a sense totalitarian, they had lived under what was, in fact, a system of political dictatorship. Their whole economic structure was planned and laid down by Imperial Spain, and imposed by the power of that Empire. The people were obedient to the commands given; seldom questioned those commands; were content to be governed by laws made, as in the Fascist and Totalitarian States of to-day, by an authority outside themselves which they could not question or control.

Very well. What happened, when these colonies faced the same problem that the English colonies had faced, the problem of federation? They were never able to achieve it. What had been, in one instance, one Spanish province, broke up into six or seven separate States, which have, with variations, remained separate States ever since, fearing each other, arming against each other. Similarly indeed in most of the Hispaño-American area. If you want a real example of Balkanisation, political disorder, hateful tyranny, dreadful bloodshed, poverty, utter breakdown of society, examine with some realism the nineteenth-century history of Mexico, Guatemala, San Salvador, Costa Rica, Venezuela, Colombia—to mention no others.

In order to establish themselves after their independence, they applied the methods of military dictatorship. In a sense they had to apply it since they had had no training in parliamentary government, self government, democratic co-operation. They applied the method of military dictatorship logically. Military dictatorship was their first and last resort. Their more dynamic citizens were usually on the look-out for chances of becoming at least a local Mussolini. And there were chances. If a State can be captured by an armed political party in the Fascist manner, the prospect becomes very attractive to men whose tradition prompts them to admire violence and 'to think with their blood.' Dictatorship may for some time show a certain external order, as it did in the Spanish Empire. Spanish America lived for three centuries without revolution or much civil war. But the moment order broke at all, it snapped so completely that there was for nearly a hundred years in Spanish America little else but revolution, civil war, bloodshed. And that arose because the principle of dictatorship, the rightness of capturing a State by an armed party over-ruling the constitution by force, was accepted as a sound political method. But it occurred to more than one bold political buccaneer that he would make a pretty good dictator. Two could play at that game. Twenty played at it; two hundred played at it, and continue to play.

After all, if you want to judge of the long term effect of Dictatorship, Latin America, where Dictators have monopolised politics for a century, is not a bad place to study in this connection. Let me read what Ernest Hamblock in his book[1] on the subject, says:

'Their domination was rooted in evil. It has produced bloodshed and tortured imprisonments, pillage, and banishment, murder, foul intrigue, and personal and political corruption—for which democracy is blamed!

'It was perhaps inevitable that the Strong Men should arise. They were

[1] *His Majesty the President* (Methuen).

the product of disorders that were evil; but they themselves cannot be classed—at the best—as anything higher than necessary evils. To elevate their status to the dignity of a system worthy to be perpetuated, and to bolster up that pretention by appealing to the material progress often achieved under their blood-stained rule, is illogical, apart from any moral considerations. For the doctrine of the infallibility of the One Man Show has this defect. The whole structure collapses directly the Man of the Moment disappears. Whereupon the strongest of the Lords-in-Waiting— like the Jews of old—sword in one hand and trowel in the other, puts up another erection on the same plan as the old one. All these successive, gaudily-painted contraptions of despotism—gilded with the savings of foreign lenders and plastered with the blood of nationals—are built upon the sand: the shifting sand of terrorism and the shifty sand of expediency. They have no political basis, except that of the forceful implantation of personal rule—mild or terrorist, according to personal whim or circumstances.'

He rejects altogether the view that the 'Latin temperament' makes dictatorship a necessity.

'It is often alleged that despotic forms of government are heroic measures imposed by dire necessity, and that it is not a question of justifying them either legally or morally. But that is mere casuistry. The alleged necessity is not a political necessity at all. Police intervention is often a public necessity; but government by policemen is no polity. The real necessity for those in power—if they are sincere in their protestations of performing a national task—is to admit that they are not supermen, and that they require the active co-operation of every citizen in that task. But this is not what happens. The people lazily hand their rulers irrevocable powers of attorney, or tamely submit to such powers being arrogated by force.'

He adds, however:

'So do galley slaves "under the persuasive tongue of the overseer's lash! The panting rowers have not even the right to turn round and try and discern in what direction they are propelling the ship, much less offer any observations on the course chosen! If the people like being chained, back to front, to the rowing bench, as a patriotic manifestation of discipline and order, that, of course, is their own affair." But slavery, even if self-imposed is not ordered discipline, which consists, not in slavish obedience to orders, but in intelligent collaboration in formulating as well as in obeying them. Even unquestioning obedience implies the right to question. The blind servility of a people under despotic rule is not a tribute to their perspicacious obedience, but merely proof of the truth of the proverb that none are so blind as those who will not see. The blindness is either an insult to their intelligence, or a demonstration of its absence.'

Because the passage is written by a man who knows those countries where dictatorship has been in action not five or fifteen or twenty years but a hundred, I cannot refrain from reading you this passage:

'When the man-in-the-street in England sees an exotic Italo-Britannic Fylfot squad marching along under its cabalistic flags, he should make no mistake as to whither those masquerading harriers are hurrying. They are marching—perhaps unwittingly—towards the civic ideal of slavish barrack-yard obedience to brutal barrack-yard truculence, of a kind that transformed Germany from the home of enlightened philosophical speculation into the grim laboratory of doctrinal philistinism which, with diabolic cleverness, staged a bloody murder at Serajevo in order to precipitate a world war—by proxy. They are—perhaps unconsciously—paying lip-service to a régime which could have a liberal patriot like Matteoti battered to death for having had the courage to speak boldly in the name of liberty in the Italian Parliament. They are—in ignorance no doubt—paving the way for the introduction into Great Britain of Latin American forms of presidential dictatorship, the highest exponents of which were Don Juan Manuel Rosas, the blue-eyed Nietzschean superman, whose praetorians so skilfully slit the throats and stomachs of Argentine citizens in the sacred name of national unity, and the taciturn Doctor Francia, the demi-god of Paraguay, whose hepatic troubles yielded only to the treat of peeping through the shutters of his Palace window at Asuncion, before breakfast, and seeing some political prisoner (whose back had already been finely laced with five hundred lashes in the Paraguayan "Chamber of Truth") fall before the rifles of a firing squad. British Fascists are lightheartedly betraying civilisation, as they strut, in their black-shirted pride to the Sanctification of the Mailed Fist, the Beatification of Tom Thumb, and the eventual constitutional Canonisation of both.'

Time alone can show whether, and in what way, that is going to happen to you as your power is extended into and over non-German States. True, Germans are not Spaniards, nor Indo-Iberians, and have a very different background of discipline and culture. But I am not sure that that fact does not make the prospect even darker.

Examine for a moment how the Fascist phenomenon is related to certain well-recognised and very powerful forces in human nature and human society, and then tell me whether we can expect Fascist foreign policy to be anything but a duplication in international affairs of its home policy—rooted in the same methods, the same political philosophy, the same way of life, the same temperamental impulses.

I have drawn the parallel between the Spanish and English experiences in America because, not only does that experience, but all experience, show that political wisdom and peace can only come if

certain indispensable conditions are fulfilled and certain habits cultivated. Peace depends on justice. But it is not easy to know what
is justice—fair and right as between the contending views of rival
parties. (Perhaps the most appallingly mischievous of all the popular
fallacies and untruths is that contained in the repeated assertion that
'all of us can distinguish between simple right and simple wrong.')
Only by a disposition of each to hear the views of the other can we
ever get even an approximation to a just verdict, any hope of knowing what *is* justice.

But this disposition to consider the views of the other party is not
'natural.' It is the result of slow and laborious cultivation; impossible without some form of training in contradictory discussion, and
can never be possessed by those who have been encouraged to 'think
with their blood,' to depend upon sheer instinct unguided by any
sense of responsibility to disciplined intelligence, objective truth. The
'natural' thing is not to listen to him who has the insufferable impudence to disagree with us, but to give him a sock on the jaw;
and, if he still persists, to knock him out, put him in jail if we have the
power, apply the thumb screw, the rack, the *auto-da-fé*. This is not
fantasy, mere vague generalisation in psychology. It is history; a history which is simply littered with sickening stories of the infamies
perpetrated by men often passionately convinced that they were right;
sure that they were performing a painful duty, destroying the enemies
of the fatherland, or of society, who would undermine the one true
doctrine and so the foundations of all morality. The Torquemadas
have usually been convinced beyond all question that they were doing
the will of God.

Very slowly the West had come to recognise that toleration for
contrary views, 'government by discussion,' was the condition *sine
qua non* of any dependable political (or for that matter, moral) judgment or wisdom. Think what would happen in the laboratory or in
technology if men were taught in those spheres to 'think with their
blood.'

It is vital to distinguish in this matter between democracy and
liberalism. Democracy is not indispensable to good government, but
liberalism is. A small oligarchy, applying to their own discussions the
principles of toleration for contrary views, the need of hearing the
other side, of developing in some degree the inductive method and
the objective habit, applying, in a word, the scientific spirit to politics,

have given the world admirable civilisations. The Roman and the Greek oligarchy did; the agrarian oligarchy—very disputative and argumentative—which ruled England in the seventeenth and eighteenth centuries did; the American colonists, so much of the same temper, did. (The Greek spirit which explains so much of Anglo-Saxon political success has animated many peoples other than the Nordic.) Those Greek, or Roman, or eighteenth-century communities were not democratic, or only very partially so; but they were liberal in the philosophic sense. Democracy was not necessary; liberalism was.

And you—Fascists in general—are much more the enemy of liberalism than of democracy. Indeed, you are democratic in the sense of being demagogic, of relying so much on mob passion. You are democratic in the way that a lynching party is 'democratic,' much more obedient to public passion than is a court of law, tied down to codes, procedures, argument, reason.

What is the essence of the Fascist and Nazi process?

A Leader, a Chief—dominating, self-willed, ruthless, clamouring for 'action,' that is to say, the violent assertion of his own views as against those of others; impatient of law or constitutional order, forms, and attaches to himself a party of like-minded fanatical, ruthless and intolerant men. Experience shows that such a party, or junta, soon becomes ready to use assassination, terrorist plots, false accusation, and the Chief to exploit every demagogic trick, every popular fallacy and weakness, every prejudice, every hate, every envy, every malice, on which he can lay his hand or tongue. (If you deem that an over-statement, just recall for a moment incidents which marked not only the beginnings of the Fascist and Nazi Revolutions, but continue to mark the regimen whether in Japan, in Italy, or in Germany.)

But this self-will, this dislike of the restraint of law or constitutionalism, the intolerance of others' views, the impatience at the discussion of any such views, the preference instead of quick and violent assertion of superior Power, cannot possibly stop at the frontier. It must, in the very nature of the regimen and the temperamental and material forces which underlie it, also be applied in your contacts with other nations. Why not? If you are prepared to use the ruthless force of an armed party with your own people, to impose your own views by any sort of terror upon your own countrymen, why should you hesitate to employ the same methods as against mere foreigners, scruple about whom nationalist passion can so easily smother? Indeed, the thing is happening on an appalling and ever-increasing scale already. Need one mention Austria, Spain, China? Spain with its Italian armies and German arms, the pirate ships, or the vast quantities of Italian and German arms now being unearthed in France, the intrigues in Northern Africa, in Palestine; to say nothing whatever of the kind of thing which the assassination of Dollfuss or the Rosselli Brothers suggests.

You say you stand by Nationalism—the right of each people to its own form of government without interference from foreigners, whether, as one of your people put it, 'they sit in Geneva or come from Jerusalem.' You reject the League or any other form of internationalism because the nationalist doctrine under which each shall mind his own business is both more sound and more practical.

So be it. How have you applied this nationalist doctrine under which each is to attend to his own business and all to be free from foreign interference? In a few brief years your nationalist regimen reveals a degree of interferences in the affairs of other States more sweeping, more brutal in its disregard of all and any morality, more cynical in its tongue-in-the-cheek disavowals, more cruel in its disregard of human life and suffering, than anything modern history can show. A Dictator in one breath announces that he will not tolerate the slightest interferences by outsiders whether seated in Geneva or elsewhere in the affairs of his State, and in the next breath proclaims to the world at large that he will not tolerate anywhere in the Mediterranean a Bolshevist State—he (having sent his forces against an established government which did not contain a single Communist or a single Socialist) to be judge of what Bolshevism is. On Monday he accepts solemnly the principle of non-intervention, gives by implication his promises not to intervene, and on Tuesday publicly congratulates his armies in Spain and proclaims his intention of destroying a government which has never in any slightest respect attacked or injured Italy—or Germany.

With all your worship of theories, political principles have ceased to have meaning for you. You have repeatedly repudiated the right of one nation to interfere in the government of another. Yet you do it from one day to another. You have in effect announced that Spain shall only have such government as the Führer approves. What becomes then of your principle of nationalism? You make it subject per-

haps to another principle, that Communism is the enemy? But again
the government which you and Italy set out to destroy in Spain did
not contain a single Communist. And if the principle upon which you
have acted in Spain is sound, you are certainly as entitled to apply it
to France where the influence of organised Communism is very great,
where Socialists co-operate in the government and where a Socialist
Jew has been Prime Minister and is likely to be again. You say the
Spanish Government was tolerating Communists, refusing to suppress
them; and that on that ground you were entitled to repudiate your
principle of Nationalism. But, again, exactly the same charge lies as
against the French Government for they too tolerate Communists. So,
if your actions go for anything, you have asserted the right to destroy
any government which permits the preaching of doctrines you deem
mischievous. Well, the British Government permits the dissemination of doctrines which in Germany would send their exponent to a
concentration camp. Would you be prepared to make the fact ground
for suppressing the British Government by means of aid to a Fascist
Party in Britain—as your government has certainly aided Nazi parties
in countries outside Germany? Communists are not the only enemies
for you. There are the Jews. And Britain not only tolerates Jews, she
proposes to establish a Jewish State which will doubtless permit its
subjects to examine, discuss, preach any economic or political doctrine it chooses. It is quite certain that the government of this new
Jewish State will—like the British, and the French and the Spanish—
tolerate Communist parties, who will try to obtain a majority in their
Council or Parliament. Would that in the view of the Führer or his
colleague in Rome constitute the 'danger of a Bolshevist Government
in the Mediterranean,' which we have been told, your two governments will not permit? Would you find any moral obstacle at all to
doing in Paris or London what you have done in Guernica, Valencia,
Barcelona, Madrid, providing 'the larger interest of the Fatherland'
demanded it? After all, the Basques and the Catalans are not so great
an obstacle as is the British Empire to the growth of your power in
Europe. Why should we British, who, unlike the Spaniards, have
recently been your armed enemies, be better treated? Or better treated
than the race from which we continue to take our whole religious
foundations and literature—the race of Jesus Christ and the Virgin
Mary?

On a thousand occasions your spokesmen have proclaimed with

great pride, and as an expression of the supremest patriotism, that you know one law only: The safety, growth, power and might of the German folk, their interests and right as interpreted by the Führer.[1] That overrides everything else whatsoever, all other law, all other morality, all bargains, all contracts. To that one supreme rule of the Führer's interpretation of Germany's interests, all international law or usage, the law of ancient churches, or creeds, Catholic, Lutheran, Christian, Hebraic, must yield. And the German conscience is now so conditioned that when, under that one supreme law, the Führer or his colleagues resort, as on that fateful June night, to methods which the modern world had come to believe were confined to the Al Capones, to the Dillingers, to the Chicago gangsters, it is all accepted without questions—without murmur.

This is the policy on behalf of which you ask our aid and our alliance, or, at the very least, our acquiescence, even though its unfettered pursuit (which acquiescence implies) may give you preponderant power over us; may create a situation in which our political independence, the security of Britain and young democracies scattered over the world, shall be at the mercy of your good judgment, your discretion and that of your Italian and Japanese allies. You imply that some affinity of 'blood' makes it safe for us to place ourselves, our institutions and social and political preferences within your power.

Do you expect us to believe it—permanently?

You say—by the event, by what you do added to what you say—something like this:

'Let us be friends; let us make a bargain. Allow us, by eliminating States that might later be your allies, to be so powerful in relation to yourself that we could at any moment impose our will upon you.

---

[1] In his speech of February 20th the Führer said:

'I cannot allow our natural claims to be coupled with political business.' While pledging that Germany would impose upon itself 'wise moderation in its interests and demands,' he made clear that the Reich would be the sole judge of the justice of its own claims and would never again subject itself to the restraints and direction of an international institution like the League of Nations. Instead of the League, the primary instrument of German diplomacy will be the Rome-Berlin axis as fortified by the anti-Communist Pact to which Japan is also a party. The Führer expressed his earnest wish to see co-operation with Italy and Japan 'more and more extended.' Mussolini was praised for his defiance of Geneva, and Japan was hailed as the bulwark against communism in the Far East. As a further gesture towards Tokyo, he specifically disclaimed territorial ambitions in the Far East or any desire to re-acquire the former German colonial possessions now held under mandate by Japan.

In return we will promise to respect your rights, to treat you fairly and justly.'

When you come to us with that proposal is it altogether irrelevant for us to inquire what you mean by fair treatment and justice in your relations with others, since it is *your* view of those things backed by your own preponderant power which you ask us to accept? (You see you reject, in your foreign relations, the idea of umpire, third-party decision, arbitration.) Germany, your Führer has so often told us, will not make herself subject to the judgment of foreigners, or any foreign tribunal. 'Germany alone shall be judge of Germany's rights.' In the circumstances you propose, that means that Germany will also be judge of ours.

So, far from your views of right and justice being no concern of ours, they are precisely the things upon which our whole future may depend. It is true that our Garvins and others who want an understanding with you, say that the German theory of political morality does not concern us. That might conceivably be true if they and you did not propose to enter into a political contract. But as they and you do, the statement is precisely equivalent to saying:

'Since Germany announces that she will keep no bargain when she deems that it is to her interest to break it, let us make a bargain with her and trust to it.'

An insulting distortion of German doctrine? But it is textually what your authorised spokesmen (all public spokesmen in Germany are exponents of German doctrine or on the road to a concentration camp) daily go on proclaiming. Only they put the statement in a context which they are careful to avoid, but which is for us the vital context. Your spokesmen have said on a thousand occasions that there is one supreme consideration which, with Germans, must outweigh all others whatsoever, even their loyalty to ancient Christian doctrine or Church or the deepest religious conviction. That consideration is the might and power and domination of the German folk and fatherland. When you announce that you are nationalists, insist that all nations should be free from the interference of any authority outside their borders, and then proceed to a degree of interference in, e.g., Spain which is far in excess of anything which the League of Nations would claim the right to do, your conduct is not so inconsistent as it might on the surface appear. For every doctrine you proclaim, every contract which you make, is subject to the one supreme consideration or qualification I have mentioned.

You see I pay the Führer and his colleagues the compliment of complete honesty and sincerity. His friends in England keep arguing—when his writings are cited—that he does not mean what he says. I am not so uncomplimentary. I think he means exactly what he says, namely, that he knows but one law, one morality, one truth: the interest of Germany as he, Adolph Hitler, conceives it.

Well, you may say, do not patriotic Englishmen put first the interests of Great Britain?

Yes, but I would once more call your attention to the very issue we are discussing. The British doctrine, in which the more enlightened Englishmen are at long last really beginning to believe, is that British security can only be achieved and British welfare ensured by the creation of an international order, by international co-operation. Without the keeping of contracts sacredly between nations there *can* be no dependable co-operation. The conditions in which alone Britain can survive cannot be created without the keeping of faith with foreigners. You in Germany do not believe in international co-operation as the basis of your security and welfare; you believe that only by German power, German domination, can Germany be made secure. In demanding preponderance for yourselves you deny—obviously—the same right to others. You do not believe in being partners with other nations, subject to the bond between you. You believe in being masters of other nations, so that there need be no bond but your good pleasure. Under our doctrine there is no conflict between probity and interest. Under your doctrine there is.

Let me summarise the main points of my reply to you, adding a hint as to certain others, thus:

1. Your economic creed of indispensable territorial expansion must lead to war because that form of expansion means that one expands at the cost of some other. There can be no equality of right. It is cannibalistic. If one is fed, the other goes hungry, or is eaten.

2. The grounds upon which the colonial claims are made are mainly fallacious and are sustained by distortion of the simplest facts and figures. When Dr. Schacht talks about colonial raw material being a life and death matter, the German people do not know that Germany drew one-half of one per cent of her raw material from colonies

and that if she could multiply that twenty times, it would not constitute a life and death matter. As to population: They are never reminded that Paris before the War possessed more Germans than all the German colonies put together.

3. But under totalitarianism there are no means by which a fallacy can be exposed if the government desires to sustain it. Indeed the Leader may himself become the very victim of the false propaganda which his machine turns out. The conditions for sound political judgment, even on relatively simple issues, are not present.

4. This bad political judgment is worsened by deliberately inculcated racial hatreds and a new paganism which places the State above truth, fidelity to pledged word, above mercy or compassion.

5. The economic and political cannibalism involved in the expansionist theory is thus rendered acceptable to a whole people by a process of moral conditioning, that is to say the universal inculcation of a creed of fighting, of struggle, of war for ends which may not be examined.

6. The nature alike of the economic and moral doctrines held by the German people is not something which concerns merely Germany. Quite obviously it concerns her neighbours. I may have no mission to reform the cannibal and his morals may be a matter of indifference to me until I happen to come within the range of his cooking pot; and then his morals concern me very much indeed.

IV

THE PSYCHOLOGY OF DICTATORSHIP

We must credit the Dictators with really believing their own doctrines which so many of their apologists in Britain insist that they do not. They will act on those beliefs. We cannot assume that the Dictators' creeds are mere 'flourish,' for even if they themselves did not believe them whole peoples are now being 'conditioned' by all the forces of suggestion contained in modern instruments like a controlled universally read Press, a universally heard wireless, and universally seen cinema, to respond violently to convictions which are never allowed to be questioned, and which are likely, therefore, to have a power of fanaticism comparable to the fanaticism of religions like Islam of the past engaged upon a Holy War. This does not mean that the Dictators are monsters, or the Germans, Italians and Japanese fundamentally different from ourselves, or that we are fundamentally any better. Neither understanding, nor conciliation, nor permanent peace is possible if we gloss over plain meanings, plainly declared beliefs and intentions. These manifestations are not merely capitalist manœuvres. Behind the ponderable material claims lie deep psychic forces. 'Human nature' so often invoked by the 'practical man' includes forces of wild fanaticism we ignore to our peril. The Russian problem.

One or two of our members had pointed out that in almost every one of the public declarations made, whether by Hitler or by Mussolini, there is an emphatic pronouncement in favour of peace. Also, in every one of these declarations there is usually a re-assertion of the doctrines of complete nationalism, repudiation of third-party judgment. The question arose: Are the Dictators 'sincere'?

One of the group essayed an answer to that question. Here is his paper:

The answer to the question is that the Dictators probably *are* sincere; and that if they are not, their peoples are; and that it is precisely this sincerity which constitutes the greatest danger, for we are confronted, not with rational claims that can be satisfied, but with a passionate fanaticism presenting claims which can never be satisfied.

But please note that this is not because the Germans are fundamentally any worse than we are. It only means that they guide their conduct by different doctrines—doctrines which in lesser or greater degree have guided our conduct too at times.

During the War, and for some years after, we divided the peoples of the world into the 'good' nations who had fought for democracy, and freedom, and right, and honour, and peace, and justice; and the 'bad' nations who had plotted against the peace of the world, and whose violence, ambitions, lusts, had launched the Great War upon mankind.

That is not a travesty of how the 1914–24 generation thought. It was the homily that you heard daily. The War had been caused by the wickedness of Germany. This theory of the War's cause was expounded repeatedly by learned professors, editors, publicists, divines. Literally hundreds of books were written to expose and explain Germany's plot against the peace of the world. Not only so; the theory has actually been embodied in the great historical document of the Treaty of Versailles. There it stands to-day, and will stand for all time as a monument to the degree of that generation's understanding of the forces which swept it into the catastrophe; the nature of the forces which govern the conduct of men.

There was, of course, no German plot. The world staggered and stumbled as one of the statesmen most nearly concerned has put it, into war.

If one had to indicate in a phrase the error, the idiocy of that kind of interpretation of events common in the period I am referring to, one would say this: that we then tried to find out *who* was to blame instead of trying to find out *what* was to blame; what policy, what principle of statecraft, what group of ideas lay behind the actions taken.

Of course, we would far rather explain a thing in terms of the wickedness of definite persons than in terms of common human errors. If you can find a villain to explain your troubles you feel very righteous and superior. But if you have to explain events as the result of bad policy, wrong ideas, wrong political or social theories—well, that is a different form of entertainment altogether and apt to give one a headache as well as likely to bring home the fact that we are as much to blame as anyone else. It must be immensely consoling in a distracted world to have the unshaken conviction that all our troubles are due to the Jews, or the Freemasons, or the Communists, or the Pope of Rome.

But I suggest that we are still the victims of this dreadful habit. We assume that if only men are 'good,' sincere, animated by peaceful intention and goodwill, are 'men of principle' that peaceful settlement with them will almost take place of itself.

This too is an effort to save ourselves the trouble of thought, an attempt to make things more easy than they are. Particularly does it bedevil our treatment of the problem of peace. Tens of thousands of honest folk believe that if only nations would be 'good,' play fair, do justice; if only friendliness could be cultivated between them; if only they could be 'brought into human contact,' see more of one another, spend their holidays together, these quarrels would not arise. Well, the Spaniards now waging against each other as cruel a war as any in history have presumably been brought into 'human contact' in the past; as also have the ever-quarrelling Hindoos and Mohammedans; as were the mutually torturing Catholic and heretic. Cannot we keep in mind the fact that the very fiercest quarrels are between those who live in the same street and see each other, or could see each other perhaps, every day of their lives?

As to this idea of keeping the peace if only men were 'sincere' and 'good'—have we really forgotten the wars of religion, the Inquisitions, the fire and sword of Christian and Mohammedan religions, the ferocities of every revolution that ever took place? Do we suggest that the great theologians who gave their approval to the burning of little heretic children, the Reformers who let loose the Massacres and shed oceans of blood in the name of the Brotherhood of man, the Purgers, were just human monsters? They were not monsters. They were fanatics, and fanaticism is not a rare phenomenon in human affairs, it is an extremely common one; it is a fact in human nature; perhaps the most portentous of all facts when we come to problems of government and human relationship.

And the German and Italian airmen who bombed those sleeping cities and disembowelled the school-children and the women in Spain in order to destroy a government which had never lifted a hand against Italy or Germany; the Japanese airmen who month after month do similar things—is the cause of these Satanic abominations the wickedness of the men who do them? Are the men who do them human monsters? We all know that they are not, that they are men just like you and me. And if men like you and me can do these things, we could do them if we found justification in the same theories or principles which animate them. It is the nature of those theories or principles which we must face. The errors, the wrong principles of passionately sincere good men, have done infinitely more of harm to the world, than the acts of bad men acting against a code which they knew to be wrong, crimes which the world had agreed were crimes.

Some similar confusion arises when we ask whether this or that nation 'wants peace.' A nation no more 'wants war' than the Inquisitor wanted *autos-da-fé*, or the Reformer wanted massacres. We often hear people dividing the nations into the 'peace-loving nations' and the others. But the difference between ourselves and Germany (or Italy or Japan) is not that Germany 'believes in' war and we do not. For we are arming, arming enormously. Are we never in any circumstance to use instruments in the feverish construction of which we are coming near to bankrupting ourselves? We are fully determined to use them—for defence. Germany would say exactly the same thing, has said it on a score of occasions. Germany wants peace, says the Führer, but she is determined to defend herself. We want peace, but are determined to defend ourselves. The difference between us then, if difference there is, is in what each respectively means by defence. It is clearly not that one will defend himself and the other refuses so to do.

When we say 'of course we would fight for defence,' we imply that it is quite easy to know when a nation is acting defensively and when aggressively. Is it? The Italian people were quite honestly convinced that they were acting defensively in making war upon Abyssinia who begged again and again and again to have the points Italy raised arbitrated. We British have fought all over the world—literally in almost every country of the world this last few hundred years— every country that is, except one, this country. We are quite sure the wars were defensive. Perhaps they were because 'defence' necessarily means the defence of interests, rights. Is it not possible for two parties honestly to differ? And is it right that we should be the sole judge of what our rights are when someone else takes a different view? Yet this is in fact precisely what we do when we claim the right to judge when we act defensively.

Yet these confusions, so dire and so dangerous are to be found even amongst the best of our writers. Here is Scrutator:

'The only way in which we can master the drift of events is a conversion of the mind of all countries, including Germany, to the view that war can settle nothing, and that a compromise is possible which reconciles the legitimate ambition of Germany with the rights of the newer nations. The danger to peace is not in a cold calculation of its interest by any Power. The danger is in an outburst of sentiment which overrides calculation—in sympathy with a nation's struggles for its freedom, or in anger at the oppression of a bully, in the loyalty which bids democratic nations to stand together or in the superstition that violence can cure violence or end war.'

But does Scrutator really believe it to be a superstition that war or the threat of war can prevent war? Then why is he so ardent an advocate of rearmament? That armament is for the purpose of waging wars, is an intimation to certain foreign States: If you do certain things which we regard as aggression, as injurious, that is, to what we regard as our interests, we shall use these instruments—that is to say, fire off guns, drop bombs, sink ships. If it is utterly useless for us to do those things, if we have decided that such violence is futile, why are we so feverishly creating the tools for doing precisely those things?

If we are to be even moderately honest intellectually in this matter, those are very important truths too often ignored by the friends of peace in the past which must be kept in mind. If the peacemaker is to be effective, he must face sincerely and with the coldest realism the fact that, while nearly everyone—certainly President Roosevelt's ninety per cent, probably even most of the remaining ten per cent— want peace, they also want things incompatible with peace without realising that they are incompatible; and that because of this fact, the line of least resistance for political leaders, the line which will most readily secure them popular support is to follow a policy which, in the end, will make war inevitable. It is not a situation in which 'the people' want peace while their governments for some unexplained reason, want war, but one in which the easiest course for governments to follow, the course for which they can always count upon popular support, is precisely the course that if indefinitely continued must, without doubt, lead to war.

The case is simple enough. Everyone—including a large section of the German people—says quite sincerely and quite genuinely, 'We want peace; peace above everything.' We keep on repeating, 'Britain's greatest interest is peace.' Plainly, we don't believe it; for if we did, if peace really did come before everything, if it were really Britain's greatest interest, we should not have a navy or an army at all. We should say: 'Foreign invasion, or government by foreigners, or the destruction of our trade, are bad. But as we have decided that war is worse still, worse than anything, they decided to place peace above everything, we will accept them rather than create a condition of war by resisting them.' We do not say that. When we say we want peace above everything, we mean above everything except the defence of our rights. We place defence above peace. We do not see it very clearly, and that is not what we say, but it is plainly what we all mean.

But if we do not always realise very clearly the implied qualification which we all make when we declare that we put peace above everything else in international politics; if we make there an assumption which we have not quite faced, we make yet another assumption still more important, still more fundamental, and of which we are still less conscious.

When you point out that it is not quite true that we place peace before everything else, since the very maintenance of our navy and air force means that we would fight for our defence, and that therefore we place defence before peace, you are apt to get the retort:

'Well, of course, we would defend our rights. But that does not make us disturbers of the peace, any more than a man who defends himself against a footpad could be described as a disturber of the peace. As well plead that a householder creates housebreakers by locking his doors and windows, since if he left them open technical housebreaking could not occur.'

(This latter argument was actually used by an eminent man of letters on one occasion.)

The assumption there, of course, is that the question of what are our rights, is as self-evident, as settled, as agreed, as that the silver spoons Mr. John Smith has honestly bought and paid for belong to him and not to Mr. William Sykes. This assumption concerning the agreed and self-evident nature of the differences about which nations fight, begs the whole of the question which constitutes the problem of war.

Wars arise because nations disagree—honestly, sincerely, passionately—as to what their rights in a given quarrel are. Men cannot usually be persuaded to die for what they know to be wrong; nor to give their fortunes, their sons, their happiness in such a cause. The more sincere, the more passionate each side is in believing its own view to be the just and right and honourable one, the greater is the likelihood of war arising out of the dispute.

When educated men say 'Of course we shall defend our rights' and assume thereby that there can be no dispute as to what those rights are, one wonders whether they have spent even an hour in considering with an impartial mind the other side of any dispute in which our country has been involved: the dangerous disputes with America about sea rights, for instance, which led to one war and so very nearly to others; whether they have ever considered both sides of any of the numberless territorial disputes of the Balkans and elsewhere. How is it possible, when going into the pros and cons of these interminable quarrels, to say that right and wrong is as clear as the ownership of the silver spoons which Mr. Sykes would take, that 'national defence' approximates to the action of Mr. John Smith protecting his property with a poker, and that the issues involved are as simple?

If we saw clearly that demand for preponderance of armament 'to defend our national rights' was *not* analogous to the demand of Mr. Smith to resist the burglar, but to the demand of a litigant in a civil action to be made also its judge, then we should see that the competitive arming of the litigants, each convinced in the complete justness of his cause, could only end finally in their 'fighting it out,' and that justice and peace alike demanded that neither litigant should be judge and both have the right to impartial judgment.

We who can look back upon the wars of religion—or look to-day upon the bitterness of some of the religious conflicts of the East— simply cannot understand why men should slaughter each other generation after generation, for tiny doctrinal differences which we find it difficult even to understand; why men should be burned alive because they put a plate of bread in one position instead of another; shaved one part of the head instead of another; ate one kind of meat but regarded the eating of another as deadly sin; or, as sin if eaten on one day of the week instead of another—taboos to some of us as strange and mystifying as the taboos of Polynesia, or of Australian tribes where it is a sin punishable by death for a woman to eat the hindquarters of an animal but quite permissible to eat the forequarters. (The introduction of tinned bully beef brought their social system toppling to the ground.)

It does not seem to occur to us that in our opposing ideologies of Capitalism, Socialism, Communism, Pacifism, Collectivism, Imperialism, Nationalism, we are doing pretty much the same thing to-day and rationalising the doing of it in pretty much the same way as did the old Inquisitors of whom Stalin so forceably reminds one.

The way the educated Inquisitor justified his ferocious punishment of small doctrinal errors was that you must have moral discipline; that if men began to wander on small points they would begin to wander on big; that the uneducated public would be unable to distinguish between the two and the only way to prevent a moral degeneration which would disintegrate all society was to impose a 'rigid party discipline,' and to have no part of the doctrine questioned or discussed.

In reality it was not society or general social needs which the Inquisitor was considering more or less coldly, and the populace resenting heatedly and passionately when both demanded the ruthless repression of heresies. What moved the Inquisitor, plainly, was a deep resentment that any should be guilty of the discourtesy, the impudence, the infamy, of disagreeing with him, of implying that he was wrong, that his doctrines and opinions were challengeable. He would soon teach them. And the enmity gave his life purpose. Here was an enemy. Here once more was a 'cause.' Here was something 'we, the faithful' could fight, hate, make war upon. Once more our great Institution had something real and stirring to do; once more life had meaning, and was good.

Two facts must strike any impartial observer of the young Nazis in Germany or the young Fascists in Italy. The first is their real sincerity, their passion of conviction. To deny the sincerity of these hundreds of thousands of young men is to make all scientific analysis of the phenomena of our time impossible. But if it be silly to deny their sincerity it is sillier still to assert that they have arrived at their hatred of Communism or Liberalism, by any impartial or objective examination of Communism or Liberalism. Their 'convictions' consist in a parrot repetition of incantations the meaning even of which they plainly do not understand. They hate the Communist in the same way that the Catholic peasant of the fifteenth century hated the heretic or both hated witches.

When Britain and America were very near to war over the Venezuelan Boundary incident ('this time,' wrote the young Theodore Roosevelt to his friend Lodge, 'I hope we shall not be defrauded of our war with Britain, for which I nightly pray'), when, that is, President Cleveland declared himself ready in effect to go to war on behalf of the Monroe Doctrine, the late General Horace Porter, at that time American Ambassador in Paris, made a genuine contribution to peace by telling at a public dinner a story which may be a chestnut but worth recalling. A certain very patriotic American was met by a friend who questioned:

'What's this I hear, Jones, about your not believing in the Monroe Doctrine?'

'That story is a wicked libel. I never said I did not believe in the Monroe Doctrine. I do believe in it. Of course I would have us go to war with Britain for it. I would enlist, die on the battlefield for it. What I *did* say was that I didn't know what it meant.'

It is, of course, quite unnecessary to know what our doctrines mean in order to be ready to die for them. Indeed it is nearer to the truth to say that if you are to be ready to die for your doctrine—and to kill others for it—you must on no account know what it means. That only by *not* knowing fully what it means can you create the conditions in which the killing can be done. Those conditions being a cause to serve, a herd to belong to, a doctrine, irreconcilable with some opposing doctrine to defend; an enemy who can be pictured as dangerous and malignant, to feed that psychological hunger for something to hate. Perpetually to feed this hunger seems to be increasingly the main basis of the power of dictators, alike of Left and Right. The doctrines which they proclaim may be completely absurd, and the enemy completely mythical; they will usually provide quite adequate substitutes for any proof that the needs of welfare are being served.

The method is not in the least, of course, the exclusive patent of re-action. On the Left side of the doctrinal frontier we see dictatorship exploiting the same psychological hunger for enmity, for maintaining an object of fear and hatred. It being inexpedient just now in Russia to turn hatred against Capitalist nations whose help may be needed for the purposes of military defence; and anti-semitism hardly serving the end, 'Trotskyite plots' are made to fill the need. Few things suggest more disturbingly the spiritual cousinship of Communist and Nazi than the way in which most Moscow trials suggest the Reichstag fire trials, and the Ogpu the Gestapo.

You recall how a year or two ago a journalist in Paris drove an able and competent Minister to suicide by stories that he had been guilty of cowardice during the War.

It will seem strange to the observer of the future that an intelligent people like the French bourgeoisie, often described as avaricious and money grubbing, should so easily be aroused to passionate hatred of a man like Salengro, who in fact was not serving badly their economic interests while the alleged offence which so stirred them had no relation in any case to his political or economic activities; and stranger still, the way in which, among a highly educated, erudite, 'scientific' people like the German, the most outrageous myths can so easily be made the basis of bitter struggle, war itself. Nordicism, Aryanism, 'non-Aryanism,' the ascription to a tiny minority of Jews of responsibility for most of the troubles that have fallen upon Germany; the ease with which all the passions of a holy war can be whipped up against Communism, when National Socialism itself is, by its own professions, based upon a large measure of Communism all illustrate the point.

Which brings us back to the point made earlier, that a separate doctrinal 'herd,' or 'tribe,' can be made on the basis of very small differences—like those which made us in the old days hate the heretic, go to war with him, exterminate him by our inquisitions. If we could be clearer as to what we want of politics, which presumably is welfare; that doctrines, theories, parties are means to that end; could remember that they are means and not an end, then we might avoid falling into the psychological state which makes an enemy where none need exist, engage in civil wars without intending to. For it is even truer of civil than of international war that it comes not because men want it, but because they pursue policies which make war inevitable; policies which do not have war as their intention but as their unforeseen result.

Sometimes the more doctrinaire Fascist, Nazi, Nationalist will admit that his ultimate values are not material but mystic; declare that 'patriotism' has little to do with welfare. And, of course, the great demagogues have based a quite conscious technique upon this fact that men are less readily interested in welfare than in certain emotional satisfactions related to the exercise of power and coercion. The author of *Mein Kampf* explains that if you are to move millions profoundly and secure their support for a policy, you must not talk to them about things economic—daily bread, welfare. And many a Communist disapproves his own theories of economic motivation by devoted sacrifices (and ferocities) revealing motives quite other than economic. And we had in the Saar the supreme example of our time perhaps where welfare comes after—*longo intervallo*—certain political considerations. For there the choice was fully conscious and deliberate. (What was true of the Saarlanders is now true of the Sudeten Germans.)

Here was a population overwhelmingly proletarian—coal and iron workers—largely Socialist and Communist, who had seen their fellows in Germany subjected to appalling oppression. Until the transfer to Germany they lived in what was one of the most stable, the most prosperous corners of Europe, and one in which the individual, particularly the individual worker, had been freer than in any other German-speaking territory. And most of these half-million workers deliberately voted themselves into danger, uncertainty and poverty. Let an American witness—Dorothy Thompson (Mrs. Sinclair Lewis) in the territory while still under the League give her testimony:

'If one listens to the radio addresses which are broadcast through the ether from Germany to the Saar, one would think that the Saarlanders have been living for the past fifteen years under the most appalling terror and oppression, and that reunion with Germany would mean their liberation.

'In reality, as one hard-headed Saarlander said: "The Saar for fifteen years has been an isle of the blest."'

When the League took over the Saar, it was in a state of disorganisation, due to the War. Saarbrücken, the capital, was a provincial town, and in bad weather you could drown in the mud of the streets. Throughout the whole territory few roads were paved. There was not a single up-to-date hospital in the territory. There was a total population of 600,000 souls.

After cession to the League Saarbrücken became a lively city, full of handsome buildings, and from one end of the territory to the other all the main roads and most of the subsidiary ones were paved and kept in excellent shape. The hospitals were first class, the schools were modernly housed. Mrs. Lewis points out that 'The Saar is probably the only governmental entity in Europe which has not a cent of debt, but, on the contrary, owns a small, well-invested fortune. The tax rate is lower than that of either powerful neighbour; the railroads, linked up with the French and German networks, are absolutely solvent, although both German and French roads are heavily in debt. The population has grown by 200,000.'

The Saar Germans escaped the German inflation, because they had a common monetary and Customs Union with France. When Germans were starving on paper wages worth a billion marks to the dollar, Saar coal miners bought themselves pianos and bathrooms with good gold francs. For a long time—until 1925—they enjoyed free trade with both Germany and France, and always the essential Lorraine iron has come in duty free.

Mrs. Lewis remarks:

'If the world were ruled by reason, and not by prejudice, ambition, special interest and all the other qualities which play a role in governments—whether they be democracies or monarchies or dictatorships—then the government of the Saar would probably be regarded by the world as an ideal, and we would all hasten to adopt something similar for ourselves.'

That all the economic advantages for Saarlanders were on the side of retention of the League status there can be no question. Mrs. Lewis adds:

'On the side of the League is the economic welfare of the Saarlanders, for there is not a thinking person who does not know that the day the Saar rejoins Germany, an era of great prosperity comes to a close. Even the Germans admit it. At the great demonstration in Ehrenbreitstein across the border in Germany, where Hitler assembled half a million people in one of the most impressive public ceremonies ever held, the word went around: "Better black bread with one's own than white bread with the foreigners !"

'There is no question at this moment that the average Saarlander, worked upon for fifteen years by patriotic German propaganda, will choose the black bread to the white, but some of them think and some of them wonder where patriotism really begins and ends.'

If we continue to wonder long enough patriotism will not remain for ever the enemy of welfare; the nature of patriotism, as of other motives which underlie politics, will certainly alter.

The common attitude towards these emotional phenomena is that 'being human nature it is just so, and talk won't alter it.' Nothing could be more untrue. These emotional values are perpetually altering; they are no more stable than fashions in hats, and far from talk not altering them, talk is the one thing that does alter them. It is indeed largely talk, 'propaganda' which has produced the present feeling. The tiny Saar territory possessed thirty-eight daily newspapers, most of them financed from Germany, all busily engaged in propaganda. Had the thirty-eight papers been talking in another sense the feeling would have been very different.

It would be entirely in keeping with the main lessons of the last twenty years that having voted themselves back into Germany the Saarlanders will in a few years deeply desire to be back under League government. Few things are more unstable than the 'imponderable' motives of politics. It is so, even in England. The ends which furnished our chief slogans in the War become, after the War, things which we do not want at all; the autocracy we fought to destroy seems to many of us now the most desirable form of government.

Perhaps the first thing most needed in politics to-day is to know what we really want of our political efforts, of organised government. If, indeed, it be welfare, economic security, then problems like that of the Saar will take a quite secondary place. The Germans talk of 'self-government.' But the Saarlanders had certainly more self-government under the League than they now have under Hitler. But did they want self-government, democracy? That desire is a very ancient urge with Teutonic people. Yet we saw the German in 1933 'pray to be delivered from the burden of freedom and self-government,' as one of them has put it. What is unique in recent German history is that autocracy and tyranny is a preferred, invited autocracy and tyranny. As Dorothy Thompson puts it:

'What actually happened is unique in that dictatorship was accomplished by popular will. The German people have not had Mr. Hitler thrust upon them. He recommended himself to them and they bought him. More than fifty per cent of all Germans politically minded enough to exercise the right of suffrage—and nearly eighty-nine per cent of them went to the polls—deliberately gave away all their civil rights, all their chances of popular control, all their opportunities for representation. The German people went over to autocracy in March 1933, in a body, burning all their bridges behind them. They bought the pig of autocracy in a poke, because they did not even know or ask exactly what form it was going to take.'

But, again, there is no assurance that another generation of Germans will not demand something entirely different.

Turn to the other side of the world. The forces which have drawn the government of Japan into the hands of the most reckless and fanatical Japanese are also the forces which marked the Fascist uprising in Germany and in Italy, and which animates movements of Fascist character in France, to say nothing of similar lesser movements in some half-dozen other countries. It is the element which, in the usual analysis of these movements, is both the most ignored and the most menacing of all.

That factor is not the pursuit by powerful economic groups of some anti-social interest. It is the essentially destructive character of certain doctrines which are both anti-social and irrational, but which have wide appeal and are sincerely, disinterestedly, unselfishly held as profound social truth; held with the same blind passion that has animated the religious fanatic in all ages. It is precisely the disinterestedness and sincerity which makes the doctrines dangerous. These differ, however, from the more ancient fanaticisms, in that though the creeds which the old religious oppressions upheld or spread with fire and sword may sometimes have been absurd, they were not usually in themselves necessarily destructive: the heretic was offered the chance of salvation by recantation. Mahomet welcomed the world. The infidel could escape destruction by embracing the Faith. But the characteristic of certain post-War political doctrines is that the infidel has no escape and that the more widely the Faith is disseminated the more destructive it must become. A man cannot change his race or nationality as he changes his religion. The essence of Nationalism is its exclusivity.

Hitler (though not Mussolini, who is much more sophisticated and much more capable of objective thought) may tell us, as he does in his attempts at justification, that the true Nationalist respects the rights of other nationalities. But he respects those rights in the same way that Hitler respects the rights of Jews and Liberals. It is not possible for one Nationalism to accord to others the rights it claims for itself. For an essential part of the creed of Nationalism is absolute independence of all other groups. (Even Mr. de Valera will not have the faintest shadow of obligation to any existing political organisation but 'Ireland.') But in the modern world we all have to travel on the same world road in high-powered cars, and it is a physical impossibility to continue to move on that road and live without some commonly-recognised rules. They must be built up either by free co-operation between the users, which means that each surrenders his 'independence,' which no good Nationalist will do; or the powerful, in order to live at all, must impose rules upon the less powerful, which is what all good Nationalists love to do. 'Independence,' which is the heart of Nationalism, if granted to more than one, becomes incompatible with order, security, self-preservation.

Let other races embrace for themselves the doctrines of the Nordic Nazis, other nations for the Sacro egoismo of Italian Nationalism, other political parties that right of heresy-extirpation by torture and murder which Fascism and Communism have claimed, and the inevitable outcome must be mutual extermination; an extermination for which, for the first time in history, we have now entirely adequate tools—tools only made possible by the past work of that scientific spirit of scepticism, freedom of thought and discussion, toleration of contrary opinions which Nationalism everywhere is destroying; destroying as the logical prelude to the destruction of all the other most precious human goods.

The pursuit of some concrete, measurable, ponderable selfish economic interest would be far less dangerous than the unselfish religious passion which characterises so much of the rank and file of the Nationalist and Fascist movements throughout the world. Economic interests are not served by universal destruction, and the strictly economic interpretation of suicide presents logical difficulties. But your Nationalist seldom calculates the cost in terms of any understandable or concrete standard.

It is quite clear that that Japanese uprising of a year or two since

was no 'capitalist plot' any more than the coming of Hitler was
mainly or fundamentally such. The hatred which has inspired the
murders in Tokio was very largely hatred of the financiers and the
big industrialists, as well as a hatred of capitalism generally. A *Times*
writer puts his finger upon this point when he says:

'The epidemic of political assassination four years ago, when two Prime
Ministers and a Minister of Finance were murdered, roused only a passing
indignation. Sympathy was freely expressed for the young officers who
had resorted to murder as the most effective means of expressing their
political convictions. The sincerity of their patriotic fanaticism was held to
explain, almost indeed to justify, the crimes. . . . This toleration for
methods of violence is a curious trait in a nation possessing so strong a
feeling for discipline in most departments of life. Perhaps it may be
explained in part by the widespread distrust of politicians, and of the
financiers and big industrialists, who are believed to control them. There
is little labour agitation in Japan; but there is a general disillusionment
over the result of industrialisation, a disillusionment which is felt most
strongly among the agricultural classes, from whom the officers are mainly
recruited. Some of the patriotic societies, while fiercely opposed to Communism, demand that profit-making in finance, industry, and trade should
be curbed by methods which are practically indistinguishable from Communism. They all resent the contrast between the great fortunes made in
business and the poverty and austerity of life which is traditional among
the military classes in Japan. The feeling that much of the modern development has not been healthy or in accordance with the national spirit
may account for some of the toleration, even sympathy, shown for the
agitation among the younger officers which has now culminated in a tragedy
which has horrified the whole world.'

Almost every word of that interpretation might be applied to explain the Hitlerite phenomenon. Where economic interest enters it
is not primarily that of Capitalism. The predominance of the agricultural as distinct from the industrial interest, the glorification of
the peasant, is notably common to the two cases. More than one
correspondent has pointed out the importance of those 'planks' in
the reported platform of the rebel officers, which deal with the dis-
tressed condition of the peasants and the claim that the interests of
the peasants should come first. The Washington correspondent of
the *Times*, who has evidently taken the trouble to inform himself,
says:

'The general movement of opinion here is towards attribution to the
rebel soldiers of a conviction that the scales are weighted too heavily in

favour of industrialism in their country, that some correction in favour
of the peasant farmer must be made.'

Compare this interpretation and its attribution of prime importance to the soil and the peasant as against industrialism and the
finances, with what Madame Keun (in the extremely notable little
book *Darkness from the North*,[1] which everyone ought to read)
writes as to the outstanding points in the Hitlerite appeal:

'The peasantry enjoys particular privileges, for "Blood and Soil" plays
a predominant role in the Nazi ideology, and the peasants have been put
on a footing with the soldiers, as the "first and nobles" of the German
classes. Although the promise of dividing the great estates has not been
realised, agriculture is protected by a sort of State-socialism, subsidised
by means of very high Customs, and the *droit d'ainesse*, the right of in-
heritance by the eldest son only, has been established for small peasant
properties.'

It is in the behaviour of the young men who make the backbone
of these movements, and the state of mind, type of motive and impulse, which the behaviour reveals, that we see the underlying common factor. In Tokio were young soldiers, passionately convinced
that their view of what constitutes patriotism is the right view, the
only view which could possibly be sincere; that any view which
differed from it was obvious treason. Just as in the German case the
young Nazis were quite convinced that their opponents, whether Liberals, Social Democrats, Socialists, or Communists were conscious
enemies of Germany, betraying her, usually as the result of Jewish
bribes. The sincerity of those Fascist and Nazi convictions, no one
who studies the behaviour of the insurgents can doubt.

It is common for writers analysing the Hitlerite phenomenon to
compare the subordinates employed by Hitler to Chicago gunmen;
to picture these youngsters busy bumping off 'traitors' as Dillingers
and Capones. But while the physical behaviour may be similar, we
shall miss the point and the real menace of that moral epidemic of
which Tokio like Berlin and Vienna (to say nothing of Moscow)
have all been examples unless we give full weight to the passion of
sincere conviction which animated the assassins. We are guilty of
the very error of which the assassins were guilty—an error which
really now does threaten the foundations of all organised society—
if we pretend that these youngsters are insincere, that they commit

[1] Published by H. and E. R. Brinton, 102 Shoe Lane, London.

these crimes for money at the behest of pay-masters, in the shape of financiers or industrialists, or bankers, or Jews. Such an explanation does not begin to explain the most serious fact about the whole business. Leaders may use as instruments men of a type indistinguishable from Dillinger; sanction horrible and bestial torture. So at times did the Roman Catholic Church. But one does not really explain the survival of that institution during two thousand years, or its acts, by saying that 'somebody paid to have it done'; or even by the desire of priests to retain their jobs. What we have to explain is not the readiness of priests to receive money, but the readiness of vast multitudes to give it. What we have to explain in the Nazi phenomenon is not the fact that here and there some capitalist or industrialist may bribe a Nazi government to do certain things or come to terms with it; but the readiness of millions of youngsters to die for a system or ideal which deprives their country of its freedom, its welfare, the rights and security of its people. To explain why a system which has those inevitable results can be regarded as a highest expression of patriotism.

We are indeed witnessing a social revolution over a large part of the world, it is a social revolution hardly according to Marx. The only successful Communist revolution which has taken place did not occur where, according to the Marxian thesis it should have occurred—in a highly industrialised country. It occurred in the least industrialised of all the nations, and the factors which counted most were the personal character and genius of three or four men, not the mere material forces of 'economic determinism.' In the highly industrialised countries—Germany, Japan, and to a lesser degree Italy—the revolution has not been made by the industrial proletariat, and it has been a movement, in some of its elements more against industrialism than against capitalism, and in others not against capitalism as such, but against big capitalism, big business, although the hatred of 'the capitalist' has been freely exploited. The feeling against big business, high finance, the international financier, 'the bloated capitalist,' has resulted in something far nearer to a counter-revolution, to undoing the results of the French Revolution, than to 'the' Social Revolution. It is a revolution of the *petite bourgeoisie*, supported by the peasant and the rural interest. Its ultimate explanation is more psychological than economic; in part a psychological protest against 'the burden of Civilisation'; the revolt of 'the country lout,' as someone has said, against urban complexities, the puzzling problems which a complicated urbanised life involves, and a preference for the old familiar simplicities where intellectualism is not necessary, and where a man may safely 'think with his blood.' 'Glandular thought,' the desire that 'blood,' passion, violence, emotion, shall suffice for life; the desire to be relieved of the burden of rationally weighed decision, is perhaps the greatest common factor.

In Leon Feuchtwanger's novel, *The Ugly Duchess,* occurs this passage:

'Prince Friedrich's principles pleased the violent young knights of the order extraordinarily. They were there, they were young, they were the lords of the world. They were filled with a boundless arrogance, bursting with a need to lay about them, to shout, to yell, to make an endless joyous hubbub. To fill the world with their youth, which did not know what it would be at, with their strength, which was without direction or goal; with their thirst to undertake something, to act. Now Prince Friedrich had given this vague impulse a beautiful and sonorous name and something that resembled a meaning, an idea, an ideal. The young, insolent, swashbuckling lords felt suddenly that they were the bearers of a mission, they had God, justice, power on their side; and they were happy.'

That was written long before the 'young, insolent swashbuckling lords' in Brown Shirts, Black Shirts, or the uniforms of Japanese officers took to murder and torture with the feeling that they were 'the bearers of a mission, had God, justice, power on their side, and —were happy.'

And note, please, that they were 'young lords'; that this type of revolution is not explained by economic misery of the severely physical kind. We talk of Germany, or Italy, or Japan being driven by economic need, poverty, hunger to the political excesses which have marked their policy, internal and external. But the initiating and dynamic forces in the government of those countries do not derive from hunger. Those who constitute the driving force of these movements, and give to the Mussolinis, the Hitlers, the de la Rocques, the Mosleys the power to act, are well-fed, well-to-do usually middle-class. We confront a mainly middle-class revolution, into which enter passions of grievance, of frustrations, but also sheer love of violence for itself. What attracts so many who rally to Hitlerite or Fascist banners is precisely the opportunity to be 'a young lord,' dominant, 'laying about him' with powers of life and death. And it is this love of power and violence for itself, as an intoxicant ('the heady wine of power' was a phrase once used by a man who had possessed power for many years), which accounts in large part for the revolt against reason, against free discussion, against thought, and for the claim that the true patriot should 'think with his blood.' For reason, thought, rational analysis would undermine the whole claim of Nationalism and its psychological cousins Fascism, anti-semitism and militarism, and reveal the 'young lord' as a drunken lout and bully, usually too congenitally stupid to understand another's point of view. His 'intuitions' are protective at least to that degree; reason or free discussion would deprive him of his intoxicant, would sober him by showing him the truth; so reason and free discussion must be banned.

That this urge to violence has very deep roots biologically, we cannot doubt. Men love violence, love to become intoxicated, and whatever the scientific psychologist may ultimately have to tell us about this impulse, we are obliged to accept it as fact for the time being, and face the problem it presents, to answer the question, What are we to do about it?—the 'we' being organised society or those in organised society who desire to preserve both order and freedom—who, indeed, desire to preserve order just because they desire to preserve freedom.

Thinking with your blood cannot, of course, give either order or freedom. For when the Fascist or the Nazi has captured power with his truncheons, knuckledusters, automatics, floggings, torturings, and got his Totalitarian State, his victims will begin to think with their blood also, also to resort to violence. If intuitions, feelings, emotions are to be the guide to what is justice, what is right, what is patriotism; then violence, assassination, murder will become the instrument of all political and social change—as indeed they were yesterday in the Balkans, in Eastern Europe, in the whole of America south of the Mexican border, and the day before yesterday over most of the world, ever since night closed upon the Roman Empire.

The fall of that older civilisation was marked by the incursion from without of barbarians, which the Empire had lost the power to repel. What are we of the present to do about the incursion, rising from within, of armed barbarians deeply convinced that they represent a higher civilisation? This arming of drunkards drunkenly convinced that they are sober?

The first thing is to face the fact, and not to burke it. Man is subject to mental sickness, to intoxications with dangerous psychological drugs. The drunken driver in charge of a car convinced that he is sober *is* sometimes found upon the roads. The political group, that may be only a small minority armed to impose upon the whole community its rules, its doctrines, its creed, passionately convinced that those doctrines are divine, and that it is entitled to act upon the principle that 'one and God make a majority,' *does* arise. What is the community to do?

It will not do to say that these are hypothetical questions relating to hypothetical circumstances. They are the precise circumstances which have arisen in three great States, half a dozen lesser ones, and may arise to-morrow in France. And the question confronts us now, this week or month, at longest this year, as the major problem of international politics. To pretend that this question of the right and wrong use of force does not exist, that there is some perfectly simple solvent known as the principle that 'force' must never be employed, is simply to evade, disastrously, fatally, a difficult decision.

The trouble about the 'no force' doctrine is that it does not dispose of force or the force problem. If France, for instance, refuses to apply the sanctions of the State against the armed Leagues, or the followers of Colonel de la Rocque, or the Camelots *du roi*, the refusal would not have eliminated force from French politics or the French State. The effect of *not* using force against the armed parties would mean that in exchange for the kind and degree of force which a Liberal State employs we should get the kind and degree of force a 'Totalitarian' (Fascist or Communist) State employs.

A member of the group rather more to the Right than the others showed signs of great indignation.

'I would make,' he said, 'only two main points. The speaker seems to desire a world of cold-blooded rationalism. It is an impossible world and predicates impossible men. It would be perfectly horrible if it were possible. Secondly the speaker has dealt only most casually with Russia, its barbarisms and its illiberalisms, certainly as horrible as those of which the Fascist States are guilty.'

A reply was forthwith vouchsafed in some such terms as these.

This old notion of a clear distinction between thought and emotion is psychologically out of date. What we feel depends upon what we see, the interpretation that we give to events. The savage may be terrorstruck by phenomena which arouse in the civilised man no fear whatever. As to Russia: I agree that the barbarities of Russia are just as great as those of Germany, but Russia was always a pure autocracy, which Germany was not. Russia had not, at the time of the coming of the revolution, emerged from Asiatic barbarism; at the time of the German revolution Germany was a highly civilised state. In other words a condition which is on the whole for Russia an advance over a former barbarism, is for Germany retrogression from former civilisation. The tendency and direction in the one case need not greatly disturb us, but in the other, the German case, is a dire menace.

There is of course, a further point as bearing upon the international problem. Russia is not an expansionist state, does not desire the territory of others; both Germany, Italy and Japan are all alike declaredly expansionist, are actually engaged in the absorption of the territory of others. We are not concerned with the internal policy of any state except in so far as it bears upon its external relations, its behaviour in the international field.

As these were points, however, that future discussions would probably deal with, the matter was left at that.

V

CAN WE GIVE THE TOTALITARIANS WHAT THEY WANT?

It is fashionable now to attribute the post-War unrest to the injustices of Versailles. But the Treaty of Versailles did not cause the Great War; nor are the States—Japan and Italy—that have been very potent elements of post-War disturbances victims of that Treaty; they are among its beneficiaries. The root of our trouble with the Totalitarians lies deeper, particularly in the fact that if we satisfy their supreme grievance it will be at the cost of creating a grievance just as severe elsewhere. They claim a form of defence which in fact kills the defence of others; rights which if granted would make it impossible for others to have similar rights. This is not a specifically 'German' fault for we have in the past committed it in equal degree. But if both sides persist in this attempt to square the political circle, there will be war, whatever revisions and remedying of specific grievances be made.

Giving full weight alike to the German case and the Englishman's reply the first question which naturally arose was 'Can we give the Totalitarians what they want? If so, how?' The English case as presented raised some criticism. One member particularly desired to put certain questions, make certain qualifications. Here they are:

Our spokesman for the British side has made out a case for democracy and liberalism. I don't doubt that it is sound. But after all, these abstractions do not make a very immediate contribution to the solution of the problem, which, unsolved may blow us sky high.

I want to submit certain suggestions which I think bear on the problem of settlement with the Totalitarian States.

The first is this: That the settlement of specific differences, or specific grievances which Germany may nurse, will not solve that problem. Revision is necessary but most tragic experience proves completely that it is not enough, and that brought about without reference to larger issues, as an isolated act that is, may leave us in a worse situation than ever. In those conditions it will not be a step towards peace but towards war—and I speak, remember, as one who was and is a very severe critic of the Treaty of Versailles.

The second point I would make is that what Germany wants really is preponderance of power. It is what she wanted in 1914 and which we refused to grant, standing by our balance of power policy. I think we are prepared to grant it now, to surrender the policy which we fought the War to uphold, to reverse the whole theory of the War.

Having established these two points I will then ask the question: Suppose we reverse the policy which brought us into the War, acknowledge that that War was a mistake and grant Germany preponderance as a good many Englishmen desire that we should, will the outcome be peace?

The unmistakable experience which most conclusively condemns efforts at mere territorial re-arrangements as an adequate cure for war, is precisely the most overwhelming and tragic experience of our time—that of the Great War itself. We know by the proof of that unique event that a very great degree of revision of territorial boundaries, like those demanded by protagonists of the revision of the Treaty of Versailles, would not necessarily give us either peace or the solution of our economic problems.

Let us suppose that the treaty could be so thoroughly and radically corrected that Germany could have restored to her everything which she possessed in 1913—not only her African colonies but all the territories in Europe now under other rule—the rule of France, of Denmark, of Belgium, of Poland, of the League. Such revision is probably beyond even German dreams. It could never be as complete as that. But supposing it were actually effected, to that thoroughgoing extent, why do we know, by unmistakable experience that it would not ensure peace? Because when Germany did possess all that territory and all those resources she was a gravely disturbing factor in Europe and the peace was not kept. Concessions, such as I have described would be concession indeed. Would it, in the absence of any fundamental system, mean peace? Then why did it not mean peace in 1914?

To this it is sometimes retorted, quite falsely, that the argument implies that the main guilt of the War was Germany's. But the appeal to the experience of the Great War becomes stronger still, if we assume that the major guilt was with Russia or with France or with Britain. For in that case it is clear that the mere fact of possessing adequate territory, possessing it to such degree that States become, like the three just mentioned, sated—even this degree of territorial satisfaction is no guarantee of peace. In that connection it might be pointed out that whereas before the War Russia was reaching out for more territory, after the War, having lost much of her territory, she ceases to be an expansive or expanding or dynamic State. Further, if we assume, as we must, that some share of the guilt is with us and our allies, if, that is, we shared the temper which led to war, how can we ascribe that temper to 'the injustice of the Treaty of Versailles'? *We* were not the victims of such a Treaty.

Not only so. In 1914 we had no quarrel with Germany on any specific point of policy. Morocco, the Bagdad Railway, and all the other differences had been settled or were out of the picture. Half a dozen statesmen most concerned in the events have testified that Anglo-German relations had not for years been as free from specific differences as they were in 1914. There was no specific demand which Germany felt she had to make (as to-day she is making demand for more territory) and which we felt we must refuse.

What then was it that she wanted and we refused?

Europe's disease is, after all, a little older than the Treaty of Versailles and its sins. The one nation which actually has gone to war—in a particularly vile fashion—as the result of a political philosophy similar to Hitler's, is Italy, a nation which was not among the vanquished but among the victors, and which, if revision of Versailles were brought about, would as a first step have to disgorge, not receive, territory. Mussolini after fifteen years of great personal success, at the very moment that he is able to declare, as he did, that 'we have conquered an empire in seven months and pacified it in three' and that 'it has all been done in the face of everybody and everything,' goes on in the same speech to add that 'certain other accounts are open' and that 'we Fascists reject the unthinking fairy tale of a perpetual peace, which never existed in the world, and which never can exist.' Of course, he hoped that others would be prepared to settle the 'open accounts' to his satisfaction in order that such peace as we could get in a world of eternal war would be 'as long as possible.'

This sort of thing is not the outcome of humiliation, defeat, injustice, or need of land or outlet. British aggression before the War —as in the conquest of the Boer republics—was not the outcome of those things; nor was the American conquest of the Philippines (marked, incidentally, by abominations not less horrible than those which marked Italian conquests in Abyssinia); nor certain phases of Russian expansion before the War; nor French imperialism and militarism; nor Japanese; nor Fascist aid to Franco.

We are dealing, of course, in the case of Hitler not with a new philosophy at all, but a very old one which has prompted German, Italian, British, French, Russian and American policy sometimes at the very height of prosperity and glory. To assume that this philosophy will be abandoned if 'justice is done' or needs are met, or that in the case of Germany it would disappear if she were put back to where she was in 1914, is to refuse to face plain fact and very tragic history.

The Germans want certain things. They believe passionately in their right to have them, and if they do not get them, will fight for them. Questions which therefore arise are whether the things they demand can be granted so that we may avoid a fight; whether, if they cannot be granted, they will accept some other alternative; and whether, if what they really demand were granted it would satisfy them and be a step towards peace or a step towards further demands ending in war.

Our German friend has made pretty clear what it is Germans ask. They ask for what he calls the means of life—space, food, access to raw materials on the economic side; and also, on the political side, security. But the vital German demand is not merely for these things. It is for these things under Germany's absolute control so that Germans shall not be beholden for them to the goodwill of foreigners. 'Autarchy,' for Germany means not merely an economic self-sufficiency but a defensive one; a demand made for psychological, moral, quite as much as for material reasons.

Our German member very rightly and very honestly stressed the demand for security, defence. But always, be it noted, it must be defence which does not depend upon co-operation with foreigners; does not depend upon that internationalism for which he, like his countrymen, as a whole, has such contempt. The Germans feel that if their defence is dependent upon co-operation with foreigners they are deprived of their independence; they feel that it makes their national life a matter of partnership—as our friend puts it—with copper-coloured gentry from Sambo republics; possibly with Communist States like Russia; possibly with international Jewry established by Jews in a State of their own to-morrow in Palestine.

Germany does not want defence, does not want security on such a basis.

Now it is possible to give the Totalitarian States those things—a very large degree of self-sufficiency; adequate materials which are under her complete political control; security which shall be based upon her own military power, and liberated from dependence in any way upon international machinery—those things can be given to Germany. But it is still more important to note that fact because it has a very direct bearing upon the persistence of her demand for them. It is just as important to note, that those things can only be given to Germany if they are taken from others. They are 'rights' which cannot be given to Germany if others are to enjoy the same rights. If others also are to have the means of life, national security, then those common rights can only be enjoyed by all by means of that international co-operation which Germany rejects as immoral and debasing.

It is also unhappily quite clear that if nations like Germany, Italy, and Japan are to be even relatively self-sufficient economically in the sense that all the main indispensables of life are to be within their political control, subject to the managements of their governments in peace-time, brought within the particular system of national socialism, and are to be freely available to them in war-time so that, again, they shall be free of all foreign control just when in their view they need those things most—then, once more, that degree of self-sufficiency can only be brought about if others are deprived of it.

There results, therefore, this curious fact: while all the three States mentioned are intensely nationalist, both economically, politically, psychologically, it is a nationalism for themselves alone, necessarily bought at the cost of depriving others of the very conditions which they claim for themselves as the most elementary and most valuable of human rights. That is why, I take it, in his reply, the member of our group charged with presenting the English case, spoke of the Totalitarian philosophy as 'cannibalistic.' He meant to indicate, I assume, that it rested on the fact that one nation was fed by consuming the other. It is plainly true of the Totalitarian ethos. Even at this early stage of their ambitions each one of the Totalitarian States has managed to excite the deepest anxieties and fears in the minds of its national, and nationalist neighbours.

Hardly one of these latter but feels that his own nationality is threatened by the nationalism of his big brother.

What the Chinese nationalist feels about Japanese conduct, conduct prompted by the nationalism of Japan, we know. Italy has already incorporated large alien elements within her borders; and it is quite clear that Germany is prepared to purchase security of what she regards as German rights—security not only in material things, but in doctrine, creed, culture, outlook—by denying those rights even to groups within her nation that have been there for untold generations, like the Jews, Catholics, Lutherans.

This 'cannibalism' as our friend calls it, can be justified on grounds of elementary self-preservation once a certain premise is accepted—the premise, namely, that international co-operation is impracticable, impossible, immoral.

Having accepted that, it is quite certain that Germany or Japan or Italy can make out an unanswerable case for the very worst of its conduct on the ground that self-preservation and necessity know no law.

'Since we cannot depend,' argues the Nazi or Fascist, 'upon co-operation with foreigners; since we can never be sure that our access to raw materials guaranteed by international arrangement will not at any moment be closed by some intrigue of international Jewry or Freemasonry, or of enemies burrowing like moles at Geneva, or deciding that we have committed some offence, and that, therefore, we are to be shut off by "sanctions"—granted this, as you must grant it,' continues the Fascist, 'then we must assure our means of livelihood by the only method left to us: our own preponderance of power. Do you ask us to commit suicide on behalf of international morality?'

I was struck by the gibe of our spokesman when the German proposed to combine peace and conciliation with the ruthless maintenance of economic nationalism. 'Either I must eat you, or you must eat me. Let us come to a friendly agreement about it.' We know in truth that they will not, cannot, come to a friendly agreement, and that the tone of friendliness will soon be abandoned on one side or the other. And assuredly there is not much friendliness in Hitler's most recent speeches.

Like the previous speaker I do not want to imply that the Japanese or the Italians, or the Germans, are monsters for accepting this doctrine. Belief in the economic advantages of conquest was universal among ourselves before the War. The Totalitarians are no more wicked than we are; they *are* more fanatical. They are not wicked any more than the old Inquisitor was wicked. He was usually a most saintly man, quite persuaded that in his restraint of evil doctrine he was defending society, and doing the will of God.

But the good man, the sincere man of passionate convictions is far more apt to become dangerous than the man of lukewarm convictions, or even the cynic.

And what we face in Germany to-day, in all the Totalitarian States, is a tidal wave of fanatical conviction, a conviction made fanatical by the machinery of propaganda which ensures that the masses shall hear but one side of the case. We face the danger of whole nations of Mohammeds ready for their Holy War.

I thought that our spokesman the other day might have illustrated his case about the nature of the British Empire with its toleration not merely of local independence and parliaments, but of a great variety of beliefs, creeds, by recalling that that was also the Roman way, and that both were in singular contrast to the modern Fascist method. The Roman Empire, like our own, was composed of a multitude of differing nationalities, religions, racial cultures, ways of life. You had what was in fact internationalism—cultural, racial, and religious divergencies, protected by a predominant Imperial authority keeping the peace between them, preventing violence. The effort, it is true, was not always successful, but it was at least the purpose to maintain these 'independencies.' And the whole purpose of Totalitarianism, the very meaning of the word is to suppress these differences, to bring all thought, all beliefs, into the one mould of the State, and to substitute for the willing co-operation of independent groups the blind acceptance of authority by all from on high.

But there is one point which cannot be too often brought out as the key fact, as the first and last thing which Germany wants. Germany wants, and must have if her scheme of things is to succeed at all, preponderance of power. Once grant that there cannot be co-operation with others; that your means of life must be within your own control; that the means of defending those things must be within your own control—then inevitably you are asking for preponderance.

Self-preservation is, of course, the first law of life with every living thing whether physical or political. It is the first and last thing. If in ensuring it co-operation is rejected; if each says, 'I must be in a position to overcome all who presume to question my rights or my acts,' then preponderance of power becomes the first need.

We speak of remedying Germany's grievances as the road to peace; of satisfying her needs. But her supreme grievances are, and always have been, the absence of means whereby she can ensure her defence through her own power. It was out of that that the War arose.

It is vital that we should face the lesson of so tragic an experience as the Great War in this connection.

Before the War we said that if the power of Germany grew much more she would be so preponderant that we would be without defence, a position no free people could accept. So far, perhaps, we were right. Not quite so right when we went on to suggest that Germany should occupy that intolerable position by being weaker than we were. To prove to Germany that she need have no misgiving in accepting such a position, we made, when we were preponderant and had Germany completely at our mercy, the Treaty of Versailles. Looking at that Treaty Germany naturally says:

'That is what comes of being weaker than your enemy. You never get justice. On the next occasion we propose to be stronger, and when we are, we shall tear up what remains of that treaty, make a new Europe, more in consonance with Germany's rights, and with the recognition of her due place in the world.'

Who is to be judge of what is Germany's due place in the world? Herr Hitler leaves us in no doubt; Germany alone is to be judge of Germany's rights.

When, therefore, she has completely established her preponderance, it is unlikely that the new treaty which she makes will be better than the one we made. It is likely indeed to be worse, and we shall discover that we are among its victims. Then, of course, we shall do what the Germans have been doing of late: build up our power, secretly at first, then defiantly, and when, with a sufficient number of allies bribed by the kind of promises which purchased the alliance of Italy and Rumania in the Great War, promises of new territory at the victory—when we have played that game successfully we shall strike, and then, by threat of war, or a new war, make a new treaty, Treaty No. 3. (It will really be Versailles Treaty No. 4. The first Versailles Treaty, though not called by that name, was made when the Germans were at Versailles as victors in 1872 to say nothing of still earlier treaties made there.)

Will that new treaty be better than the one we made in 1919? It will be much worse as there will be more atrocities and wrongs to avenge. And if the Germans have cause to rebel against No. 1, they will have still greater cause to rebel against No. 3. New war for new treaty worse than any of its predecessors, *ad infinitum*.

Plainly, revision, correction of injustices, while indispensable and important, is not the only key to peace in Europe. It is not even the master-key, as our own political conduct in the years preceding the War most clearly shows. We entered that War, not because we had definable grievances—we had not; not because we were attacked—we weren't. We were not the victims of a Treaty of Versailles, which we were determined to alter. We entered the War for one reason only: we feared the growth of German power, and what she might do with it when it became irresistible. When we entered the War she was, in fact, extremely anxious to keep us out of the War. We just objected to the creation in Europe of a power so great that she could at any moment lay down the law to us, tell us at any moment what rights we should be allowed to enjoy; deprive us, that is, of National Defence.

What *we* fought to resist—inferiority of power—Germany is now preparing to fight to resist; what made us passionate to the point of dementia before the War, is making much of Germany passionate to the point of dementia to-day. Why *should* Germany accept in respect of our power a position we absolutely refused to accept in respect of hers? Especially in view of the plain fact that British preponderance of power was the main element in producing that Treaty of Versailles which even we now declare to be iniquitous; of the fact that it could never have been imposed but for British naval preponderance, British blockades, British determination to prolong the War to the bitter end; British refusal to discuss an agreed peace.

There was in 1914, as there is now, a curious disinclination to face this bottom fact of the situation. We seem to want, as an explanation to ourselves and others, something more tangible, more ponderable as a motive than mere desire for power to resist the power of others. Before the War we 'rationalised' our motives by fantastic stories of dark designs on the part of Germany to invade and conquer Britain itself, to seize her Dominions; by description of the Kaiser as the anti-Christ; theories of a very special wickedness attaching to the German race. We had nothing to fear, we said (we really did say these things), from French power, however great; or Russian power, or Japanese power. These people, unlike the Hun, had become civilised, and their power would be beneficent.

We can judge the worth of all those theories by the fact that great sections of our people to-day are more disposed to support Germany against France, than France against Germany, despite the fact that Hitlerite militarism is certainly no more civilised than *Kaiserlich* militarism. Just as we found grounds for our fear and hatred of the superior power of a foreign combination before 1914, although we had no tangible ground, no Treaty of Versailles to revise, so will a modern Fascist Germany find still more easily grounds for fear and hatred of superior foreign power, even though every inequity of the Treaty were revised.

What is to be our attitude in face of this situation? In 1914 we fought to destroy German preponderance and replace it by our own; decided to compel Germany to accept a position which we refused to accept. As a consequence, Germany suffers gross injustices (for which we are partly responsible). She is in a position now to begin building up her power to redress those wrongs, and by our own power we cannot prevent her. We are urged to keep out. Suppose we do and France, deprived of our support, of America's, perhaps of Italy's, suffers the fate we fought in 1914 to prevent? France is crushed and the hegemony of Europe is once more Germany's. 'We are not concerned.' Then why did we fight the War? And should we not be concerned? Once more dominant Germany would need to settle accounts with us. Germany, which in defeat had suffered Versailles with all its memories, would necessarily in victory be more retaliatory than one which did not possess those memories. Apart from the fact that such a Germany would certainly ask for the return of her 'stolen' colonies, she could hardly disregard the fact that it was *our* power which made the Treaty of Versailles possible; *our* Navy which starved her people, even when all the fighting was over; *our* power mainly which had exposed her to those miseries, humiliations, dismemberment. And she would undoubtedly take the Treaty of Versailles and apply its disarmament provisions to those who during ten years tried to impose them upon Germany. A favourite argument during our making of the Treaty of Versailles was: 'What would Germany have done if *she* had won the War?'—the suggestion being, of course, that her policy (which for years we had declared Satanic) ought to be ours. On the morrow of German victory the most popular argument in Germany undoubtedly would be: Do to the authors of Versailles what they did to us. Again, why should we expect Germany to be wiser or more generous as a victor and conqueror than we were?

We did not call our struggle before the War a struggle for preponderance, but for 'maintaining the balance.' We now ask for 'parity' as the condition of safety.

But no man can ever know, no expert can ever say, when two alliances are equal in power. One has larger armies; another a larger population. But the latter, owing to increasing birth-control, declines. In order to establish equality you have to equate present military effectives to the future influence of birth-control—army corps to Malthusian text-books. This nation has more battleships; that more coaling stations. How many of the first go to how many of the latter? It was once said that you could never establish equality of power until you could equate 'Bogs, fogs and hogs.' And, of course, the elaborately erected 'parities' of the technician which may have taken years to devise can be destroyed overnight by some new alliance combination of the diplomats. The ultimate factor is political: Who will be for us and who against in the conflict which armaments envisage? The answer to that question will determine whether our armaments are adequate or inadequate.

Yet we evade political commitments clearly indicating how our power is to be used. We fear to say that in such and such conditions we shall use these instruments and in such and such will not use them. Yet we insist on retaining and increasing them (by an addi-

tion this year amounting in cost to many hundred times our contribution to the League). No one knows really what our armaments
are for; when they will be used, when not; whom they will protect,
whom they will not. We funk these clarifications because they seem
to commit us to war in certain contingencies, which, says the First
Lord asking for a stiff increase in the naval tools of war, is a thing
so horrible that only 'blood-thirsty pacifists' would contemplate it.

If he does not contemplate war in any circumstance, will not fight
to defend the country, why is he asking for increased estimates?
The difference between himself and the 'blood-thirsty pacifists' is
as to the best means by which arms can be made effective for defence, the method most likely to ensure that they will never be
brought into play.

When it is said so easily that the lesson of the War is that we
'must do justice,' there is an implication that justice is easily recog-
nisable and that we can easily do it if we have the will. But the truth
we have to face is that men differ passionately as to what is justice;
that actually to-day in Europe what one side of a frontier regards
as an obviously fair settlement, the other side with equal sincerity
regards as an infamous outrage. To say to both, therefore, be just,
be fair, is to be guilty of a fatuous over-simplification of the problem,
to reveal what one might term ethical illiteracy.

We know, indeed, that there never can be a settlement satisfactory
to all the Nationalists of Europe, for the reason that what would
be satisfactory for one group would be fanatically resisted by another. Even with real effort at fairness, what is fair in the Hitlerite
view would be grossly unfair in the French or British view. The
difference might well be a passionately sincere one. It is of the essence of the kind of Nationalism that rules in Hitlerite Germany
and Pilsudski Poland that each would be quite certain that the other
was guilty of conscious unfairness, injustice, wickedness; and persuaded that resistance to such a criminal was a holy obligation of
patriotism.

In such a circumstance we have to discover some principle of
justice which is equal for both. That principle of justice is clear
enough: it is the principle of third-party judgment.

So long as each of two parties demands that he shall be judge in
any dispute between them, there can be no justice, because each de-

nies to the other the right each claims. It is a claim which no party
to a dispute with a sense of fairness would make and so long as it
is made there can be no peace.

It is clear indeed that we may find the explanation of that weary
see-saw of struggle for preponderance just sketched, in the fact that,
say, Germany appears at Versailles in 1872 as victor, imposing its
judgment; in the same place forty-five years later as vanquished and
has judgment imposed on it; to appear again as victor it may be later.

That series of wars with its threat of never-ending repetition is
due to the fact that however passionately both parties may believe
themselves to be right, both are wrong in that each is claiming a
right—right of defence by superior power, right of judgment in disputes to which he is a party—which he denies to the other.

Defence must be defined henceforth as the right to third-party
judgment, not, as heretofore, as the right to deny it to the weaker.
Germany insists upon her right to deny third-party judgment for
those with whom she may quarrel as Italy denied it to Abyssinia,
Japan to China.

The idea that 'defence' can be left undefined, unclarified, without
creating the fears which create armaments, must surely, at this date,
be seen for the nonsense that it is. We tell Germany that we entered
the War against her and brought upon her the Versailles Treaty 'as
a measure of defence.' And Germany is then entitled to reply with
truth that our defence may be her destruction. If our defence means
not allowing some other to become more powerful, and that other's
defence not allowing us to be, then there is no end to it. There can
never be general defence. We walk in a fatal circle.

By this refusal to say what we mean by defence, how and in what
conditions we shall use our power, we create the fears which are
the cause of war and armament competition.

There is sinister significance in the fact that precisely this sort of
evasion of the real questions marked the relationship of Britain and
Germany before the War. There was, it is true, everlasting discussion of respective naval equipment. Germany could not lay down a
submarine or mount a new naval gun without the British Press setting up outcries and the experts calculating elaborately the effect
upon the balance of the two forces. Novelists produced stories dealing with the landing in Britain of great German armies. More than

one play gave us scenes of that invasion. The Press from time to time produced thrilling accounts of the discovery of secret plans for such invasion. (As a matter of fact, of course, invasion of Great Britain was the very last thing of which the German rulers were dreaming.) But what object did each assume the other was aiming at in these alleged plans of aggression? That question, which should have been the first, was never really raised.

We tried to get agreement about our forces; tried to equate navies with armies, to discern how many ships went to a coaling station or a refitting harbour. But no one either on the German or the British side seems to have said: 'What do you want ships at all for? Ships are the instrument of war, and war the instrument of a policy. What policy?' Why did each side fear the other? What purpose did each suppose the other was pursuing? No German diplomat explained why British preponderance at sea damaged the welfare of the German people, or for that matter of the German capitalist. German trade was expanding, even in British colonies and Dominions Germany possessed very considerable overseas' territory of which she made little use commercially, largely for the reason that expansion was much easier into non-German territory.

Instead of attempting to arrive at the grounds of fear, the real nature of motive, we tried to get agreement upon our respective forces, as though force itself, not its purpose and what its user hoped to achieve by it, was the issue. Neither side said to the other:

'Supposing you beat us completely in this contest for armament and we had to admit ourselves completely in your power, what would you ask us to do? Is it something we could easily grant without injury to ourselves, or is it something that would constitute an intolerable burden?'

A dozen statesmen and historians of the first rank have testified that never were there fewer specific differences dividing Britain and Germany than on the eve of the War. We had no unresolved difference. Yet we went to war. Why? Because Germany, adding to the greatest army in the world the greatest navy, threatened to overtop us completely by her power. What would she have done had that predominance been established? What did she desire to do? No one knows.

While some writers of the time alleged that the whole motive was economic, the fight for trade, others—usually with a great display of moral indignation—denied that trade or economics had anything to do with it. Many financiers and capitalists greatly feared the War, and quite a considerable number, alike in Germany and Britain, foretold, with some accuracy, the ruin and devastation which would come upon their order and economic system. Incidentally, does anyone believe that the main motive of intervention in Spain is economic in the sense of a struggle between Capitalist governments for markets and investments? If so, why do the Capitalist governments of Germany, Italy and Japan (to say nothing of others) agree, and if three can agree why not thirty? If the struggle is as between Communism and Capitalism, why is there danger of war between Capitalist governments, as the whole idea of war over Spain implies?

Before the War this present speaker asked one of the diplomats concerned in the Anglo-German dispute why it was that the discussion of the underlying issues, the ultimate purpose of power, could never, somehow, be brought to the surface. The diplomat replied: 'We are concerned with the discussion of facts, and acts, not motives or theories.' As though motive did not explain acts, and theory policy, and policy were not the very fact with which he was dealing.

There is, of course, some tiny progress since then. We are nearer to-day to asking Germany 'What do you want? What can we do in order to give you satisfaction, so that you may get without war what you hope to obtain by means of it?' So far it is a gain. But such is the prevailing ignorance of elementary facts in economics, and their relation to international politics, that, as soon as we get to grips with specific cases (e.g., throwing open the Ottawa preferences to all nations that will give us terms as good as those given by the Dominions) passion and propossesion will take the field.

We must begin perhaps by an understanding between great States, because they are the States that have the thing about which the agreement has to be made: armaments, power. Agreements as to how power shall be used made between States that don't happen to have any, will not get us much further. If war is a misuse of power, the first parties with whom to deal in preventing such misuse are those who possess the thing likely to be misused. If it is a question of refraining from the use of coercion, the first agreement to obtain is from those who hold the means of coercion. If it is a question of restraining the use of coercion, the first co-operation to be secured is that of those who have the means to apply such restraint.

But this, it may well be objected, will in fact make of any pact a new Holy Alliance for dictating such revision as the Big Four may like and opposing the revision they don't like, and undermining the rights of the lesser States.

That, of course, is a danger, but it will be a small danger if we are fairly free of illusions as to what power can and cannot accomplish in a positive sense.

If the power of any new alliance is used for the one purpose of imposing peace, we may welcome it.

Dictation of peace is the only form of Dictatorship which civilisation ought to welcome, for it is the prevention of dictatorship by one litigant to another; the cancelling out of force as the arbiter of disputes. If, when you resist the force of another who would rob you, and overcome him, that other complains that you are 'dictating' to him, you would probably agree he abused language. But, if having overcome him, you used your power to rob him, you *would* be dictating.

The whole question is whether an alliance is to dictate peace or dictate frontiers. If it says: 'Obtain change of frontiers by any means you like except war,' it will be good. If it says: 'Should you attempt to change your frontier by war we shall defend your victim,' it will be good. If 'Change your frontier or we go to war,' it will be bad.

The phrase 'fighting for the strict maintenance of frontiers,' implies confusion which has bedevilled understanding of this matter from the first. We have nowhere 'guaranteed frontiers.' What we have done is to give guarantees against their change by war. We guarantee not frontiers, but peace. Far from guaranteeing frontiers we should, in many cases, work energetically for their change—change by means of making them of less importance, by attenuating some of the obstacles to free movement across them which they constitute at present; by securing greater respect for minority rights within them; by developing the principle of equality of right for all nations in colonial territories; as well as change in certain cases, perhaps, by actual change of sovereignty. But while working to such ends we should make plain that their attainment by the war of one interested party against the other will be so resisted as to make the way of the transgressor exceedingly hard: resisted not necessarily by fighting, though the whole method collapses if we say beforehand, as we said in the case of sanctions: 'Nothing will make us fight.'

My reply, therefore, to the question which I have put is that we cannot give the Totalitarian States what they want now without accepting an impossible position for ourselves. For what they want now is preponderance.

Whether they could be brought to accept collective security if we made it clear to them what it means and that it really would give them security because we are prepared to fight for it, I leave to other speakers. I would like in closing to make an attempt at definition of collective security. It is this:

Collective security means the pooling of the power of a group of States to ensure by their combined action the right of each to third party judgment of its disputes with others, to peaceful settlement, that is; which means defence from the aggression of a State that will not accept third party judgment. The essential element of the method commonly overlooked is that the group offers to those against whom it arms the same rights which those arms are created to defend. It is in this last element that it differs from the old type of alliance.

VI

DO WE THEN SURRENDER DEFENCE—TO THE TOTALITARIANS?

It is clear that we have given up our historic Balance of Power policy; chiefly because to maintain it would involve association with the Soviets, though we were prepared in the past to ally ourselves with the Czar or the Sultan. We are in consequence prepared to grant to the Totalitarians—particularly to Germany in Europe—a position of potential preponderance which we fought the War to prevent. What is our substitute for the now abandoned 'Balance'? Surrender of defence to the preponderance of just those Have-Not expansionist States whose policies, ambitions, political creeds, constitute the gravest menace to the 'owner' of a quarter of the globe? There is a large and perhaps growing school of thought in Britain which demands just that thing because the alternative involves associations which are to some more distasteful than a strategically dangerous situation for the Empire.

The question then arose whether in fact we were not, while waiting vaguely for the collective system somehow to come into being, surrendering our defensive position to the Totalitarian States. One member addressed himself to the question thus:

The last speaker showed, I think quite clearly, that what really brought us into the War was our refusal to accept the preponderance of Germany, a preponderance which would deprive us of any means of defence. We fought for our old friend the Balance of Power.

Although we fought in 1914 to resist German preponderance in Europe, German hegemony, we are—or very many of us, very important influential elements in the country—prepared to accept Ger-

97

man preponderance, and admit the whole policy of the War to have been a mistake. I will give my evidence in a moment.

Before doing so I want you to consider the significance of this fact: In 1914 the preponderance which we feared, was just an Austro-German preponderance in Europe. But the preponderance we face to-day is something infinitely more portentous: it is the preponderance of an Austro-German-Japanese-Italian combination, the preponderance of a combination which, so long as it can act as a unit, will be able to dictate to us in the Far East, in the Mediterranean, on the Suez Canal, on the road to the Antipodes and to India—and in the Channel. The lesser danger prompted the incalculable sacrifice you know. The obviously greater danger we are prepared to accept without any real attempt to face it or to fight it. We now argue that the thing which was a deadly danger in 1914 is the thing we can quite well and safely live with to-day.

Let us get the point clear. The last speaker has demonstrated that it was no particular or specific difference between us which brought us into the War. It was a general one. I know that early in the War the whole thing was most usually explained—or dismissed—with one word: Belgium. Subsequent discussions have at least served to make it clear that Belgium was an incident in the quarrel of the other States, that if certain other issues had not been involved the Belgian question would never have arisen. That is precisely why Belgium is not quite content to see the devastation of her country take place as a mere incident of the quarrels of others—though it is what is likely to happen, not alone to Belgium, but to any of us in a badly managed world.

If it be true, as the present claims of Belgium make clear, that if certain other issues had not been involved the Belgian problem would never have arisen, why did Germany raise it? And why, if our object had been the protection of Belgium, did we not do in 1914 what we did in 1870, and say to Germany 'Keep out of Belgium and we keep out of the War'? That would probably have saved Belgium. But we could not say it because quite other considerations would, we felt at the time, compel us to come into the War against Germany. And as that realisation grew upon Germany our power ceased to have any value so far as preventing war against Belgium was concerned.

The previous speaker is quite right when he insists that one supreme consideration moved that part of our public opinion which is decisive in these things, as the same consideration later moved the same kind of opinion in the United States: Germany's victory in the War would place us at her mercy, render nugatory that 'national defence' for which nations, any nation, will give everything. German victory would, we felt, place our most vital interests and rights in her keeping, not ours, enable her to dispose of them at her pleasure, at her discretion. More specifically, a Germany which had annihilated France as a Great Power, overcome Russia, opened the roads to the East through the Slav territories, established complete hegemony of Europe and the Near East, was in a position to occupy, when she would, the Continental ports of the narrow seas—such a Germany would have been master of our policy; irresistible. (She proved to be nearly irresistible, anyhow.) In any future dispute with such a power we should not talk on equal terms. We might as well, in such a contingency, have had no armament at all, because the outcome of any attempt to use it against such a power would have been a foregone conclusion. (Under the code duello a fight was stopped immediately one of the duellists became 'placed in a position of manifest inferiority,' for then the fight would become mere butchery by the stronger combatant.) Such a position of defencelessness was, we felt, particularly paralysing for a world-wide empire. It is indeed one which even little States will not accept without struggle, without at least the gesture of defence (as witness the rearmament of all the little States, including Belgium, this last year or two) although the final outcome of isolated resistance against the stronger power may be tragically certain. Even distant America, at the period of the German onslaught, was stirred by the same spectre of this growing Germanic power. One of the most effective bits of war propaganda in the United States was a map of Europe showing pan-Germania dominating the whole.

There was nothing new or apologetic in this theme that such domination as Germany threatened was incompatible with the defence of the British Empire. As the *Times*, among other serious newspapers, repeatedly pointed out after our entrance into the War, to resist domination of Europe by a single power had been our declared policy for two centuries. We, like other free peoples, had stood by it in the Napoleonic era, and it had gained in force since national had replaced dynastic considerations. Indeed, it is clear that

if defence means the defence of political independence and sovereignty, so that no external body can exercise its will upon us, then
that body must not be stronger than we are since then we would
not be independent. We would be subject to the dictation of others,
with no means of effectively resisting that dictation. And during the
War it would have been, in the prevailing view, a treasonable surrender of national and imperial security to allow the creation abroad
of a power, or a combination of powers, so great as to make resistance to it impracticable.

All this, in the War years and before, was almost universally accepted as political truism. In one respect at least the War confirmed
certain of the underlying assumptions of the common view. The
power of the Central Empires proved to be enormous—infinitely
greater than had been generally anticipated. And if the view that
only an equilibrium of opposing forces can secure the defence of each,
to say nothing of justice or peace, is sound, the danger of which the
enemies of Germany made so much, was a real and portentous danger.

But to-day, this whole theory, accepted in the War years and before the War as so obviously true and the underlying justification
of our entrance into the War, is rejected almost as generally as previously it was accepted—rejected sometimes by those who were its most
prominent and persistent advocates.

It is strange to reflect that politicians, newspaper writers, authors
of distinction, who for years before the War did their utmost to
make our participation in it inevitable, now by implication (sometimes explicitly) declare that the whole policy which lay behind that
participation was mistaken. Those who previously described so luridly
the dangers of German power now tell us that an enormously strong
German Mitteleuropa, dominating the Continent, or an overwhelming combination of Continental powers, does *not* constitute a menace
to our defence and that we should welcome and encourage it; that
the ends which it was the whole purpose of the Allied forces of the
War to frustrate (e.g., absorption of Serbia into a Germanic Confederation or Hegemony) are in fact desirable ends, or inevitable;
that, in other words, the War was a tragic error and need never
have been fought; as tragic an error in its realistically political aspects
as in those more idealistic aspects embodied in the popular slogans
about 'ending German militarism,' 'making the world safe for de-

mocracy,' the 'War to end war,' where failure is so patent that in very decency we try to forget that these so loudly proclaimed purposes moved millions to their death.

If, however, the thing is true, if the failure is a fact (as at least in the ultimate sense it is), it is wise to face it and try to discern its lessons. And if those who stood for the War in 1914 and for certain policies which led to it, now avow change of opinion, only fools would find ground for disparagement therein. Capacity to change one's opinions in the light of new facts is proof of wisdom far too rare in our changing world. But conscious and deliberate change of policy and opinion is very different from an unnoticed slipping from one policy to an entirely opposed one, without knowing why the change is made, without even knowing that such a change has taken place, with no clear realisation of why the old policy failed, and what elements in it must at all costs be avoided if the result of the new is not to be as bad as that of the old.

Take one indication:

Mr. Garvin's articles in the *Observer*. They are sufficiently indicative of the degree of change which characterises a great deal of Conservative opinion. Recall for a moment, not only what was until yesterday our attitude towards Mitteleuropa or Pan-Germanism and its dangers, but the fact that the direct occasion of the War was the Serbian resistance to Austro-German absorption; that our action was directly designed to support, among other things, the right of small States to be free of German domination, or suzerainty or compulsion; that this cause was supported with a passion and idealism for which some hundreds of thousands sacrificed their lives. And set beside that fact Mr. Garvin's recommendation of to-day, which is that Poland, Austria, Czechoslovakia, Jugoslavia, Rumania, Hungary and Bulgaria be brought under German domination constituting a German Federation. He recommends it presumably on the ground that 'the German race should have a scope comparable to that of the Soviet Empire.' (Why, then was not pre-War Germany entitled to a position comparable to Czarist Russia? Of this new German Empire he says:

'It would comprehend most of that great geographical sphere in farther Europe, dislocated and disorganised by the War-treaties in the name of emancipation—"Balkanised" as the vivid and true phrase went amongst all intelligent pacifists. The second of the main conditions of constructive peace in Europe as a whole is that a large part of "Eastern Europe" proper shall be reconstructed under German leadership.

'The eastward sphere concerned lies between the Germanic centre of the Continent and the Soviet boundaries. The most vital part of it stretches down the Danube. Not for nothing in the politics of to-day as in past history does the Danube, that longest river-artery of Europe, draw its headwaters from the Reich before it flows far onward through or by many nations to the Black Sea. Through or by Germanic Austria, mixed Czechoslovakia, dismembered Hungary, redoubtable though ill-united Yugoslavia, penalised Bulgaria, and New Rumania. These far-stretching territories, naturally connected, but now split up beyond all reason by racial antagonisms and the consequent restrictive economics, are the seismic region or "earthquake zone" of European affairs. Their present conditions contain more acute causes of future war apt to spread into general war than all the rest of the Continent put together.'

So he would unite them economically by a customs union, though, unlike the old German Zollverein, not on the basis of full free trade within the Federation, but something it would seem along the lines of a Central European Ottawa. Thus:

'The precedent is furnished by the great network of preferential treaties which, in the twenty years before the War, were negotiated by Germany throughout all the areas we have mentioned, and to the remarkable advantage of all concerned.'

He adds:

'For illumination on the nature of the present case, though not on its extent, let us all remember the profound prophecy not of a German but of one of the founders of the modern Czech revival, Francis Palatzky. "If Austria did not exist it would have to be invented." And this holds true in the spirit though the reconstruction necessary would now have to be carried out on a magnified scale, as we have seen. The historic Hapsburg monarchy, though an obsolete political structure in its last period, was an admirable economic system, with far better conditions of general human welfare and progress than now exist where it stood among the disrupted fragments and the "Balkanised" discords of the separated States. They ought to be as efficiently connected with each other and with Germany along the whole course of the Danube as are the American States along that other "ole man river," the Mississippi.'

In other words, the whole plan is pretty much what we accused Germany of desiring to do before the War, and which we entered the War to prevent. She would probably have achieved just such a purpose as that described by Mr. Garvin if we and our Allies had not made war upon her with the deep approval of the pre-War Mr. Garvin.

But please don't assume that Mr. Garvin is a voice crying in the wilderness. Such straws as this show the wind. Dean Inge—who by the way accepts the anti-Christian push of the Hitlerite State with surprising complacency—prefaces one of his evening paper articles thus:

'No Englishman who has visited Germany with his eyes open has any doubt about the fine spirit of patriotic exaltation and disciplined self-sacrifice in that country, nor about the sincere wish of the Germans to be good friends with us.

'Twenty-three years ago, when we were thinking of nothing less than of war, we were dragged at a moment's notice into a Balkan quarrel which in no way concerned us, because agreements had been made behind our backs with France, and we were more afraid of France, if we stood out, than of Germany.

'If we want to make sure that this monstrous folly will not be repeated, we must make it clear to the Government that the country would not stand it a second time.'

A similar pronouncement during the War would have lost the Dean his deanery.

This straw is just one of many. I have made, quite casually, not at all systematically, a collection of comments appearing in our Press during the last few years revealing (though this feature has recently dropped) dislike of and hostility to France; passionate prejudice of course against Russia; but liking and admiration for the Totalitarian Dictators and the expression of a determination on no account to oppose their purposes. It seems strange, but it is true. If it had been English generals fighting in Abyssinia, their victories could not have been more rapturously welcomed by Mr. Garvin; the Japanese action against China in 1931 was warmly applauded throughout nearly the whole of the Conservative Press; Germany was never so popular as when she occupied the Rhineland; Franco has warm adherents, the advocacy of his cause being undertaken by a British Society, a prominent member of which recently joined the British Government.

Going back a year or two, here are expressions of opinion which indicate with sufficient clarity the attitude of many of our papers to the threatened Totalitarian preponderance:

Thus the *Daily Express*:

'The British nation is not going to get at odds with the Germans for the sake of the French, who want to maintain their military domination of Europe.

'This attitude on the part of the public is not due to any love for the

Germans. It springs from a fixed intention to preserve "peace in our time," so far as we are concerned.

'We will not fight again in a European cause. The future of Alsace-Lorraine makes no difference to us now and henceforth.

'We must stay at home and cultivate our garden, far from the militarist frets and fevers of Europe. . . .'

So, if France is crushed by Germany and French hegemony gives place to German, we are unconcerned.

At a later date the same paper feared Mr. MacDonald may have been 'committing' us[1]:

'He is committing us in Rome and Paris to defend the indefensible frontiers of the Continent against those who seek to change them. If he succeeds in his purpose he may involve us, within a few weeks, in armed conflict on foreign soil . . .

'The House of Commons must make it plain to the Chancelleries of Rome, Berlin and Paris . . . that at all costs Britain is resolved to keep outside the embattled lists of Europe.'

In the *Sunday Times*, 'Scrutator' gives aid and comfort to Japan:

'This country is determined to incur no responsibility for the sanctions under Article Sixteen, in no circumstances to run the risk of war for the sake of Manchuria, or to allow ourselves to be diverted from our first and over-riding duty to recover for our own country its freedom from oppressive taxation, for misery of slums, the decline of international trade, and the demoralisation of enforced idleness. What is Jehol to Southwark, or Chaoyong to Salford?'

From another quarter, *Truth,* comes this:

'. . . There is a strong, though unexpressed, current of feeling in England in favour of forming some sort of alliance with Germany in Europe and with Japan in the Far East to keep the peace of the world against all assailants. And why not? There is a strong and general revulsion of feeling on the part of most of us in favour of post-War Germany—there has arisen a very general feeling that we get on better with the Germans than with the French, and that if ever there were to be such a calamity as another European war, Great Britain and Germany (including Austria) would be allies, not enemies. . . .'

The constant stream of encouragement which the Imperialist Press gave to the Japanese conquerors may be indicated by these extracts from two typical representatives of that Press: the *Morning Post* and the *Daily Mail*. The following are characteristic extracts from the *Mail*:

[1] March 21, 1933.

November 5, 1931

'Japan's presence in Manchuria has been a benefit to the world. . . . Not for a moment would the people of this country permit an attitude of hostility towards Japan.

February 27, 1932

'Japan's case is a very strong one. It is that China is not an organised people with a responsible government as the League of Nations assumes.

'Ignoring the realities of the situation, our pacifist warmongers are re-doubling their shrieks for British intervention. They are clamouring for the British Government to carry out an "economic boycott" and "pacific blockade" of Japan. Their aim, they say openly, is to "bring Japan to reason."

'Once more we must remind them that "economic boycott" and "pacific blockade" are impossible in the modern world without war, and of that war the brunt would have to be borne by the people of these islands.

'The duty of the government is clear. It is to have nothing to do with action, whether diplomatic or "economic" against Japan.

November 21, 1932

'The Japanese reply to the Lytton Report *re* Manchuria was issued last evening. It is an exceedingly able document, which will convince all reasonable people that Japan has right on her side. The essential passage in Japan's reply is that she has treaty rights and vast economic interests in Manchuria, and that having a large number of her people settled there, she is vitally interested in the country.

'As everyone knows she won those rights by prolonged struggle with the Russian Empire in 1904-5, and will never tamely surrender them.

'It would be an outrage on humanity to bring about such a solution in order to save the face of the League of Nations. But the misguided idealists who have so openly taken side with the Chinese war-lords and communists mean to make strenuous efforts to force Great Britain into some wild scheme of economic and financial boycott of Japan which they hope would drive Japan from Manchuria.

December 10, 1932

'Japan is rendering good service to civilisation by restoring law and order in Manchuria. She means to stay there and Great Britain has not the slightest intention of turning her out.

'Fortunately Sir John Simon's wise and moderate policy prevailed with the Assembly of the League of Nations.

February 6, 1933

'The attempt of the League of Nations to force Japan out of Manchuria, where she has vital interests and where she is creating order and peace, is a thoroughly mischievous one.

February 27, 1933

'Any embargo of arms to the combatants must be applied equitably to both sides. But any embargo would mean ominous interference with British industry. To impose an embargo at all would absolutely wreck our trade in the Far East.'

The *Morning Post* editorial comment is in similar strain throughout. Thus:

November 9, 1931

'We have no cause of difference with Japan as long as she observes the rights of British subjects in Manchuria, and we have even reason for gratitude (as for admiration) in the strong stand she is making against anarchy, brigandage and murder. If the Chinese Republic were to establish order and good government south of the Great Wall she might then have real ground to claim non-intervention in these outlying parts of the ancient Chinese Empire. As things are, it would be both futile and inhumane to espouse her quarrel with the Power which is putting one room of her house in some sort of order.

November 16, 1931

'But even if the Japanese case were less strong than it is nothing could be more foolish than any attempt on the part of the League Council to invoke against Japan the "economic sanctions" stipulated in Article Sixteen of the Covenant. . . . A policy which risked embroiling the world for the sake of peace would be a mockery. What is at issue is something more important than the dignity of the League of Nations.

January 30, 1932

'But to suggest that Great Britain should enter into some sort of agreement with other Powers to intervene on behalf of China seems to us fantastic. . . . We say plainly that Great Britain would never consent to be dragged into the danger of war on such an issue.

'Japan, we hope, is our good friend: apart from a possible error in the weapons used, she is acting under the sort of provocation which has forced Great Britain into similar action before now.

January 30, 1932

'For our part, although we do not believe in peace at any price, we value it enough to beware of entering into superfluous danger in a doubtful cause. Japan, broadly speaking, is the only element making for order and good government in the Far East.

March 3, 1932

'Those politicians whose credit is involved in the League of Nations were ready to drive the world to war in order to vindicate the machinery of peace. To the plain man the lesson of these dire events will remain obvious: an appeal to Geneva is no satisfactory substitute for the power of self-defence.

February 21, 1933
'Yet the League which might have used the occasion to lesson the Chinese, is behaving as if they were the innocent as well as the injured parties. We do not see how this partiality is going to benefit the world at large or any British interest. Nor do we see how it is going to help the cause of peace. On the contrary the Chinese politicians have foolishly persuaded themselves that if they make war with Japan in Jehol, the League which has taken their side in the argument will also take their side in the fighting. . . . The League of Nations would best serve the interests of peace by making it clear to China, without any further delay, that there is no prospect of such intervention.

April 24, 1934
'The intervention both in Shanghai and in Manchuria, whatever may be thought of the methods employed, were invited by China, if not forced upon Japan, through the anarchy and misrule which threatened every foreign interest.'

Lord Beaverbrook indeed comes near to declaring, in terms, that we should never have gone into the War at all. Referring to the comment raised by the daily publication of the most grisly pictures of the War, the *Daily Express* says in its leading article on March 16, 1934:

'Deplore it as any person not utterly mad must do, the deadly fact remains—the Continent is making ready a new vast battlefield, digging an immeasurable grave.

'We are engaged, by present commitments, to attend on the day that the European armies clash. These pictures tell you what happened the last time we fulfilled the obligation.

'They ask the question: *Are you prepared to face all that again?*

'A great moral issue is raised and put before the people.

'It is stated in this way: Shall British citizens be subject to an order to lay down their lives defending the possessions of another people? Or

'Shall they declare their freedom from such a fearful bond, resolving never to engage in war again, but to preserve peace in the British lands?

'The people can choose whether their sons shall live out their lives of useful labour and be buried at last in their native soil. Or hurry them in a new untimely expedition to the graveyards of the Somme and Aisne.

'Who doubts what will be the resolve of mothers and fathers who face that?'

If words have any meaning, that tells us that we should have denounced the Belgian Treaty before the War, declined all 'consulta-

tions' with France, and remained indifferent to German victory over
that country.

For several years before 1914 the coming aggression of Germany
—envisaged usually in the form of invasion of this country—was
the commonplace of daily talk and discussion. Plays were produced
(*The Englishman's Home* was one), based upon the time when the
German army would make a sudden descent upon these shores. The
more popular Press constantly published stories of the discovery of
secret plans of invasion. The *Daily Mail* published a serial, based
upon the forthcoming German invasion, describing the battles that
were to take place on British soil. Writers like Robert Blatchford
were engaged to enlarge upon the theme. His articles, re-published,
sold by the hundreds of thousands. We were all told how the German navy made a practice of solemnly toasting 'The Day' when
Britain would be humbled by Germany. The late Lord Roberts took
an active hand. Political writers made us familiar with the great
German Trinity of Treitchke, Nietzsche and Bernhardi. Day by day,
week by week, month by month, the fears and apprehensions of the
country concerning Germany's intentions were sharpened and in-
tensified.

The justification presumably was that Germany *did* constitute a
danger and that to awaken the public to the danger was indispensable
to our safety. To the extent that other nations joined in our apprehensions, we rejoiced. At a later stage in the development of the
situation very great efforts were made, to bring home to others, particularly America, the dangerous nature of German policy. We felt
it to be of obvious advantage that other nations should also see the
character of that policy, because in the event of war it would ensure
their friendly neutrality—prevent them becoming allies of our enemy
—and possibly even lead to them becoming our allies in resistance to
him. If, in the years immediately preceding the War, a great world-
gathering of States had solemnly pronounced German policy to be
dangerous and provocative, we should have regarded that as of immense value to us, a fact which no one but a madman or someone
desiring the success of his country's enemy could possibly deplore.

Yet when that very thing did take place in the case of Japan the
Press which had been so belligerently anti-German in the pre-War
years found the spectacle a distasteful and irritating one, and came

to the defence of Japan. Japan should not be scolded. The world should mind its own business. And even when Japan, having already violated undertakings solemnly given to us, bombarded peaceful cities, slayed and destroyed without declaration of war, in a way which if done by Germany before the War would have provoked instant war by us, the selfsame papers who had so consistently made the most of every incident of German hostility, extenuate and excuse; and even applaud.

The popular Press of our day, in facing the Japanese danger, reverses completely every argument which it used in facing the German danger before the War. Why?

If the growth in power of the orderly Germany of the pre-War era, a Germany of culture, traditions, race, so closely allied to ours, was a menace that we had to fight to the death, what shall be said of the danger presented by the sudden growth of an Asiatic power of such immense potentialities threatening the security of India, Australia, our Eastern interests as a whole? If that pre-War Germany, aided by Austria and Turkey, was so grave a menace to our Empire and trade, what would be the threat presented by a Nazi Germany, allied, as she would inevitably be in the event of a Russo-Japanese war, with a Fascist Japan?

Until 1913, Germany was a State with which, never in all its history or ours, had we had a serious quarrel. We had, on the contrary, for centuries been political and cultural allies of the Germanic peoples. To German culture we owed much of our religious Reformation; the later Reformation of that Reformation; much of our metaphysical thinking; most of our music; a great part even of our social services, like the Health Insurance System—to say nothing of our Royal Family.

Until 1914 itself, Germany had scrupulously respected all her engagements with us; had, in fact, made resistance to the expansion of the Slav on the Continent, not resistance to British expansion overseas, the major element of her foreign policy. Yet, nevertheless, in a year or two, because of her threatened domination of the Continent, Germany had become in the mind of the average Englishman, especially apparently in the mind of popular newspaper proprietors, the gravest possible menace, the mad dog of the world, who must be chained as the price of saving mankind from an evil and intolerable tyranny.

Compare the conduct of Germany in the decade which preceded the War—without a single breach of a single international treaty, a single breach of the peace—with the conduct of Japan this last five years: the establishment in power of parties wedded to a 'Prussianism' which has not hesitated to resort to widespread assassination to eliminate opponents at home; the sudden and ruthless bombardment of peaceful cities which were partly British cities; the cynical disregard of solemn Treaty obligations; a claim now to what amounts in effect to the right of conquest of China and the exclusive right to intervention in that country, which foreshadows the possibility of organising four hundred million Asiatics as an instrument of power for further Japanese objectives, not likely to be more 'moderate' than those already announced.

Even the moderation of a *Times* leader can hardly soften the grimness of the situation:

'The British Empire has a large and increasing trade with China. Hong Kong, a British Colony, is one of the most prosperous ports in the Far East, and its University is doing much for the education of the Chinese youth. More than a third of the foreign ships that enter and clear Chinese ports fly the Red Ensign. British capital has been invested in a multitude of undertakings in almost every province, and in Shanghai British interests are only second to those of Japan. The work of British officials in the Chinese service, of British teachers and missionaries in China, cannot be assessed in material terms, but it is not to be dismissed as of no account. America, too, has large trade with China, and American education has done much to make the "Young Chinese" what they are. French Indo-China borders on the Southern Chinese provinces; French capitalists have an important position in the Chinese Republic; and there is a large French concession at Shanghai. Other European nations trade extensively with China; and it must not be forgotten that in British North Borneo and Malaya, in the Philippines, and in the Dutch East Indies Chinese colonists form most important communities. The political and economic importance to Japan of her relations with China, and the needs of her geographical position, are universally recognised. They entitle her to a foremost place in any international conference that may deal with Chinese affairs. But they do not justify the claim to a monopoly of influence, and it is because recent Japanese statements seemed to make this claim, with an arrogance that recalled the days of the Shoguns and the "closed Empire," that they caused such widespread uneasiness.'

To which consideration the *Observer* adds certain others:

'In effect, Japan now claims an exclusive influence over the 400,000,000 Chinese people, despite the seven other Powers who signed the Nine-

Power Washington Treaty. She has inspired an expectation that she will further claim naval parity with Britain and the United States. On the evidence of a Japanese newspaper she even contemplates protesting against the Singapore base as a "menace" to herself. These are portentous things, a sign of Japanese unwisdom. Neither Washington nor London can or will ignore them. The immediate result has been a spurt on Mr. Roosevelt's part in naval construction.'

The above is noteworthy for several reasons. It goes further in criticism of Japanese policy than most of the Conservative or popular press of Great Britain is even now prepared to go; it gives some hope that we may at last face, not in panic and haste, as a newspaper or party stunt, but deliberately and in time, the fact of the Japanese-German challenge.

Consider the most probable contingencies and their relation to Britain's interests. Quite obviously it is part of Japan's hope and plan to do in China what Britain has done in India: to make internal disorder of a large part of the Asiatic continent a means of its conquest; to conquer China, not so much with Japanese power, as with Chinese power, to use Chinese forces of one part for the conquest of the remainder. It will not, of course, be done in a day, but that the plan will be followed persistently Japanese history of the last thirty years reveals quite plainly. The attempt, whether successful or not, will inevitably bring Japan into conflict with Russia—much more certainly than British conquest of India made of Russia a potential foe. And if that Sino-Russian conflict produces war, then just as surely will Germany become the ally of Japan.

But the engagement of Russia in a great war would be precisely the opportunity for the 'liberation' and 'outlet' which has become the religion of Hitlerite Germany preached with flaming fanaticism and all the power of an all-embracing State. The offer of Ukrainian lands to Poland would afford to Germany the means of a 'deal' with Poland about the Corridor, and the defeat of Russia mark for the Germany of Hitler an immense achievement in prestige, in the removal of what Germany regards as her gravest 'moral and political' menace. It would be regarded as a supreme triumph for new Germany, wiping out all past humiliations; the winning of a great battle in that 'eternal war' against Communism to which Nazidom is sworn.

That is why it is true to say that the problem of German power, in so far as it ever was a problem, was not solved in 1918. The problem of a potential German preponderance which faced us in 1914 has become the problem of potential German-Italian Japanese preponderance now, of infinitely greater urgency. The growth of German power in 1914 did not present us directly with any immediate threat to our Far-Eastern or Antipodean Empire; the Japanese-Teutonic possibility does. The triumph of Teutonic over Slav influence, of German over Russian civilisation, would not have confounded us in 1914, despite the nonsense written at the time, with the triumph of a culture utterly alien to European tradition. But the preponderance in Europe of a Hitlerite, Nazi Germany backed by a Fascist-militarist-autocratic Japan triumphant in the East, would present Western civilisation with a threat much more fundamentally disturbing.

'It is plain, therefore,' a Martian observer might remark, 'that an Empire like the British, as much Asiatic as it is European, will be even more disturbed at the growth of the Japanese-Teutonic power than it was at the growth of the Austro-German power in the years preceding those events of 1914 which compelled Britain to stake her whole existence as an Empire upon the defeat of that combination.'

And therein the Martian, as we have seen, would be entirely wrong. The self-same groups which before 1914 saw in the growth of Austro-German power a menace to the Empire, to Britain's political freedom, to democracy, to Western civilisation, look quite benignly upon the growth of Japanese and German power twenty years later and resent bitterly any proposals for political combinations which might hold it in check.

The explanation, the reader may object, is simple enough: We are afraid; afraid that any act by us might expose Hong Kong to the same bombardment which Shanghai suffered; London to the fate of Barcelona. We have not power enough to take a vigorous line.

Well, Germany in the years preceding 1914 was a powerful and redoubtable enemy. The fact did not have the effect of producing the sort of submissiveness or acquiescence in aggression which we adopt in the Japanese case; German power had the quite contrary effect. And as to not having power: it is clear that America, Russia and China are all potential allies, and if a combination of the United States, Russia, China, Britain, with other States at the very worst benevolently neutral does not constitute power enough for decisive resistance to attack upon our rights and interests, what power would?

That does not mean that America is now ready to act with us or that we should form an alliance, even if we could, to declare war. But the drawing together of Britain, Russia, America, China would present a potential aggressor with the possibility of a combination sufficiently great to make aggression look less attractive and might well cause Japanese policy from becoming too aggressive.

Does the alternative mean that so far as Japan and her ambitions in China and the world generally are concerned, we are to take the line of non-resistance? Is our policy a notification that anything that Japan cares to do would be unopposed by us? (Japan, in fact, seems to have interpreted our policy in that sense, for her claims have steadily and remorselessly stiffened, as recent acts reveal.) A policy of non-resistance would have had a very great deal to recommend it. But non-resistance plainly is not the motive behind the policy of those who support Japan. For they are the very groups most insistent upon increase of our armaments for the protection of the national interests.

The kind of situation which we face, the way it has developed, the logic of the process, the weight and nature of the forces behind it, can only be grasped if we take the story as a whole since, at any rate, 1931, see to that extent at least the whole picture.

In that year Japan, faced (like the rest of us) grave economic and social difficulties, due largely to the growth of an economic nationalism, which made it extremely difficult to obtain the exchange necessary for the purchase of raw materials which she needed for her industry, the food and life of her people. One way of escape, even if only a temporary one, temptingly presented itself. Japan might do in China on a much bigger and more effective scale what Britain had done in India, find alike, raw materials, a market and enormous sources of military power. In China was a nation of four hundred million people having drifted into disorder, division, chaos, one section fighting another; but a people which was, nevertheless, more sturdy and vigorous than many of the Indian peoples and not riven by religious and caste differences such as those which divide Mahommedan and Hindoo; a people almost maniacally industrious—and splendid fighting material, once properly trained. More than one British historian has explained that India was not conquered by Englishmen: it was conquered by Indians, by one group being used to fight another. *Divide et impera.* Assuredly the principle could be applied to China.

But what of the nations, other than Japan, having important interests in China? It was true that here the weight of power against Japan seemed at first sight overwhelming. Japan was challenging not only four hundred million Chinese, but the interests of Russia, with its hundred and fifty million, of the United States—sufficiently powerful of herself if her strength were put forth to crush Japan utterly—of Great Britain, with its world-wide Empire, embracing Australia, India, Canada, all this leaving out such power, economic or financial, as might be exerted by some fifty members of the League of Nations. Could any one nation challenge such a combination?

But Japan was perfectly aware that the *divide et impera* principle could be applied, not only to China, but even more successfully to the West, to those whose interests were opposed to a Japanese domination of China.

For European society, as a whole, was even more divided than China itself, and to Western society could be applied the same principle as to China: one section could be played against another, used to fight another. Indeed, not merely were the White Nations struggling one against another, but there were deep fissures and divisions within each nation. Each nation was deeply divided about the very instrument that would be used in any restraint of Japan. The latter was aware that great sections in Britain would not desire to see the League of Nations succeed, would certainly refuse to take risks on its behalf, especially at a time when the country, just being pushed off the gold standard and forming its first post-War 'national' government was deeply preoccupied with domestic concerns.

All these Japanese expectations were fulfilled, fulfilled to a degree that must have been beyond Japanese hopes. The suggestion of the United States to the Government of Britain that these two countries give the lead in resistance to the Japanese challenge was curtly rejected by Britain, where Japan found many very vocal defenders, some even suggesting an Anglo-Japanese Alliance, rather than an Anglo-American understanding.

One consideration was, of course, the fear that defeat of Japan might hand over the control of China to Russia, and mean the extension of 'Red' China, and the influence of Communism throughout the world. Upon all these factors of division and disintegration Japan successfully counted. Britain and America did not begin that building up of a system of resistance to her (employing such means as the money market, bill discounting, refusal of loans, boycotts, embargoes on materials necessary for armaments, might offer), about which we are now talking six years later. Had the United States and the British Empire then started upon it and combined it with steady aid to China, we might by this time have created a situation in which the renewed conquests that have so appalled us, would not have been possible.

Instead of which, the Japanese defiance of immensely superior power was so successful as to inspire, as he has avowed, the Italian dictator to go and employ the same method of *divide et impera* in Abyssinia. Discontented tribal chiefs were bought. France was detached from support of British leadership or initiative. Abyssinia is to Italy what Manchuria may well be to Japan: not a great source of raw material or of area for redundant population, but a source of further military power, furnishing a *point d'appui* or useful base; the means for furnishing Italy with a black army of a million men, just as other parts of Africa furnish an immense force for France and India furnished for Britain a million and a quarter men in the Great War.

And just as Japan had found defenders in sections of British opinion, Mussolini found even more. If Japan had been able to nullify and defy immensely superior power by dividing it against itself, so was Mussolini able even better to play that game.

But note what follows. When Mussolini established himself in Abyssinia, a British soldier remarked somewhat naïvely: 'We now have him where we want him. If he plays any tricks, we can bottle up as much of his force as he chooses to put into Abyssinia.'

But is it not just possible that that thought has occurred to Mussolini too, and that his next step begins to give us a hint of 'Why Italian forces are in Spain'? Mussolini has just acquired a colonial empire, a much bigger one incidentally than he ever expected to possess at this juncture. (For it is known that he did not at first intend the conquest of the whole of Abyssinia.) He has succeeded beyond expectations; boldness, recklessness, even, had, from his point of view, paid extremely well. Is he likely, therefore, to be in any mood which would leave this surprising gift of fate at the mercy of Great Britain, or British seapower? If Abyssinia is to fulfil its purpose, if it is to be aught but a liability, he must protect his communications with it, as much as France must protect her communications with Northern Africa.

And Spain furnished a heaven-sent opportunity for applying the same technique of setting one section of a country to fight other sections for the benefit of an intervening third party, and of completely dividing those whose interest it is (and whose power, if invited, would be adequate) to resist the intervention. Franco, as the instrument of Italy and Germany, has many and vocal partizans, both in Britain and in France. So much so that Mussolini has no hesitation in avowing his whole purpose. History will have to say of Mussolini that he had such amazing confidence in his own ability as a player of the diplomatic game that he did not in the least mind revealing his cards to other players. Thus while a member of a Non-Intervention Conference he publicly congratulates his armies in Spain, which, officially, are not there at all. In the same way one of his journalistic spokesmen has announced that Italy has not the least intention of annexing any part of the Spanish Peninsula, but will loyally respect the integrity of Spain 'just as Britain has respected the integrity of Egypt.' And in order to dot the i's and cross the t's, the spokesman goes on to say that Italy's purpose is to occupy in Spain the same sort of position that Britain has occupied in Egypt.

In other words Italy will have in future such bases on both sides of the Straits of Gibraltar as she may deem useful or necessary. And if, as was argued the other night in the House of Commons, the mounting of large calibre guns on both sides of the Straits does not close them so long as Britain has command of the sea (Mr. Lloyd George pertinently asked why then the forcing of the Dardanelles during the War had not been feasible), then Italy (with Germany in the background) will of necessity be pushed to strive for the complete command of the Mediterranean. For the alternative would be to make Abyssinia or the new Italian African Empire worthless for the only real purpose which it might serve—a source of increased power for Italy. And if the technique of using discontented minorities has succeeded so well in Abyssinia and with hopes of such large results in Spain, why should it not be used throughout most of the Arab world, as an instrument against the British Empire, as a means which would help towards complete Italian command of the Mediterranean?

Just after the Italian occupation of Addis Ababa, Mussolini gave an interview to the *Daily Mail* (which someone has rudely described as 'his unpaid British organ') in which he announced that henceforth Italy took her place with the satisfied and sated nations, the implication being that she would indulge in no more ventures of expansion. Within a few months Italian armies were in Spain. There is no reason to doubt Mussolini's entire sincerity. Conquerors seldom seem to grasp fully the fact that in a world where relative national power is the criterion of self-preservation, it is impossible for the process of conquest to stop. Britain, heaven knows, was a 'sated' Power at the time of the Versailles peace making; but she could not reconcile herself to seeing pass into the hands of others vital strategic points, or sources of power, which could be used to embarrass her defence of a world-empire already difficult enough to defend. And Italy has not yet begun to secure any overseas empire of any real use as an outlet for population, a source of materials.

She has had immense success in the preliminaries of empire building. Can we expect that she will stop at the beginning? Why should she? The assumptions and principles upon which she is acting (e.g., 'the need, for expanding peoples, of new territory') have been accepted in the past all but universally, are still largely accepted by opinion in this country and are now being re-enforced by groups whose purpose is appeasement and conciliation. These latter, from the very highest motives, declare by implication that the old ideas of colony-owning and imperialism as the condition of survival for an expanding people are valid; not something from which the world should make every effort to get away, but the moral and material validity of which should, for the sake of peace, be conceded to Germany and Italy—and so, presumably to other Have-Not States, of which, once such claims begin to be made we shall find there are quite a number. (Poland is one of the more recent claimants.)

There are those who are so insistent that everything depends upon the conciliation of Germany that they do not want the facts brought out or even mentioned. Some propose apparently unconditional return of German colonies. The very fact that this school is vocal and influential will make it extremely probable that Germany will insist on nothing less than such return, or—quite as probably—upon compensation which she will regard as equivalent in economic and military value. Then there are those who, while insisting that Germany must at all costs be conciliated, also insist that the colonies must not be returned and that we must preserve the right not only to maintain preferences in the Crown Colonies, but to stiffen such preferences. Their general idea seems to be that we should recreate the old eighteenth-century Protectionist Empire and placate Germany, Italy and Japan by encouraging them to go and do likewise—first getting their empire.

Note the situation if we ever got to discussion of return of colonies, accepting the assumptions of the Rothermere-Beaverbrook-Garvin-Amery-Astor school of thought. We should be abandoning the internationalist solution looking to the abolition of preferences, the establishment of the Open Door all round in the colonies. We should presumably be attempting a 'fairer distribution' of colonies imperially 'owned,' the sovereignty therein unqualified by international obligation, attempting to render a twentieth-century world workable along the lines of self-sufficient empires, economic nationalism. This is in accord with the feelings of our own neo-Imperialists as it would certainly be in accord with the general sentiments of the Fascist Dictators since their whole system is based upon government control of production and economic life generally. This unqualified control is only possible in a system of autarchy, self-sufficiency. So far agreement. But self-sufficiency for Germany can never be achieved merely by the return of her colonies. It would not even make any considerable contribution thereto. Only by that Pan-German hegemony, a virtual dictatorship over Czechoslovakia, Hungary, Rumania, Bulgaria, Poland, which Mr. Garvin among other English writers has been advocating, could there be anything approaching a successful autarchy; and even at that it would have to include extension into Russian territory.

Here we touch the real core of the policy of territorial redistribution. It could only give a prospect of working if China in the East and Russia in the West were sacrificed upon the autarchic altar. Does anyone believe that we could help forward the peace of the world by giving Japan a free hand to absorb China and Germany (together with Japan) a free hand to 'remove the Bolshevik menace' by destroying those foreign Governments, which in their view, were too tainted with Bolshevism? That vision deeply disturbed even President Roosevelt looking at it from distant Chicago. Those responsible for the Governments of Germany, Italy and Japan believe evidently that empires can be conquered and made profitable; believe in the international anarchy of unfettered national sovereignty and independence; that this free-for-all struggle in which the best nations will come out on top is the right and natural method of determining the relationships of peoples; that the idea of any constitutional system which would equally restrain an Italy and an Abyssinia, 'Bolshevik assassins' and the Government of the Reich, placing them all on a level, is silly, offensive, unworkable. This conviction has been stated emphatically a score of times by both Mussolini and Hitler, and there is no imaginable reason for doubting their complete sincerity in the profession of those particular opinions. They have added furthermore that with goodwill and friendliness anarchy can be made compatible with peace, not peace with barbarians like the Russians and the Chinese or Bolshevik Spaniards, but as between the Totalitarian States and the British and French democracies. Nor need we doubt their sincerity in this respect either.

Why in the name of reason should Japan, for instance, want to quarrel with us if we are prepared to refrain from interfering with her designs? It would be idiotic on her part, once granted that condition; and she has emphasised and will continue to emphasise her friendliness towards us—provided we keep off her newly acquired preserves. In 1931 many in Britain (including the Foreign Secretary) were quite prepared to accept this condition. The Japanese invasion of China was 'a distant dispute that did not concern us.' Similarly in the Mediterranean. We can maintain the peace in effect says Mussolini if only you will not talk law at me. And recently Von Neurath, speaking to the Academy of German Law, said that the very first condition of peace in the Far East was to drop towards Japan the attitude of moral judgment. We must not, if we want peace, talk about Treaties or Law or Constitutions, or codes, or rules. As against such ideas he put friendliness, day-to-day adjustment applied to each particular and specific case. There must be, he said, 'no standardised arrangements' or principles.

There is plenty of response to those ideas on this side. The newspaper correspondence to which reference has been made above reveals the fact that many, here, too, believe that with 'friendliness,' by setting aside that is all question of law or morals, anarchy can be made to work; that day-to-day accommodation is infinitely more important than the building up of any constitutional system.

If this is true, if return to an anarchy even more complete and an amoralism more stark than any we knew before 1914, is the road to peace, then it is safe to do what we have been doing for six or seven years: conceding some principle of Right because it gives us peace for to-day, and repeating the process every time a Dictator takes a new step forward. But if it is true, then do not let us pretend that we are not surrendering Right and Law and hope of such. And if it is not true that indefinite sacrifice of the law is compatible with future peace, let us face that fact too, and make clear what our aim really is, even though we are unable for the moment to pursue it.

On one ground only could we justly assume that a new and larger German hegemony would work where the old one failed, namely, proof that the Germany of Hitler shows greater capacity for the management of minorities, racial, religious and national, for reconciling them and securing their willing co-operation, than did the Germany of the Kaiser. Well, the history of the German Totalitarian State during the last few years in dealing with non-German elements within its borders, answers that question too. Answers it so completely that it need hardly be enlarged upon.

As Mr. Guerard, the American writer, once put it, England has not been saved by muddle; her natural advantages were so great as to offset the muddling.

'It is only in retrospect that they rationalise their drifting into a national purpose. Downing Street and the London *Times* cover chaos with a thick coating of impressive verbiage. As a matter of fact it is impossible to chart England's course to-day. She has no single principle of action, not even "sacred egotism"; she has at least five, and they are incompatible. The result is that, whilst individual Englishmen are intelligent and honest, "England" as a character in the international drama is thoroughly undependable. It is not "perfidy"; it is inner contradiction. England was honest when she promised to evacuate Egypt, and honest when she constantly refused to do so; honest when she pledged her support to France in case of aggression under the Locarno Pact, and honest when she reminds the world that such an agreement is to be taken only in a Pickwickian sense.'

Mr. Guerard's conclusion, by the way, is interesting. He says:

'Neither England nor America can have a position and steady policy antagonistic to each other. On the basis of mere national selfishness, they cannot unite. Their one hope, and the one hope of the world, is that they shall work together in the organisation and enforcement of international law.'

To say to America 'When we fight it will be only for our direct national interests; we shall never use force to promote a general interest or purpose' is obviously not the way to secure her co-operation.

League policy, if not League organisation, is the only possible basis of Anglo-American co-operation.

VII

'WHAT! FIGHT FOR CZECHOSLOVAKIA': THE CASE FOR ISOLATIONISM

'John Smith'—the plain man who by his vote will in the last resort settle the country's foreign policy speaks up. The simple hard fact, he says, is that the John Smiths will not vote for going to war for Czechoslovakia or any other place with a name so hard to pronounce. Moreover, he thinks that the old Balance of Power policy can be made to work in another way: by letting the foreigners—particularly the Hun and the Bolshie—eat each other up while we look on, the end being that all the combatants will be so exhausted that Britain will easily be able to defend herself and empire. In any case the risks of such a policy will appear to Smith, with the memories of the Great War still with him, less than the risks of once more mixing in the continental mess. If law or its sanctions mean war then Smith will let law go by the board.

'I really do want,' said the member who so far had not spoken much, 'to bring you fellows down to realities.' He continued:

Here for several meetings you have been making these excursions into history and politics and psychology and strategy but you have given little attention to what is going to settle the foreign policy of this country, namely, the view of John Smith, Voter—the not very politically minded voter.

Do look at your popular papers. Your non-political ones, the ones particularly that the women read. Listen to the talk in trains and buses. Do you really believe that if it was a question of fighting for Czechoslovakia you could ever hope to win the support of the Smiths to it? They cannot pronounce the word, and that of itself is almost enough. How are we concerned in it? Nobody except highbrows like you people here really knows.

Nor is it any good calling the thing for which you propose to fight 'law.' That word, too, is really quite uninspiring. The law is an ass, and we are not going to bleed ourselves white for him. Anarchy is another unexplained word. The electorate does not know what it means. An anarchist, so far as he knows, is a fellow—almost always a foreign fellow—who throws bombs. Well, let the foreigners throw bombs at each other; and then both sides, likely to be mischievous if they turned their attention to us, may be rendered powerless to injure us. If 'the international anarchy' means the system which we have known internationally in the past, well, this country has not done so badly under it that we should take any great risk to alter it.

Besides, are you sure that the 'instinct' which prompts Smith to keep out of the mess is not a very sound instinct indeed for which a great deal is to be said?

What is the danger which seems to disturb you people? I gather you regard it as something like this:

'A combination of autocratic Powers—Japan, Germany, Italy—may dominate the democracies, Britain, France, the Scandinavian States, the British Dominions, and possibly at a later date America, unless the democracies stand together. Russia who might serve as a counter-balance to the power of the Fascist States will be eliminated, or even, be brought to act in common with the Fascist combination, unless we bring her first into our combination. If such a combination becomes a political fact, the British Empire will be placed in a position of manifest inferiority, so that it will be unable to defend itself, as Britain feared in 1914 that the defeat of France by a Germany that dominated the Continent would put Britain in a position in which defence would be impossible.'

That is the theory. It was the theory which moved us in 1914 though the arrangement of powers then was different.

We have come to believe it was a wrong theory. Foreigners sometimes better than ourselves see that that is our belief.

I was recently in America and said to a friend of mine, after listening to talk in the Pullman smoker: 'It seems to me that ninety per cent of you Americans believe that you were bamboozled when you entered the War. You believe now that you never need have entered it.' He said: 'If you don't know that about American opinion you don't know anything.' But he also added this: 'From a recent visit to England I gathered exactly the same impression of British opinion which you have gathered of American. Not ninety per cent, but perhaps seventy-five, of your people really in their hearts believe that the entrance of your country into the War was a ghastly mistake; that your victory has not improved the face of Europe, that it has not made you any more secure. How *could* they believe it in face of the present situation?' And do you know, I had an uncomfortable feeling that he was right?

It is not only the Garvin-Lothian-Astor-Londonderry-Round Table lot who have abandoned the Balance of Power theory of defence; for popular elements, the Rothermere and Beaverbrook newspapers, and the Pacifists have abandoned it too.

It is shocking perhaps now calmly, casually, to decide that the War of 1914 was a mistake; that instead of fighting Germany we should have permitted her with Austria to discipline Serbia and dominate the Balkans; that the greatest blood bath of all history, the episode which marks the beginnings of the end for Western Europe, was all just a vast mistake. But it will not really shock our people very much. They have already been told it by Mr. Lloyd George and others who now explain that we all muddled and blundered into the War; that, in other words, our sons perished and millions were ruined because our politicians were muddle-headed and did not know their job. That is not a new story for John Smith. War memoirs are full of reflections still more appalling, as that the dreadful butcheries that went on in the great battles for day after day, week after week, in which hundreds of thousands went through tortures that we dare not think about, were sometimes due simply to personal quarrels and bickerings of individual generals or commanders who would not take the trouble to arrive at a real understanding with one another because they did not like each other's manners, or who half thought out a military problem upon which ten thousand lives might hang, because they were anxious to get to lunch. Our public know these things; they are not particularly angry.

So now when they are asked to accept the proposition, as the basis of future national policy that the Great War was due to an error of political judgment; or that we should now abandon a position in respect of Britain's preponderance of power which we gave a million lives a few years ago to sustain, there will not necessarily be much objection.

In any study of political movements, which are so much movements of feeling, impression, temper, one fact must never be over-

looked. The only attention which the mass of men can give to public
affairs is a spare-time attention. From the very circumstances of life
they are compelled to judge hastily, from headlines, careless chatter,
momentary impressions. To be presented on one and the same foggy
morning with puzzling questions about the gold standard and the
proper value of the dollar, the French quotas and the sacrifice of trade
with Russia for that with Canada; the price of milk, and the position
of the co-operative societies, our concern to protect the independence
of Austria from German Fascism and that of Britain from Lord Rothermere's; Japanese competition and the Indian White Paper; disarmament, aeroplanes, sterilisation of the unfit—all in one day's headlines,
means that no one subject can get very long consideration when a
man's personal affairs are likely to demand all the vigilance he can
summon.

And John Smith has a case, when he proposes not to mix any
more in the Continent. You tell us, he says, that if Japan conquers
China, Germany dominates the Balkans and the Danubian States, and
perhaps Russia, if Italy is placed in a position which will enable her
to close the Mediterranean, our position will be such that we can
no longer defend ourselves.

Not quite so fast, says John.

What will China, Russia, the Balkans, the Danubian States, Abyssinia, the African territories that Italy is to take over from France, be
doing all this time? He suggests that the farther these fellows go into
their conquests the greater will be the difficulties into which they will
get. China in all her thousands of years of history has never been
conquered, has always rather conquered the conqueror. The attempt
to conquer Russia undermined the greatest military Power that the
world till then had known, commanded by the greatest military genius
that the world till then had known. After all neither Hitler nor his
generals have the brains of Napoleon; yet Russia was too much for
Napoleon.

Note the experience in Spain. When Italy promised help to
Franco, Franco was to do the trick in a week or some such time, you
remember. That is getting on for two years ago. Japan was to smash
China in a series of rapid hammer blows. She is not doing it and more
and more people are coming to believe despite the Chinese retreats
that Japan never will do it. Even the Abyssinian tribes—just naked
semi-savages—are able to immobilise great Italian forces. Austria may

not be for Germany quite the simple before breakfast task of annexation that the Nazis would have us believe. The Balkan States are jealous of their independence. And then, what of internal trouble within these States if only we have the sense not to interfere with them? Perhaps it is true that the Italian people would have made their opposition to the Abyssinian conquest felt if only Mussolini had not been able to use the imposition of sanctions as a means of welding them together. Are the British and French Empires the only empires where trouble is likely to embarrass their governments in the future? Consider for a moment what, with all our moderation and liberalism we have had to face during the last twenty years or so: civil war in Ireland, virtual civil war in India, war in Palestine, serious trouble in Egypt, wars on the Indian frontier. Yet we are old hands at running Empire, not likely to make errors that Hitler, Mussolini, Japan can almost certainly be counted upon to make, are indeed already making.

And something more. While we do not want Fascism to sweep the world, neither do we want Communism. The victory of Russia, if it came to war might well be as disagreeable as the victory of Germany.

It is all very well for our German friend to say that we shall be obliged to take sides. I doubt it. We can very well not take sides; we can in truth sit on the fence and let Hun and Bolshie chaw each other up to our very great moral and material advantage. Give the Japan-Germany-Italy combination rope enough and if it does not hang itself it will at least so entangle itself in grave difficulties that it will be no particular danger to us.

Such is John Smith's case. I recommend it to your attention, for when the time comes I believe it to be the policy which has in it less of risk than any attempt to establish law, maintain the collective system, defend the European Constitution, or any of the other rather vague things which we have been discussing in our circle.

A spokesman was appointed to reply to John's case and that reply will follow in due course. But first of all it was decided to hear from the American.

VIII

THE AMERICAN OBSERVER OBSERVES

---

*The American member of the group shows that the American
John Smith has not only a more plausible but a genuinely stronger
case for Isolationism than his British counterpart. Yet it is not
strong enough, because it ignores the totalitarian technique of
domination which can be applied to America as to others and
which is not open war upon powerful democratic nations but their
weakening by (a) fomenting internal divisions (as in e.g. Austria,
Czechoslovakia, Spain and to some degree in France); (b) exploiting their fear of Bolshevism and (c) their fear of war.*

*Terrorism based on these fears has been employed to prevent
the democratic states from combining for mutual, collective defence, the only method which would give them equality of power
with the totalitarian group and effective defence against it. Americans, like others, are unconscious of the degree to which their
policy and moral standards are re-shaped in obedience to the
threat of war. The ways in which the totalitarian methods might
and probably will be applied to the United States are indicated.*

The American member of our group, who had preferred
so far to be regarded as an 'observer' rather than as an
active participant in our deliberations, was asked at this
point to contribute a paper on America's concern in the
problems we had been discussing.

I had rather do that, he said, than do what, however, I am tempted
to do—to undertake an apologia for America's policy since the war;
for her summersault of policy in the matter of the League, which
her President in a sense imposed upon Europe and then when the
Europeans accepted, the Americans repudiated; for America's eco-

126

nomic policy—protectionism combined with maintenance of debt claims; for her isolationism; for her, at times, rather comic fear of being entangled by British propaganda, and much else. As some of you know all those things can be explained, and not altogether to the discredit of the American people. Had more weight been given in Europe to the American point of view, the position to-day might not be so desperate.

It is not merely totalitarian policy which has been revealed here as bad. The policy of the European democracies has been shown in none too good a light. I do not take the view that the Fascist phenomenon is simply due to the Versailles Treaty, or we should have difficulty in explaining either the Italian or the Japanese manifestations, or indeed the Great War itself. That anyhow was not due to the Versailles Treaty. As some observed the other night, war is a little older than that much abused document. But what is true is that much of the development of Fascism is the direct outcome of mistakes made again and again by Britain and France ever since the war.

For that and other reasons America's apologia might be of use to you. But it would lead us rather away from the main purpose of our discussion which, I take it, is to uncover the significance of the Fascist phenomenon, our concern in it, and right policy towards it.

There is just this which, as a preface, I would like to say: Assuming, as it would seem we must, that the nations can only get peace and order and security by constructive and co-operative effort (just as individuals within our respective nations have discovered that peace and order between them can only be secured by constructive co-operation), assuming in other words that orderly society must be organised—even assuming all that to be true it is clear that America cannot come over and save Europe if Europe refuses to be saved; she cannot do for Europe what Europe refuses to do for itself. If Britain cannot manage to co-operate successfully with, say, France, why should you expect America to do so? Unless Britain, or Anglo-French or European policy attains to a certain degree of wisdom and success there can be no American co-operation. If the nations of Europe cannot prevent descent into the pit, then you are not going to be saved from outside. After all, you are much nearer to the problem than we are, ought to know better how to handle it. If it is beyond you, it is beyond us.

But it is not that aspect with which I would like to deal. I have been trying to see how far the fact which has emerged from this discussion—the danger which the growth in the relative power of the three great Fascist totalitarian states constitutes for the future of democratic nations—applies also to America; whether what we have been saying here concerns also my country, and if so, in what way.

The spokesman for John Smith has made out a case for British isolationism based mainly on the view that the further the totalitarian states become entangled in their conquests, the less power for mischief against Britain do they possess. The recent experiences of Japan in China, Italy in Abyssinia and Italy and Germany in Spain would seem to give some confirmation to his thesis. Those conquests are not going to be a walk-over and by the time they have been digested— if indeed they ever are—it may well be that little energy will be left over for the conquest of the British Empire.

But if that argument appeals powerfully to the British John Smith, think what its appeal must be to the American who, after all, is not concerned as are you in the defence of a world wide Empire. For you the Mediterranean is a vital artery through which runs what is for Britain economic life blood. If Italy and Germany manage to place themselves in such a position that they can cut that artery, you do indeed suffer—you and India and your Dominions. Yet, as these discussions have shown, great sections of your people, including your Conservative Imperialists—or Imperialist Conservatives—remain indifferent to such a contingency and would regard a German-Italian victory in Spain (as they regarded the Italian conquest of Abyssinia) with equanimity, with indeed satisfaction. But if you are not disturbed at such an advance of totalitarian power, why, in heaven's name, should we be?

If the British Smith has any case at all, our case is many fold stronger.

In this connection I would call your attention to the curious position taken by some protagonists of Anglo-American understanding or alliance, protagonists of the type of your Mr. Garvin and your Lord Lothian and in some respects your Lord Beaverbrook. Although of the 'Anglo-American Alliance' School they are also of the School which deprecates collective action in resistance to totalitarian power, of the school which—if Mr. Garvin is an example—are prepared to argue that Germany's hegemony of Europe would constitute no particular danger to civilisation or democracy in Europe; who are opposed to using power to prevent such aggressions as that upon Abyssinia, opposed to the use of force as the instrument of international order, of any Covenant or law. But if force is not the right instrument or sanction of an international organisation, or for an international purpose, and if you are only prepared to fight for the direct interests of Britain, as you so frequently proclaim, with what sort of grace can you ask our alliance? What is the purpose of the Anglo-American power which this school of 'force only for British interests' invokes? It hardly lies with those who declare that British power should never be used except to promote a British interest, either to reprove American isolationism or to appeal too insistently for Anglo-American co-operation.

This parenthetically. My concern for the moment is to ask in what way, if at all, America is concerned practically in the extending power of totalitarianism; whether that case for Isolationism, plausible as the British John Smith puts it, much more plausible when put as the American John Smith can put it, is indeed sound.

Lately, by the way, one has heard the usual arguments buttressed by the question: 'Why should the Fascist states *want* to challenge the power of America?' Well, that America, and American public opinion generally feels some challenge is reflected in the big efforts at re-armament made by my country. Whence is the danger, against which that armament is a preparation, most likely to come? Britain? France? No one believes it. Some years since perhaps some might have replied 'Russia,' vaguely 'the Bolshevists.' But no one whom we need consider would urge that to-day.

But this question, Why should the totalitarian states be concerned with America at all? needs a word or two. Consider the matter in its elementary aspect. Any state, even a liberal one, may find itself in a position of having to make demands—diplomatic, economic, commercial, matters of tariff, or shipping charges, or exchange control, or immigration restrictions, or refugees, or what not—upon another. In those circumstances its relative power in respect of that other may make a lot of difference. Indeed the final argument for all struggle for power is that we live in a world in which in the last resort a nation depends for its security, its independence and survival, upon its own *relative* power. That relative power is increased to the degree that the power of others is diminished. And the totalitarians have developed a very elaborate technique, as I shall try to show in a moment, for weakening the power of resistance of other states.

We recognise that the totalitarian triumvirate is a very powerful combination. Serious differences with it arising out of Japanese or Nazi or Fascist demands are by no means inconceivable. After all, the real enemy of Nazism is not Communism with which it has so close a doctrinal cousinship. Its real enemy is successful democracy. The continued success of democracy is a daily denial to seventy million Germans of the kind of doctrine daily dinned into their ears by their mentors. Yet if the millions whom the Dictators rule do not accept with conviction the dictatorship dogma, the position of the Dictator can never be quite secure. Democracy represents for the totalitarians a heresy; and where religions are dictated by authority, as political religion in Germany is, an evidently successful heresy may become very dangerous.

This continued denial, by the event, of a fundamental article of the Fascist credo, is of itself a standing encouragement to any anti-Fascist movement which may arise. The more that the democracies around them forsake the democratic principle and adopt Fascist methods (particularly if in the process powerful foreign states become weakened) the more does the position of the dictators in the totalitarian countries become strengthened, rendered secure from subversive movements within or inconvenient resistance to adventures abroad.

The argument for isolationism in its more familiar forms runs somewhat along these lines:

'Whatever Germany, or Italy, or Japan, or the three in combination may attempt to do, they will certainly *not* attempt the invasion of the United States. Given the military advantage which attaches to the defence in our day, particularly the defence of a country like the United States, the invader would face an unsurmountable military obstacle. Invading armies, even if they could gain a foothold, would be swallowed up. And though foreign trade, sea rights, freedom of travel, might be grievously interfered with, this need not vitally affect the well-being or the freedom or the way of life of the American people. These things will remain secure however great the power of the totalitarian states may become.'

Certain elementary military considerations are often invoked. Although Britain in the war had complete command of the sea and the coast of Belgium, occupied by the Germans, was only thirty miles away, Britain was never able to turn the German flank by a landing in Belgium. What chance of a successful landing in the United States would be possessed by a foreign army with its base three thousand or six thousand miles away?

It took England three years and over a quarter of a million men to conquer the territory of the Boers, who could never put more than about fifty thousand men into the field, who could not manufacture a rifle or a cartridge. On such a basis, taking into account the population and industrial resources of the United States, how long, what number of men would be required to conquer it?

So the argument of invulnerability, and the isolationism based on it, is at least plausible.

Nevertheless, reflecting upon our discussion, I am convinced that the growth of totalitarianism deeply concerns us; that it may prove a fatal menace to American freedoms, institutions, way of life; that we too may be coerced to living under totalitarian terror, though conceivably not a German or Japanese soldier ever landed on our soil.

The kind of isolationist argument I have tried to outline to you really ignores all but completely the particular technique which the totalitarian states have employed this last few years for the extension of their own power and the weakening of the power of those who might stand in their way. That technique does not include at this stage formally declared, or open war upon nations that come near to being their military or naval equals. This for two reasons: (1) None of the Dictators is very sure what would happen to him at the hands of his people after a period of warfare in which victory was uncertain, and in which suffering endured by the people of the aggressor state would be immeasurably greater than any endured in the very cheap military victories so far obtained by the totalitarian powers. And (2) since the totalitarian states have had such amazing success in extending their power without major war, by the mere threat of the use of their power, why should they abandon that method for a much more hazardous one?

Full appreciation of these two points is obscured by lurid stories of coming attempted invasions, and the destruction of great cities from the air. At this stage in the development of totalitarian tactics that is probably a quite remote contingency. The real danger is less dramatic and much nearer.

It consists in the relative ease with which much of the power of resistance of any democratic state which it is proposed to dominate can be weakened beforehand by what is in the first instance a profound moral change produced by terror, that moral change in its turn creating internal divisions that reduce the victim to powerlessness.

Let me expand this a little, for there is no reason in the world why the technique should not be applied to America in ways which I will indicate.

The totalitarian states have proved that terror, the threat of war, can be used in such a way as to frighten great masses of a country's population out of one moral code into another; and to the fear of war the totalitarians have known how to add other terrors by exploiting the fear and dislike of 'Bolshevism' and by developing latent racial animosities. Having produced by these varieties of fears and hatred and by terror this change of moral code (I will particularise in a moment) it becomes quite easy for the totalitarian state to produce in the people whom it proposes later to dominate a disunity, an internal conflict which, in turn, makes it easy to apply what we have called here the Spanish technique (which is, of course, also the Austrian and Czechoslovak technique) and provoke subversive movements against the constitutional government of the country which is to be the next victim, and so render it in fact helpless in the face of any powerful external aggression.

That is the method Germany is applying not only to lesser states like those of Southern and South Eastern Europe, but is actually applying before our eyes to France (about which I will say a word in a moment). And I see no reason why it should not be applied to the United States.

Note first the method and significance of its application to the lesser states.

A totalitarian state like Germany, great as it is, would be hopelessly out-balanced in power by the neighbours whom it threatens, so long as those neighbours can act as a unit, can maintain a co-operative collective defence. If, to put it in an extreme form, one could imagine Britain, France, the British Dominions, Russia, China, Belgium, Czechoslovakia, Rumania, Jugoslavia, Poland, Greece forming themselves for purposes of defence into one state, one defensive confederation, they would form a power much greater than that of the United States and just as impregnable, and much greater than that of the dictatorship group.

Such consolidation of power would form an insuperable obstacle to the ambitions of expansionist totalitarian nations. And, as has been pointed out in our discussions, this defensive co-operation is the only means by which lesser states *can* possibly protect themselves against the more powerful. This right of combination for mutual defence is assuredly a very elementary social right, it is indeed the principle upon which all organised society is based, and upon the answer to the question whether we can now extend it to the society of nations, to the international as it has already been applied to the national area, depends the answer to the question whether the democratic nations can preserve their civilisation.

But the democratic peoples have been terrorised by the threat of war even from trying the experiment. Why have the lesser states one by one withdrawn in what one of our speakers has called 'a pathetic skedaddle' from this system of mutual defence, of hanging together in order that they may not hang separately, which constituted their only real method of effective defence?

It is quite undeniable that the lesser states have been frightened out of their right to combine for self-defence by the threat of war upon them.

I don't, of course, mean that a German Ambassador has said to a Danish, or Swiss, or Hungarian Foreign Minister: 'If you link up with any system of mutual defence, Germany will make war upon you.' But it has nevertheless been brought home to the lesser states that the totalitarian powers are far readier to attack a small nation that displeases them, than League states are to defend their fellow members. Now my point is that this threat of war, blackmail, is working just as effectively in frightening the great states (including America) from adopting the only political principle which can effectively defend them against the power of the totalitarian group, as it has proved in threatening the small. The totalitarian states have said to the great as to the small: 'You may defend yourselves separately, individually, but not collectively, by common action; if you do so, we will make war upon you.' By submitting to that threat the democratic nations place themselves within the power of the totalitarians.

This truth is disguised for us by the fact that in applying their threat the totalitarians are helped by confusions and prejudices like those operating in the Spanish business. But the decisive factor in causing both Britain and America to retreat from the collective principle is the argument that any attempt to defend law would expose us to risk of attack from the law breakers. 'Sanctions mean war.' That slogan really meant 'law means war.' And as a commonly defended law is the only means by which ultimately the democracies can defend themselves effectively, to surrender law and the right of combination involves ultimately—for America as well as for you—submission to Nazi power.

I know that some of you will regard much of this as far-fetched. But let me point out how an incident like the Abyssinian business supports my contention.

It will be recalled that that affair developed to the stage where it was formally agreed by fifty nations in conference assembled that Italy was committing a crime, a felony. In that verdict America had concurred by her action in initiating the Kellogg Pact which agreed that henceforth war as an instrument of national policy was a crime. Italy not only admitted but very boastfully proclaimed that her war of conquest in Abyssinia was on behalf of national policy, national expansion.

The feeling in Britain as to the enormity of this offence was deep and passionate, as your Peace Ballot at the time proved statistically. Feeling was deepened by the cynicism with which Italy violated one solemn treaty after another, notably the one which forbade the use of mustard gas. She used it against half-naked and unarmed peasants.

People in Britain consequently said: 'We can have no part nor lot in this infamy.'

It became evident that Italy could not continue these abominations unless Britain and other democratic nations supplied the means, the tools. And Italy in effect said: 'Please give me the instruments wherewith to commit what you have all declared to be infamous crime.'

The reply at first was simple and clear. Your people in effect said:

'If we did that we should be partners in your offence, your burglary and murder; we should be making profit from the crime we condemn. We should be as bad as you. What you do is an abominable thing and we will have no part in it.'

The moral foundations of 'sanctions' were, after all, just that, and for the moment your people saw it and refused to supply such instruments as oil, knowing that they would be used for murder. True, at first certain childish confusions as to what were instruments of war arose. Had it been a question of supplying Italy with the actual

bombs and poison gas, not a baker's dozen of public men in Britain
at the time would have dared advocate it. When Italy said: 'I don't
want the completed articles for I have factories in which to make
them. What I want is that you should let me have the raw materials
and the oil wherewith, once made, the bombs can be transported to
the villages where they will kill most effectively'—the moral issue
certainly was not changed in the least. And in fact there was not any
doubt as to whether oil was an instrument of war which caused the
oil sanction to be lifted. It was a consideration of quite another order.
Your people were frightened out of the position they had taken by
threat of war.

Italy said: 'If you refuse to let me have oil, I will go to war with
you; I will do to your cities what I propose to do to the Ethiopian
villages and which I cannot do unless you supply the oil.'

Whereupon the British public began to say: 'This changes the situation. Evidently the oil sanction means war and we must at all costs
avoid war. So Italy had better have the oil, without which she cannot
make war.'

And there entered into British public discussion a slogan fathered
mainly, it is true, by the government and government supporters, but
adopted in large part also by Pacifists, in these terms: 'Sanctions
mean war.' On that ground sanctions were abandoned and Britain
was led more and more into becoming Italy's partner, not only in the
Ethiopian business but in other enterprises as well.

Note that this is not at all the Pacifism of the Quaker or the Early
Christian. When to the Early Christian the Pagan Oppressor said:
Renounce your faith or die' then the Christian as a matter of course
accepted death. The Quaker, asked to take part in war, or suffer all
the penalties the State could inflict, accepted without any question
whatsoever all those penalties—even though in so doing his family,
his children, might suffer hardly less than he himself.

I admit that there were certain intellectual confusions which made
it easier for Italy's threat of war to be effective, but those same confusions exist in the American public mind, and at the appropriate
moment can be exploited with the same ease. Note what those confusions were.

What the slogan 'Sanctions mean War' really meant was that while
you were quite prepared to see Italians kill Abyssinians without risking war to stop it, you were not prepared to see Italy seize British

territory or property or oil wells without going to war to stop it, and that as she might seize the oil if you did not let her have it, it was better to let her have it, to become accomplices in her war against a third party, than be compelled to go to war to defend your property.

For note the situation: If Britain had said clearly to Italy: 'We shall not supply you with oil,' Italy, if really willing to challenge the British Empire (which of course she was not) would have said: 'I shall take the oil, land my troops in Haifa or wherever necessary, seize the pipe lines and help myself.'

The Pacifist of an earlier date would have retorted: 'We shall not kill your men attempting to do this, but as oil has become the instrument of aggression, we shall ourselves destroy the wells rather than that they should fall into your hands.' (The oil wells of Rumania were so destroyed on the advance of the invader during the war.)

To which, doubtless, Italy would have replied by threats of retaliation, of doing to British cities what she later did to the Abyssinian villages.

But this would not have moved the older Pacifist in slightest degree, who would have replied that he would not become partner in what he believed murder, even to save his children; for his children would not wish it.

In passing it may be noted that the whole argument behind the suggestion that effective sanctions meant war, was completely fallacious; that had you been prepared to defend the law, the Covenant, those whom you had undertaken to defend under the Covenant, with the same energy with which, it is assumed as a matter of course you would defend your property, there would never have been any question of having to fight at all. Had Abyssinia been British territory, British 'property,' there would never have been any Abyssinian war (and consequently no later invasion of Spain) for Italy would never have dreamed of challenging the British Empire. At the time you talked about the strategical situation being such that Mussolini could have 'walked into' the British Sudan, or Egypt, or Malta if sanctions had been maintained. Well, if Mussolini could have had an Italian Empire so cheaply, why did he not take it? Because he knew that in the end he would have had to face a great deal more than Sudanese garrisons. He would have had to face the British Empire. If Mussolini really had 'walked into' the Sudan, or Kenya all those difficulties about the reluctance of France, the shortage of planes would have disappeared like magic. Mussolini knew this and that is why he did not 'walk in.' Had the defence of the Covenant been regarded by Britain on the same plane of importance as the defence of British territory, Abyssinia would never have been attacked and the question of war would never have arisen. War came, and was extended to Spain and will be tomorrow extended elsewhere, because the defence of law by the democracies is placed on a plane of importance infinitely lower than the defence of territory or property.

The first great effort of Europe to organise mutual defence through common collective action, against illegality and violence, broke down utterly as the result of a threat of war by one totalitarian power. The threat be it noted did not cause the great powers to abandon force, for they began to arm more feverishly than ever. The decision not to use force did not diminish by one ship, one gun, one bomb the weight of force in the world; it multiplied those things many times. What this terrorism did was to frighten the nations from forming a society to the end that force should be limited in its use to social purposes; should not be used by the individual for redressing his own wrongs as he saw fit, but reserved for the sole purpose of protecting the innocent, the more law-abiding, against the violence of the less law-abiding. That is to say, the totalitarian states have destroyed completely the policy embodied in the Kellogg Pact which was America's particular contribution to the international problem. American policy, that is, has been at that point, as at others, defeated.

You here are not likely to dismiss that Pact as a mere empty gesture whereby its signatories 'promised to be good and not quarrel.' It constituted a very important and profound change in the juridical principles governing international relations, a very important advance in international standards. Heretofore war had been legal, legitimate, however horrible. The legality of war was one of the bases of the then accepted international code. Under American initiative this was completely reversed. America said: 'Let us agree that war shall be placed upon the same footing as the personal violence of an individual within the state—legitimate as a means of resisting violence upon himself, in self-defence, but criminal when used as a means of promoting his private interests or purposes.' We all agreed that war 'as an instrument of national policy' was a crime. And then as a next step in the development of that principle—again on American initiative—it was proposed, in the Doctrine of Non-Recognition (of changes of frontier brought about by violence) to give a diplomatic, political sanction to the new rule. This together with the development of the moral attitude which it was hoped would result from the universal acceptance of the new principle would suffice for its growth.

But yielding to the threat of war if we stood by these principles, it has all disappeared. Britain has been, in Lord Cranborne's phrase 'blackmailed' (i.e. frightened by threats that otherwise war would be made) into a series of negotiations with Italy that have ended both principles just enunciated. For the agreement 'recognises,' that is to say legitimises, changes brought about by conquest, in flat contradiction with the Stimson Doctrine, and by that fact legitimises a war of conquest, which is in flat contradiction with the Kellogg Pact.

Well, it may be argued that America was rushing things; that the nations were not ready for the new standard of the Kellogg Pact, and that we must do what we can on the basis of the old.

But note that, also under the threat of war you have not only abandoned the new, you have destroyed the old. The recognised law of the matter when the Spanish government faced a subversive movement within its own state, was that that government should be free to obtain from outside the materials it needed for its own defence. But it soon became evident that both Germany and Italy intended to aid the rebellion against the Spanish Government with which they were then in normal diplomatic relations (a gross breach of international comity).[1] The two totalitarian governments made it plain— as they continue to make it plain to France to-day—that they would regard the maintenance of the normal right of the Spanish government with disfavour. So, again you invoked the slogan of the Abyssinian situation: 'The maintenance of the Law, the Covenant, means war by those who do not like it; so we must abandon the law and the Covenant.' The diplomatic vagueness of the phrases about 'leading to war' really meant that if you abided by the law and allowed the Spanish government its normal rights, those who were breaking the law would make war upon you. It was better you decided that they

---

[1] The Franco revolt started on July 17th, and on the 28th of the same month Italian aeroplanes were wrecked or landed on the wrong side of the border between Algeria and Morocco. The pilots declared to the French authorities that they had been taken from the Italian air force at the beginning of July and received their final instructions *on the 15th*—three days *before* the revolt was timed to begin.

should make war upon the Spanish Republicans. So just as you had thrown China and Abyssinia to the wolves, you threw Republican Spain, as tomorrow we may throw Czechoslovakia or Russia to the totalitarian wolves.

Grant, if you like, that the Spanish Government was not a democratic and constitutional government in the British or American sense; grant that the situation was complicated, involved. Your interest, the vital strategic interest of the two democracies of Britain and France, was overwhelmingly on the side of the application of the ordinary international rule to this complicated situation; and you abandoned it on the declared ground that unless you did, the totalitarian states would make war on you. You acknowledged and finally helped to crystallise a situation in which they could break the law to their advantage with impunity, but you could not observe the law to your advantage with impunity. Of course, in this blackmail based on the fear of war there was made to enter this other fear, Bolshevism. The defeat of Mussolini would mean communism in Italy, the triumph of the Government in Spain, communism there; its spread to France, the close neighbour and associate of Britain. What would Britain's position be with a Communist France at its elbow, and Bolshevism spreading everywhere? And what of the painfully restored prosperity if that sort of disorder faced the world? So, as we know, a great many in Britain did not want to see the Italian government embarrassed by defeat either in Abyssinia or in Spain. To that extent the totalitarian states actually secured the support of great sections of British opinion.

It meant an enormous success for the totalitarian method—which Germany was soon to prove meant success for Germany.

But much greater success may be in store for her. The system, which Germany has applied in order to bring small nations under her dominion, is now being applied, as the result of the Spanish adventure, with every prospect of success to France herself. To France, the greatest of all the continental democracies occupying such a key position, a position upon which now will turn the whole future of democratic Europe; France, which was but yesterday, and perhaps to-day still is the greatest military power in Europe; France that a little over a century ago held all continental Europe in the palm of her hand; that for centuries has been Germany's most redoubtable opponent; France, the destruction of which the author of *Mein Kampf* insisted so strenuously must be achieved if Germany is to fulfil her destiny. It is that France which is now in danger of succumbing, so far as one can see, to the totalitarian tactic; succumbing to the fear of war, the fear of Bolshevism, to the internal divisions which the latter fear provokes in a fundamentally bourgeois and peasant nation; to the anti-constitutional movement which that fear can so easily set in motion, aided, as any such movement would be aided and indeed is already being aided from outside as part of the totalitarian method we are discussing.

I emphasise the French case because what can be done with France can, I shall suggest, be done with the United States.

Assume that the author of *Mein Kampf* really desired those ends upon which he is so violently and passionately insistent—and there is no reason on earth to suppose that he is not sincere in his expression of those desires—what are the first steps that he would wish to see accomplished? They are surely first of all a weakening of France's strategic position, then such internal divisions as would weaken her capacity of resistance to German attack.

The first of these purposes has already been achieved and the second seems likely to be. Others of our group have pointed out the very great change for the worse in France's strategic position as the result of the events in Spain; France is now threatened, as someone has put it, on six frontiers—the Rhine, the Alps, the Pyrenees, the African frontiers, the Mediterranean communications, and at the Palais Bourbon. France would have to defend herself not alone from the enemy without, but from the enemy within prompted and aided by the enemy without.

It is this last circumstance, the fact of a deep internal division, which has made it impossible for France to prevent that grave worsening of her strategic position, which others here have described. For the Spanish peninsular to be brought under German domination is something which France in the past has been ready to go to war to prevent. It was not a question on this occasion of going to war to prevent it, but of applying in the case of the Spanish government the normal, heretofore universally accepted international rule. When the totalitarian states forbade the application of the law they were, of course, fully aware that they would find support for their action within France (as in Britain) itself, so much so that both the British and the French governments would encounter violent resistance from their own supporters if an attempt were made to apply the law in the

Spanish case. I have it on very good authority that when the French government proposed to take strong action to enforce, not the law but even a real application of that alternative non-intervention which has been the diplomatic mask for totalitarian intervention (and would have operated to the disadvantage of the Spanish Government even if it had been genuine), it was faced by something like mutiny on the part of certain French army officers who intimated that if they were to be used for a purpose which would promote 'atheistic Bolshevism,' they might find the strain upon their loyalty too great. Rather than the triumph of Bolshevism they would accept the strategic defeat of France. Thus, in his attack upon the strategic security of France, Hitler has had the co-operation of forces within France itself, within the French army.

It would probably be unfair to accuse either Germany or Italy of 'plotting' the subversive movements in the neighbouring states. But they have known how to take advantage and make the most of an existing tendency, of anti-Red or anti-Jew or anti-masonic crazes which exist in every country and can with skilful demagogy be exploited—aided, subsidised.

A Fascist or Fascist-minded minority—it may be quite a small one—starts a movement in opposition to the constitutional government. (Every democracy in Europe now has such a minority.) It can always count upon help in one form or another from Italy or Germany or both. It is not necessary that such a minority should have racial or nationality affiliations with either of the Fascist powers in order to secure such help, as the case of Franco proves. (On what ground of race or nationality has Germany or Italy poured armies or material into Spain to sustain a Spanish rebellion?) Any state that the Fascist power proposes to dominate can by this preliminary process be weakened to the point of helplessness. Nor need the method be pushed to the point of actual rebellion. A democratic government may hesitate to take a strong line for the suppression of nascent rebellion for fear of calling upon itself the fate of Spain, or Austria, or Czechoslovakia, so that such a subversive movement knows it can count upon a large degree of immunity. In either case internal strains weaken the defensive power of the victim state.

Now note that Fascist movements have gone very far in at least three American nations. We have already had armed rebellion, an attempted putsch, from a million Brazilian *Integralista*. It is a little suggestive that there are in Brazil a million Germans—Germans it may be of the second or third generation but who preserve their distinctive German quality, German speech and contacts with Nazi Germany.[1]

The same week that brings news of the armed fascist coup in Brazil brings us news of an armed rising in Mexico against a government which is commonly regarded in Conservative circles in America as plainly Communist, having contacts with Moscow. It has adopted (like Moscow) a line hostile to the Catholic Church as it exists in Mexico. Mexico's conduct in that respect has created great bitterness among American Catholics. And finally, the Mexican government has lately confiscated great blocks of American oil property and has entered into a bitter conflict with the American administration.

Does anyone suppose that if a Mexican Franco arose, promised to restore Church property, re-establish the Catholics in what they regard as their rights, restore generally the rights of property, to redress the grievances of American investors, with promises to save and restore hundreds of millions of dollars worth of American property—does anyone believe that in those circumstances a Mexican Franco would not prove as popular with American Conservatives as a Spanish Franco has proved with British? Why should he not? The American concern in his success would be far more tangible, visible, understandable, than the passionate partizanship expressed almost every day in the British House of Commons for the cause of Franco.

Approximate the Mexican situation a little closer to the Spanish. If the Mexican Franco began to receive aid from abroad (from Europe and Asia perhaps) would that make much difference? At the

---

[1] A London paper of May 19 has the following from Brazil:

'Last March, on the eve of a *putsch* planned by this organisation [the integralista], President Vargas was warned from the United States that the rebels had the backing of foreign dictator elements. Promptly, Vargas arrested 1,000 Integralistas, and unearthed in the office of Fascist Werneck, a Brazilian of German descent, a complete file of Hitler's own organ, *Voelkischer Beobachter*, and a library of Nazi publications. In the basement was found a fully-equipped printing office and supplies of ammunition.

'Loyal Brazilians were last week quick to name Nazi Germany as the chief instigators of the latest plot. In support of their contention they pointed out that Lieutenant Hasselman was a German, also that in the house of Leader Plinio Salgado at the time of the previous Fascist failure in March were found all kinds of arms, including 3,000 Swastika-engraved daggers, large sums of money alleged to have been sent from Berlin, and plans for a Fascist form of government for Rio Grando do Sul.'

very moment that Mussolini was publishing his official congratulations to his gallant armies in Spain, he in his turn was receiving cordial communications from the British Prime Minister.

Of course, the Mexican Franco would receive the help of German material and German 'volunteers'—whole German armies would be landing on Mexican soil as whole Italian armies have landed on Spanish soil. And, of course, American parties would be deeply divided on the issue, as the French and British parties have been deeply divided on the Spanish issue; so divided that it would be out of the question for the American administration to give effect to the Monroe Doctrine. It would lapse, and nothing would be done about the German armies at our doors—except perhaps the establishment of a Non-Intervention Committee which would solemnly sit in Washington with German representatives upon it solemnly pledging Germany to complete non-intervention while German battleships or planes outside Vera Cruz sunk American merchant men and drowned American sailors with all the immunity with which at the present moment German aeroplanes and bombers and Italian airmen are sinking British merchant ships (two have been sunk this week) outside Valencia or Barcelona.

American quiescence, or acquiescence, would be defended in the name of 'peace.' Any administration, criticised for thus handing over the virtual control of Mexico to European Fascists would, if British experience is any guide, only have to repeat one phrase:

'The alternative to the present policy is war. Do you want war?' And ten thousand women's clubs would answer with one deafening and resounding 'No.'

So you see the Fascist danger would be brought a little nearer home. Whether what would follow in the United States itself would resemble what is happening in France rather than what is happening in Britain I do not profess to know. Whether, that is, there would arise an American cagoulard movement, a new form of the Ku Klux Klan to make common cause with Mexican Fascists to destroy communism and atheism on the Western Hemisphere using terror and arms, I do not know. I am inclined to think that the American internal situation would approximate more nearly to the French than to the British pattern.

Is there anything fantastic in what I have just sketched?

I wish I could think that certain American traditions would stand in the way.

But why should we suppose that those traditions would stand in the way when certain British moral standards just as deeply rooted have not stood in the way of a moral transformation which a few years ago we should have regarded as fantastic.

Note that throughout it has been a case of the weak threatening the strong.

Whether we examine the Japanese story of 1931 or that of Abyssinia, or the German and Italian invasion of Spain, we see the same curious situation: Those whose interests, in which 'interests' I include the survival of democracy, are thus assailed have a clear preponderance of potential power for the protection of those interests, and had there been any clear intention to use that power its use would never have been necessary; for in that case the interests would not have been assailed. I recall once more the undeniable fact that if Abyssinia had been British territory, there would have been no Italian war at all, no attack to resist, for Italy would never have dreamed of attacking.

But that argument will not indefinitely remain true even of territory, if the democratic retreat goes beyond a certain point. The bloodless use of potential superiority of power rests upon the conviction in the mind of the would-be aggressor that if he does certain things, force will be used against him. If he believes, as he has very good ground for believing, that if he leave actual territory alone he can by threat of violence secure any moral concession, those threats will be made increasingly. If he is uncertain as to what we shall resist, he may 'take a chance' and the taking of such chances may land us in war.

I come back as my final word to this ease with which moral or political standards can be surrendered to violence; the complacency with which we can avow that surrender. That is the significant thing. For, after all, the security of democracy rests ultimately upon the wish of the multitude to preserve it and the readiness to make sacrifices for it; and upon the capacity to act in unity against those who would destroy it.

The moral standards which must be the basis of that unity have been incredibly undermined in Britain. You British have surrendered bit by bit the moral basis of your political life and have begun to adopt in exchange the ethic of the very people who threaten you.

The great discovery which the modern dictators have made is a fact about dictatorship or tyranny which should have been self-evident to those who had eyes to see, but which the rhetoric of democracy has tended to obscure. It is the truth that physical force is not the foundation, only the occasional instrument of dictatorship or tyranny. Its foundation lies in the public mind. Only when a certain moral capture has been achieved can the physical force be used at all. Commonly when we think of the past struggles of 'the people' against the tyrant, we have in our minds a picture of great popular masses 'held down' by the physical force of a tiny minority. It is an absurd picture. How can one man, or two men, or a hundred by physical force, the sheer power of their sinews 'hold down' a million, or ten million, or a hundred million men? The physical force the tyrant uses must be supplied by the millions whom he oppresses, supplied in the form of armies drawn from the multitude, in armaments made by them, paid for by them. They must first of all be persuaded to do those things; their minds and wills reached.

When Hitler began with a party of thirteen persons, the victories which laid the foundation of his power were not those of physical conflict. Indeed his first putsch promptly fizzled out and landed him in jail. He realised then that his real problem was a moral or psychological one—to dominate the mind of Germany. This did not necessarily mean making all or even most Germans Nazis. He could just as effectively dominate the will of the German nation by confronting a confused, divided, hesitating and fearful majority which did not quite know its mind, or had no single mind, with a minority fanatically indoctrinated, resolute, that knew exactly what it wanted and was prepared to be ruthless in getting it. At that point, truly, force and terror entered, but it only entered effectively for his purpose because the moral preparation had been made, that moral preparation being the creation of a group of fanatics having a single purpose and on the other a number of groups which though possessing in the aggregate much greater physical power were too disunited to use it. The moral disintegration of the majority gave power into the hands of a ruthless minority.

That, of course, has been an age old dodge of tryanny since the world began. The element of novelty or relative novelty enters when fundamentally the same technique is employed for purposes of foreign policy, of foreign conquest and domination.

I hinted a moment ago at one part of the process by which the moral disintegration of the democratic states was taking place to the advantage of the totalitarians, when I implied that the ultimate effect of surrendering your political principles—like those of the League or Kellogg Pact, or Non-Recognition, or Mutual Assistance—in submission to the threat of war was to become partners in the offence, or policy, you had till then condemned.

Note what has happened this last month in your relations with Italy—the necessary sequel I suggest of what happened in 1935. Your purpose in this last deal was to placate Italy, keep her quiet. How did you propose to do it? By offering her the 'recognition' of her conquest of Abyssinia. But think for a moment what that means.

The question of Italian sovereignty in Abyssinia is a question of fact and of legal consequences arising from it. If it is fact by all means admit it; if it is right to give certain legal consequences to that fact give them. But what have bargains about fortifications in the Mediterranean to do with those questions? Italy's sovereignty in Ethiopia is a matter which should be treated on its merits, an impartial judgement of the facts and the legal situation that results therefrom. But you did not make recognition dependent upon what the facts really are, whether in truth the Italians are in complete occupation of the country (they are not) ; whether anything could be rescued in the way of Ethiopian autonomy, so as to preserve something of an independence which had lasted a thousand years, and which in the minds of millions of Africans has become symbolic. Nothing of this was even considered. Would Italy give Britain, not Ethiopia be it noted, certain advantages if Britain undertakes to facilitate the final extinction of this African Switzerland. If Abyssinian sovereignty was to be traded in this way, it should in equity be for the purpose of securing certain rights to Abyssinians, some measure of autonomy or what not. It is not mentioned. And yet one would have supposed after all that as that has happened to this little state you were pledged to support, you would have had a certain conscience about doing what you could for those people.

That is only one feature of this precious bargain. You pledge yourselves, and encourage others to pledge themselves to legalise and legitimise Italy's act. But a couple of years since you were declaring it to be one of the infamous crimes of history. The crime has become permissible. Tearing up the Covenant, and the Kellogg Pact and throwing overboard its principles you 'recognise' this conquest, and it is suggestive that you use as the diplomatic instrument of this pretty deal a very religious man, a high churchman, something of a mystic who has always insisted upon the importance of moral standards. The implication of which seems to be that if Halifax the Gentleman can do that kind of deal with Mussolini, ordinary politicians need not trouble to be more squeamish.

If means determine ends, as Mr. Aldous Huxley argues that they do, then one wonders what the ends of British policy will prove to be. For the means employed to promote them are exceedingly dirty means, as even those who employ them are fain to admit.

'Righteousness and Peace are in conflict,' said Lord Halifax arguing for the recognition, virtually the legalization, of the Italian conquest of Abyssinia. So he chose, he said, Peace, explaining:

> 'You have to choose between the unpractical devotion to the high purpose that you know you cannot achieve except by war you do not intend to have and the practical victory for peace that you can achieve. I cannot hesitate between the two when both my conscience and my duty to my fellow men impel me directly in the direction of peace . . . Refusal to recognize a situation brought about in spite of the League may, of course, keep our principles intact on paper. If that were all that mattered we might well be content with that satisfaction. But when we find that refusal to face facts does in fact keep resentments and antagonisms alive and threaten understanding, then we have to consider whether it is right to abandon the substance for the shadow.'

Lord Halifax was careful to add:

> 'His Majesty's Government do not and never have and never will condone the Italian action, nor do they ask the League to condone methods by which the Italian sovereignty was established.'

Which is quite certainly not true. Mr. Chamberlain's policy, the policy that is of the British Government, is not a policy of cold reluctant acknowledgment of the triumph of force; it is a policy of recognition plus friendship, cordiality; of flattering speeches, banquets, naval visits, of receptions at the Italian Embassy in London, the last of which the papers describe as 'the event of the season,' outdoing in numbers of guests anything London has known for years, 'a public

manifestation of the warmth of the new Anglo-Italian friendship.'
We read of the formation of a Parliamentary Group to promote the
new Anglo-Italian Entente, personal flattery from the Prime Minister,
all of which amounts certainly to moral condonation, if words have
any meaning.

Let us assume, if you will, that it is politically wise, that it helps
peace. But since we are asked to 'face facts' let us face the nature
of the means which we employ, the fact that we are lauding and
flattering and covering with honours a Dictator whom yesterday we
branded as a criminal; of whom one may hear repeatedly in that
same fashionable world which now flocks to his receptions, stories
which imply that he has employed cowardly assassination for ends
of personal vengeance. Whether true or not thousands believe those
stories to be true: and thereupon pay rather fulsome compliments to
the presumptive murderer.

The phrases of Lord Halifax about the futility of 'keeping our
principles intact on paper' comes strangely indeed from a man who
is at once a religious ritualist, who has emphasised the weight of
moral forces in the world; and a foreign minister who proposes, he
tells us, to combine realism, clear thought that is, and peace.

For he starts by stating the alternatives incorrectly, thereby begging the whole question. The choice is not as between peace and
righteousness, but whether a systematic disregard of righteousness
can be made a sure basis of peace. Very many who object to certain
methods of the British Government do so, not because they are 'immoral,' but because they are likely ultimately to land the world in war.

The very first sentence quoted above includes a complete misconception of the purpose of those who opposed recognition of the Italian
conquest. That purpose was not the reconquest of the country from
Italy, but the preservation of a diplomatic and political principle which
happened to be also a moral one. Even if we grant that it was not
within your power to prevent Italian conquest, it is certainly within
your power to withhold that 'recognition,' legalization, which Mussolini so keenly desires. And to withhold it has practical as well as
moral importance.

It happens at times—indeed it happens pretty often—that some
scoundrelly adventurer pulls off some enormous swindle by which
thousands of poor folk are ruined, and just manages to keep outside
the meshes of the law. Well, the law is notoriously defective and

later we will remedy it. For the moment let us admit nothing can be done about it. But between that attitude and the attitude which implies that because the swindler has been successful and become a millionaire the law shall therefore be abandoned and altered in his favour so that imitators may know that in doing likewise they will not be embarrassed by any legal inconvenience, that they will not even suffer social discomfort since the successful swindler is now to be given banquets and feted by society—between these two attitudes is a world of difference which is not merely moral but which has, be it noted, extremely practical consequences.

The very circumstances that Italy herself attached such enormous importance to recognition, was prepared to buy it by concessions, was proof enough that there was something more than a merely 'moral' gesture in the fact. It had practical political value or Italy would not have bothered about it. In granting formal recognition you were doing a great deal more than making a 'constatation' of existing fact; you were getting deeper and deeper into actual co-operation with Italy in both her African and Spanish conquests. As the result of recognition you would be in a position to furnish more freely the instruments with which Italy would crush Ethiopians; might even furnish funds for the purpose; hand back as 'rebels' the native Abyssinians who, in the course of their resistance to Italian invasion might be driven over the border into British territory. To refuse recognition therefore was not, as Lord Halifax implied, merely 'shutting our eyes to facts we cannot alter.' It was to refuse to do certain definite and concrete things having a bearing upon the fate of African natives whom you had sworn to protect; to refrain from a policy which would associate you more and more with the Italian political conceptions and get you further and further away from those which you had heretofore professed and to which it will be increasingly difficult to return.

Are we witnessing something of that same moral degeneration in America?

There has certainly been there a large degree of moral preparation favourable to the totalitarian design; a development due, not to Fascist propaganda but arising as the result of the same tendencies we have been witnessing in the European democracies.

Take our reaction to assaults upon our interests and security. It used to be explosive, ferocious. Recall the Maine business, the numer-

ous affairs at sea with your people. Yet when an American ship of
war is sunk by the bombs of an Asiatic state, and American sailors
are killed, our papers relegate the story to the back pages. A year
or two since the Hearst press would have screamed itself all the
colours of the rainbow in demanding war. Nobody demands war
and the Hearst press least of all.

Many regard this as an advance on the older attitude. But that old
attitude was mischievous, not because it resented violence and wrong,
but because it glorified partial and one-sided judgement of what was
wrong and what right. To become peaceful because we have become
indifferent to right; to be quiescent in infamy because we fear that
otherwise we too may become the victim of lawless violence is hardly
an advance. It is certainly not an advance towards stable peace.

Our people and yours face an armed fanaticism; gangster governments, but gangsters who have persuaded themselves or their peoples
that the robberies, cruelties, rapes and murders are justified and
right.

'Let all who do *not* believe in robbery, cruelty and murder combine to
help the victim or probable victim of such crime. The crime can usually by
this means be made physically impossible. Having made it physically impossible for the gangsters and the racketeer to follow that method they
will then be in a mood perhaps to listen to us when we suggest to them
law abiding means of livelihood, means which do not injure others. Indeed
on condition that they will obey the law we will see that it protects them,
makes their peaceful livelihood easier.'

To these proposals our peoples have both in varying degrees been
opposed. Large elements are contemptuous of such a policy; brand
it as 'idealism' which has failed. They demand 'realism.'

What is 'realism' in their view? It is to say to the gangsters:

'We don't really mind your robbing, torturing, killing, so long as you
don't rob, torture and kill us. If we promise not to interfere when you
murder and rob others, promise indeed to say that such things are really
quite respectable, to "recognise" them, to meet you socially and make professions of friendship—if we promise that, will *you* promise to confine your
attentions to others?'

Thus we indicate that Manchuria is not our concern, nor Abyssinia,
nor Spain, nor Austria, nor Czechoslovakia, nor Hungary, and south-
eastern Europe. We secure peace for ourselves by throwing some
innocent third party to the wolves.

In the end that method must fail if only because the supply of innocent third parties is limited, and the appetite of the wolves is not. Every time we sacrifice an innocent third party the number of those who might stand with us to resist the wolves when our turn for consumption comes, is diminished, until finally we reach a point where we stand alone before the whole pack, with nothing but their promise of good behaviour to protect us.

I suggest this is not really 'realism.'

IX

REPLY TO SMITH: ISOLATION MEANS WEAKNESS

Looking back over the last six or seven years it is quite clear that the process of foreigners eating each other up does not lessen but increases the danger to us. The steady advance against British interests and security alike of Japan in the Far East, Italy in the Mediterranean and Germany on our Rhine frontier, are cases in point. Isolationism is a myth, a sham. Unless we are prepared to accept the Pacifist position at least in so far as occupying the position of a Norway or a Denmark, isolation is almost a contradiction in terms. For if we renounce international combinations while the other fellow adopts them, we cannot possibly keep our end up defensively. In fact we are taking sides—against the law—and by our failure to take risks for an European law or code or constitution are accelerating the coming of the European civil war, the class war, not, however, quite according to Marx.

'Our friend John,' began the Spokesman deputed to reply to the case of John Smith, 'really has not faced the problem which confronts us.'

The question is really not whether we shall gratuitously interfere in Continental quarrels in order to uphold the Balance of Power or maintain our defensive position. The question is not whether we shall leave the Fascist States alone giving them rope to hang themselves with. The question is whether they will leave us alone and that if they do not what is to be our attitude to their interference.

Specific demands are already being made upon us; acts immensely damaging to our trade and welfare being committed. The immense rearmament we are now carrying out has some reference presumably to that fact. Our rearmament is a defensive gesture which presumably John Smith highly approves—there seems to be every evidence that he does so. In any case it is going on, and he is paying the bill.

Now the real question is whether we are to take such political precaution that it will be possible when the time comes to use that armament effectively, or whether we are suddenly to find that all our effort, our expenditure, has gone for nothing; that notwithstanding it all we are at the mercy of those against whom it was intended to defend us. If suddenly we are confronted with that sort of position and our armament is very great, we may make a sudden plunge—disastrously.

That is the real position we have to consider. I suggest that John's support of rearmament proves that he does not in fact believe in his own isolationism. For what would be the sense of pouring out a Niagara flood of money in the creation of, say, gigantic battleships, while at the same time Italy and Germany mount big calibre guns on the shores of the Straits, secure bases in the Balearics and the Canaries, eliminate one by one, allies that may be indispensable to us? The isolationists would undo on the political side what they are trying to do on the military side. The truth is that armed isolationism is almost a contradiction in terms. Isolationism is possible if we are prepared to accept the position of a Norway, or a Sweden, or even a Holland. But to say that though you are isolated you will be as strong as the next fellow, is simply to forget the conditions of so being.

We are devoting these astronomical sums to aeroplanes, shells, poison gas, gas masks, battleships, because we say we must be of equal strength with our potential enemies. So be it. You choose a yard stick. The power, shall we say, of a State like Germany. You make yourself equal. Then that power makes an alliance, comes near to doubling its potential force. What do you then do? Double our armament programme? Perhaps. The rival dual alliance becomes a triple alliance. What do we then do? We make an alliance or drop out of the race. An alliance, as someone has said, is a source of power like the air arm or the submarine. If others adopt it, so must we. We cannot renounce combinations for ourselves, if our potential enemies are busy making them. The War proved this clearly enough. We had about twenty allies and we seemed to need them. What would have been the sense of our pretending to oppose the advance of Germany to the Channel and to the Mediterranean, if France had been out of it, Russia out of it, America out of it, and Italy and Japan on the other side?

The very term 'adequate armament' is meaningless unless we can say adequate for what, to meet what political situation, whether the arms are to face one State or half a dozen and to face the enemy by ourselves or aided by others.

But, I am aware, of course, that our friend has just insisted that John Smith's point is that the members of the hostile combination will be so busy dealing either with each other, or with its own recent conquests—Japan in China, Germany in the Balkans—that they will not have energy to attack us.

Well, let us look at the facts and see whether the theory that the more Fascist States expand, the less danger they are likely to be to us, is supported by those facts.

Let us go back to the first step of Japanese expansion in 1931. We were then moved by pretty much the considerations that Smith's spokesman has advanced. Our Foreign Minister said that the Sino-Japanese quarrel, the Japanese invasion of Manchuria was a distant dispute that did not concern us. And whatever be the inwardness of Mr. Stimson's offer to co-operate with Great Britain in making the Japanese advance as difficult as possible, it is quite certain that we did not make the most of that offer. It may, as some of our Foreign Office politicians said, have been too indefinite, but what is quite clear is that we did not even try to develop it or to nurse America in such a way as to make something of it. On the contrary it was curtly declined and our Imperialists cheered Japan on.

Very well. Did Japan's advance into Manchuria render her less dangerous as a challenge to British interests in the Far East? Events are the answer. It is quite true that the Manchurian adventure did add to Japan's burdens, that she did not gain materially by it, that her internal problems became increasingly difficult. But what was the result upon Japan's policy? To make her less imperialist, more pacifist? The result was to make her more imperialist. She discovered that to make her position in Manchuria secure, she had to go on, that she could not retreat. Her commercial classes were rather against going on, as we know, but they were rapidly overcome by a vested interest which had become more powerful than capital, commerce, trade, profit, dividend—the vested interest of the military order which was so growing in its power as to be able virtually to take over the government of the country. Incidentally, when we discuss international affairs in terms of 'interests,' whether of capital or trade or what not, we are apt to forget what is becoming the greatest interest of all in the modern world—the interest of the professional soldier and his civilian satellites. Japan has shown that that interest is more powerful than that of 'the capitalist.' And the military interest has motives of action more powerful than that of calculation, more powerful than those which animate the merchant, the financier, the investor. It is an interest of passion, like the passion of those young men who, in distant Tokio, behaved in so strikingly similar a manner to their counterparts in Munich, in Berlin. We face a new force (or an old force in a new form) in the modern world, the implications of which we must not burke.

What has happened in the case of Japan? In 1931 Japanese advances into China were relatively limited. She did not so visibly touch British interests as to raise the apprehensions of our people, least of all of the City. But she has gone on, step by step. According to the theory which we have just heard expounded, British interests should have found their protection in the paralysis of Japanese power which the penetration into China should have involved. But the more she became involved in China, the greater the menace to British interests until finally we face the actual invasion of what is in fact British territory, the killing of British soldiers, the sinking of British ships, the destruction of vast quantities of British property, the exclusion of Britain from great potential sources of trade and finally the shooting up of a British ambassador. When that happened we were, of course, indignant, appalled, outraged and all the rest of it and we clamoured for action. But 1937 is too late for action. If we had intended to act, we should have acted in 1931 when the American administration was disposed to come in and co-operate, the co-operation we then so coldly rejected and which now we would give much to have offered in the same spirit.

But the Japanese advance in the Far East had immediate repercussions upon our interests and defensive position in Europe. Mussolini had for long, as we know, nursed the idea of an Italian Empire which would fortify his position among his own people. He might have proceeded quietly, beginning by peaceful methods, securing by treaty arrangements, as the nations of the British Commonwealth and Britain and America are trying to do, the enlargement of Italian trade. But when he saw the immunity which Japan enjoyed, when he heard Sir John Simon actually in Geneva so defending the action of Japan that the Japanese representative was able to tell him that it would not have been possible for a Japanese to have done it better; when he saw what collective power by the League Powers really meant, he proceeded to take the imperialist and nationalist line, the conquering line. He began with Abyssinia, establishing himself at the back door of the Suez Canal, securing a jumping off place for further expansion in the future.

He did get into difficulties. Abyssinia has not been conquered. It is expensive. But on balance the conquest has strengthened his régime. And, just as in Japan's case, it has not had the effect of keeping him away from attack on British interests. It has had the effect of bringing his threat to British interests much nearer. Seeing that large sections of the British nation excused or supported his action, that the Garvins and even the Bernard Shaws, big and little, actually applauded his conquest; facing a situation in which John Bull announced that he would apply sanctions 'unless Italy objected,' in which, that is, the British Government announced beforehand that it would do nothing which might provoke Italy to make war (Mussolini must nearly have burst with Gargantuan laughter), he was encouraged to go on. He did go on. From the invasion of Abyssinia, he proceeded to the invasion of Spain. From getting near to controlling the Suez he gets near to controlling Gibraltar.

We hardly improved things when our Imperialists explained that we were powerless to stop him. I notice, however, that though he is hungry for colonies, he leaves British colonies severely alone. He thinks we should defend them, and does not believe for a moment that we should be powerless to do so.

But the threat to Great Britain came nearer still. Hitler, realising the immunity of those who care to challenge Europe, the law, what you will, felt that he too must profit by this impotence or paralysis (why should the non-Nordic Italian derive from this condition of impotence all the advantages?). So he crossed what for a year or two we had been proclaiming was 'our' frontier, the frontier of the Rhine.

I need not continue this story because it is a familiar one. But there are two points to which, at this stage, I want to call your attention. First it disproves the theory that absorption of a conqueror in the difficulties of his conquest tends to keep him away from any challenge to our interests; the theory that if he can 'explode in the East,' for instance, he won't bother us in the West. The theory can work just as well the other way. The very fact that Japan has difficulties in China prompts her to seek a German ally in order that Russia shall not take her at a disadvantage. Russia, replying to this by increasing her power, Germany is prompted to insure her rear by action upon the Rhine. Italy having been tempted to make a conquest of Abyssinia must then protect that conquest from interference by us and so challenges our Mediterranean route with a view to insuring the security of her own line of communication. Thus the Spanish adventure.

That is one point. But there is a further one just as vital. Throughout in this story recklessness has paid. The Japanese adventure in Manchuria was opposed by the more moderate elements in Japan on the ground that Japan would get into difficulty with the League powers. She did not get into any serious difficulty with the League powers. The reckless elements were justified, and the disintegration of the League which if used might have restrained these elements began.

The effect was very greatly to enhance militarist tendencies in Japan. So with the imitator in Rome.

The experts warned Mussolini that the Abyssinian adventure would be difficult and dangerous. We know from de Bono's book and other documents that the Fascist Grand Council feared very much what the effect of League hostility and the effect of challenging vital British interests in the Mediterranean might be. Mussolini risked it. Much of Britain supported him, opposed the action of the League. So once more recklessness paid.

So again with Hitler and the Rhineland: His army officers were against him. France might be supported by Britain. Hitler 'took a chance,' and by the fact of 'invading her own country' Germany became in many British circles more popular than she had been since the beginning of the War. Again recklessness paid. Recklessness again is likely to pay in Spain.

But there is a third point more important than these two which Smith's simple theory ignores.

That point is the fact that conquerors will not proceed any more by wars of conquest in the ordinary sense. Our German friend has warned us about that. Germany is not going to 'declare war' on

Russia, even if German advance in the neighbouring States is such that Germany has direct contact with the Russian frontier. Germany will pursue in Russia as in France the technique that has been pursued in Spain, in Austria and to some extent in Abyssinia. There may in the future be a Ukrainian movement against the Moscow Government (vast sums are now being spent in Ukrainian propaganda) and there is likely to be a subsidised anti-governmental movement in Russia. Without much doubt there has been something of that sort already, and it is there that we may find some tiny fraction of truth in all the wild accusations of the Russian trials. It may be that Stalin is ruthlessly, Satanically, determined that he shall not be caught napping as the Spanish Government seems to have been caught napping; and will not suddenly be confronted with an armed movement subsidised and assisted from outside. Be that as it may, it is what one might term the Spanish technique that will be applied by Germany to Russia and we may get civil war in Russia originating conceivably in the Ukraine; a Russian Franco who may conceivably capture the Moscow Government. But even unsuccessful Russian rebellion will have served the Japanese and German purpose by immobilising Russia for a time.

That something of the technique has already been applied in France is quite certain. The British Press has grossly minimised the significance of the Cagoulard incident. The fact that very great quantities of German and Italian arms—and no arms but German and Italian—have been unearthed in what was to have been a *coup* against the French Government tells sufficiently its own story.

Now please note that this technique avoids for continental combinations the very danger that Smith's spokesman referred to. It is not the conqueror who gets into unmanageable internal difficulties or difficulties with his conquest; it is the potential victim that struggles in the toils of an internal upheaval, as Spain struggled, as France may struggle tomorrow.

Now that situation, so immensely to the advantage of the Fascist States, arises just because in truth the democratic peoples are in two minds as to what they will fight for and whom they will fight. Our German friend is entirely right there. If and when Fascist intrigue manages through larger and more successful Cagoulards to create a French Franco, when some popular figure of the Right, after the triumph of Franco in Spain, is tempted to save France from the

Communist danger, it is quite certain that opinion in England will be as much divided about it as it is about the Spanish conflict. Many of our Conservatives, much of our Cabinet, would support, morally, the French Franco as it supports, morally, the Spanish Franco. They would in this sense be the allies of Germany and Italy (as they are the allies of Germany and Italy in this respect in Spain) as against Republican France, the France of 1789. The war then would cease to be a war of nations at all. It would be a war of classes, of interests in which, again, in so far as one could any longer talk of France or Britain as national units, they would be at an immense disadvantage as compared to Germany and Italy.

Just because so many Germans have not the libertarian mentality and have that strange readiness to accept the dictatorship of the Austrian house painter; just because the Socialist blacksmith has made himself so completely master of the Italian people, they will build their power upon a national unity which in the imagined circumstances neither Britain nor France would possess.

Again, I am afraid our German friend is right. We do not believe in democracy or freedom or liberalism as much as Germany and Italy believe in the opposite, their particular political faith. Perhaps it is not a matter of belief, but whatever attitude it is that enables the dictatorial government to impose itself, they have got that element of unity, of solidarity to a greater degree than Britain or France.

If we would only accept dictatorship there would be a chance of peace with the Dictators. Some of us would almost rejoice, because so many of us now feel that for peace you cannot pay too high a price. But neither France nor ourselves are likely lamely to accept the Fascist solution or the Fascist dictatorship. And when the pinch came, when Spanish Republicanism had been destroyed, Russian Socialism had been destroyed, not as the result of a straightforward war of national conquest, but by the stimulation and subsidy of subversive movements within those countries, and when there came a danger that the Fascists were trying to do that thing in France and more indirectly in England itself, then we should get explosion.

In other words, to allow the Fascist expansion in this way to go on, to allow it to be assumed that we shall submit, will in the long run not bring peace, it will bring war in its very worst form. It will bring the civil war of Europe.

Mr. G. T. Garratt in his book *Mussolini's Roman Empire* writes (p. 237):

'The moral of the last few years has been that Italy is relatively ineffective when opposed by a united and determined people. Signor Mussolini's triumphs have been won at the expense of countries which were neither united nor determined. All through this unhappy period he has been able to rely upon sufficient support inside England to be certain that the policy of the British Government would be vacillating, dishonest, and tortuous. If the new Roman Empire develops into an organism, strong enough to hold our country in pawn, and so situated that all our present re-armament will be futile, then Signor Mussolini should raise a new altar to Janus, and offer his daily thanksgiving to those men and women in England whose divided loyalties made his gamble a success.

'The English who have supported Italy all through her period of aggression correspond roughly to the three Spanish groups—the "traditional obstacles"—the Church, the property-owners, and the army. The Catholic hierarchy naturally sympathise with *el Clero*. The slaughter of trade unionists and socialist workers and their wives did nothing to counterbalance the subsequent killing of priests. To the Catholics it was a one-sided tragedy. The equation—one priest is equal to ten workmen—is one which they cannot even consider.

'Their adhesion to the dubious alliance with ultra-Conservatives and business interests was based on faith rather than argument or interest, though the Catholic hierarchy, as opposed to their rank and file, have always shown a keen sense of property, and a dislike for any effective trade union organisation. The business men, who have been supporting Italy, are presumably urged by interests more than by faith, though it is very easy to believe in the sanctity of property until it becomes a religion. They find a natural basis for working with the Catholics in their common distrust of socialist experiments and in their desire for an ordered society, which to their mind means a State where the lower orders are world disciplined and kept in their proper place.

'There is hardly a military caste in England, but their place is taken by our neo-Fascists, supported by a large group of back-bench Members of Parliament. They have a great teaching in the Press, and in the more venal type of periodic journal. The Spanish affair has brought this group more into the open, and shown that a new kind of internationalist exists in this country.'

Let me recapitulate, noting certain further features.

The Fascist States propose to expand, as they say we did in the past: establish preponderance of power as the foundation of their national defence.

Probably they, and certainly their peoples, as the result of the power of their incomparable propaganda machines, really do believe in the 'vital need' for territorial expansion—an expansion which does not necessarily mean in the case of Germany for instance the annexation of alien peoples but does mean their control, control of policies which uncontrolled might operate adversely to German interests, economic, political, doctrinal.

All three Fascist States repudiate internationalism, any system by which their freedom of action will be subject to foreign control, by which any foreign body would be judge of their action.

What are the ways in which we can meet that situation?

We could ease it, at least temporarily of course, by material concessions. We could transfer colonies, unconditionally. We could make one-sided concessions in the matter of colonial tariffs and economic opportunity in colonial territory, renounce Imperial preferences and so on.

But it is one of the curiosities of the present situation that the very people who call loudest for understanding with the Fascist States —the Rothermeres, the Amerys, the Page-Crofts and others of that school—are also those who are most adamant in refusing that kind of concession to Germany. Though the economic difficulties of the Have-Not States arise far more from the tariffs and preferences which we impose than from lack of colonies, the 'conciliators' propose to stand firm in refusing precisely the one kind of economic aid that would most help the Have-Not States.

A much more popular alternative, the one upon which John Smith has enlarged, is to suggest diversion of Totalitarian energies. 'Let them explode in the East. The protection of south-eastern and eastern countries is no affair of ours.'

Whether in fact we say: 'Have a shot at those fellows and leave us alone' or not, our policy when we say 'We are unable to give commitments other than in the West' comes to the same thing so far as probable results are concerned. We indicate that that for them is the line of least resistance.

Let us then see what is likely to happen, what indeed is happening.

First of all, the expansion will not solve their economic problem nor fulfil their hopes. Manchuria does not pay dividends, nor does Abyssinia; yet somehow the Dictators must deliver profits or appear to deliver profits to their people as the outcome of their 'expansionism.' They go on. The conquest of Manchuria developes into an attempt to conquer a great part of China. From Abyssinia Mussolini goes into

Spain as the prelude to a larger African bite. The French are anxious about Tunis and other of their colonies. Meanwhile those whom we have thrown to the wolves are unlikely to be completely eaten, or are likely to prove indigestible morsels. Russia, despite internal up-heavals is probably notwithstanding, a more considerable military power than she was in Czarist times. Japan certainly fears Russian air power; Germany realises that, attacked in the old way, Russia is unconquerable and has an awkward tendency to prove the grave even of Napoleons who can get to Moscow. Even Abyssinia gives trouble. What follows next?

What follows next is that the 'expansionists' begin to doubt—in the absence of dividends—whether that *is* the line of least resistance. The resistance is proving pretty severe.

Meanwhile a certain other line will have weakened. Because we have thrown China, Russia and certain small States to the wolves of Totalitarianism, they will have ceased to be our allies, ceased to form part of our power. We may soon become the line of least resistance.

Take a case. Italy, disappointed with Abyssinia, turns eyes to Tunis where nearly a hundred thousand Italians are already estab-lished—more than will be established in Abyssinia in half a century. Here is a ready-made colony on the eve of paying dividends. Our Italian member gave discreet, but most interesting hints, along this line.

If you cannot persuade the British public to 'fight for Czecho-slovakia,' as little could you persuade it to 'fight for Tunis' or rather fight to enable France to keep Tunis, fight, not to keep your own property but enable other people to keep theirs. No, we abandon France. And Italy and Germany between them become the inheritors of the French African Empire.

But in that case what becomes of 'our' Rhine frontier? If we refuse to fight for France can we expect that she will fight for us? Our position in the Mediterranean, in the Near East, Palestine, on the Canal, in the Sudan, is difficult enough as it is with France as our ally and her ports open to us. But with France out of it all, that area simply goes. Here indeed is a new 'line of less resistance' for the Totalitarians who have to deliver goods, the goods of Imperial-ism, from time to time to their peoples already finding the earlier booty thin enough. Here indeed we can imagine the Dictators ex-plaining to their peoples is where the plans of expansionism begin to work, to show results. They would be saved at what would possibly be very awkward junctures.

John, I suggest, has been completely bamboozled when he swallows the suggestion that if only he will throw over all idea of law, or the collective system, if only he will refuse to 'fight for Czechoslovakia' or other countries he can keep out of continental entanglements. Let him examine what, for instance, the present dickering with Italy is likely to involve.

What indeed is actually happening now? Geneva, the League, internationalism has been abandoned or put in cold storage. Do our continental visits and conversations and talks with foreign statesmen thereupon cease? Do we in fact turn away from 'a Continental System' or policy? Why at this very moment conversations between our Ministers and foreign statesmen are going on in two capitals. Does John really suppose that those conversations are not going to entangle us in one way or another?

May I remind him that before the War the John Smiths were just as fanatically determined to have no entanglements; that our Ministers again and again got up in Parliament and announced that no undertakings of any kind had been given; that our hands were free. Everybody's hands were free; there were no commitments; the Covenant did not exist.

Clearly that freedom from commitment did not keep us out, for we were all dragged in, even isolationist, distant, unentangled America. And looking back at that world of free hands which went to war, almost every student of its causes now concludes that the world would have had the best chance of keeping out if its hands had *not* been free at all, if the Central Powers had known, that is, that as the result of their policy so much of the world would come in against them.

What is happening now as the result of getting rid of Geneva entanglements? We turn to such devices as either the Stresa front or the Four-Power Pact.

The first means that we have an 'entente' with Italy as we had an 'entente' with France before the War to resist further advance by Germany. Oh, nothing binding of course; our 'entente' with France before the War committed us to nothing. But we could not get out of it when the pinch came.

Or, we may turn to the Four-Power Pact.

Now the Four-Power Pact cannot become a reality—Hitler whom it proposes to include—has made that very clear, unless France abandons her arrangement with Russia. But Germany and Italy are not to abandon the arrangement which ties them to Japan, the Anti-Comintern Pact. So having abandoned Russia we become the allies of her enemies, which really means that we have joined the Anti-Comintern Pact.

But does John really believe that all these dickerings with Powers who have sworn a vendetta against Russia will not commit us, will leave us any freer than the 'Conversations' with France left us in the years which preceded the War?

Well, John might reply, he would condemn those conversations and make it clear that we really are uncommitted. Is he then going to denounce the undertakings given to France and Belgium? He is not. They will remain; and their implications continue to entangle us.

But there is one aspect of this problem which John has left out completely, left out presumably because at the moment it is not very visible. But more and more it is rising to the surface; shortly it is likely to dominate the whole picture. It may well prove the most vital of all.

Most plainly the disparagement of the League, the insistence that it has failed, the refusal to interfere with Japan in 1931, the refusal to take sanctions against Italy seriously, the popularity of the Duce, the strong partisanship of Franco in fashionable quarters in London, the sudden approaches to both the Dictators, and the talk of Pacts which involve exclusion of Russia, means a move on the part of re-actionary elements in France and Britain to back authoritarian govern-ments as against those of the Left, like the government of Spain.

So that in fact, while professing impartiality, non-intervention, we do take sides in the conflict of ideologies; the wrong side. One refusal to work the collective system involves just that thing. That refusal will not liberate us from foreign entanglements it will only make our commitment one to the Right, instead of to the Left. If the Collective System so strongly supported by the Left in France breaks down completely; if the Spanish Government is destroyed by the intervention of those with whom we now discuss Pacts of friendship and co-operation, something like civil war in France results. I wonder if John thinks that that would make for the peace of these Islands, whether its social stability would remain unaffected or its Empire secure?

It is quite clear that in the British negotiations with the Dictators no very ardent defence of the collective system will be made. The Dictators are, of course, perfectly aware of the fact that they will not have to pay any great price for its formal abandonment.

As to Mussolini, what he asks for the time being is mainly the formal recognition of the Italian empire in Africa; that the Abyssinia which entered the League no longer exists.

It sounds practical, sensible, the very thing likely to appeal to the British Conservative type of mind. Mussolini will certainly have no very great difficulty on that point. Yet this apparently innocent concession will mean that in the future in so far as principles govern international relations at all, the fundamental principle will be the 'realist' one: 'Prove your capacity to seize territory, and we shall recognise your right to it. Might will henceforth be the only touchstone of Right. If, in asserting your Might you violate practically every undertaking you have given (as Italy violated the conditions about poison gas and Japan has violated a round half-dozen treaties) that will make no real difference. If you are successful you will be Right.'

To refuse to recognise the Italian Empire in Abyssinia may be to shut our eyes to 'facts.' But that does not alter another fact—that to recognise the conquest will facilitate the return to all the old political immoralisms that involved the world in war before; and must ultimately involve it in war again.

About Russia it will not be necessary for France or Britain to give any undertaking at all. Germany and Italy will offer the West a complete, water-tight, absolute non-aggression pact; and they will offer it with the greatest sincerity. There is no reason in the world why at this stage either Germany or Italy should attack either Great Britain or France. The Fascist States may even consent to collective arrangements of the Locarno type, if only Russia is excluded.

Any such offer will be acclaimed by great sections of British opinion as so obviously making for peace that nothing—they will declare—but the most wicked indifference to peace, or equally wicked ideological fanaticism could prompt its rejection.

And yet note what is involved.

It means, whether we realise it or not, the surrender of all efforts to do that thing for which we supposed the Great War was being fought; it would mark the failure of the first real effort to get away from that anarchy in which each takes what he can grab in a general scramble; the definite abandonment of the effort to create anything resembling a society of nations. In our present mood few tears will be shed on that. We shall be told that the collective principle is a theory, a doctrine, an 'ideology,' and that we should not fight for ideals. Those asked to fight will duly note.

But the throwing of Russia (and China) to the wolves can hardly be considered as the abandonment of a 'mere theory.'

The first fact to be noted is that not merely is Russia excluded from the talks, but that in any state of mind at all resembling the present one in Germany, there is not the slightest hope that the inclusion of Russia will be possible, for we know that the whole psychological and propaganda method of the German régime is based upon welding the national community together by giving it a common hate, a common enemy, a danger, a scapegoat. It is the easiest and most certain road to unity for any group. 'Find me a common hatred and I will undertake to make the whole world feel like brothers,' said a psychologist. (If we were in danger of destruction by the Martians our deepest earthly hatreds would be forgotten in a month.) That common enemy for Germany is Bolshevism. The fight against Jewry itself comes a bad second.

Moreover, the psychological motive can be buttressed by strong economic motives. Russia stands there as the means by which Germany may satisfy what its propaganda machine puts forth as Germany's greatest economic need. 'What could not Germany do if only she possessed some of that territory now in such evil and Satanic hands?' as the Führer has so explicitly asked. And to the economic motive for maintaining a *casus belli* against Russia there is added a third motive, perhaps the most powerful of all—the military and the political. Germany can never be safe in the Nazi view so long as Russia exists as a Communist State steadily growing in power and resources; as not merely in herself a potential enemy, but, in the German view, still more threatening to the safety of the Reich as a potential ally of France and Britain.

So, whatever else happens, Russia is not likely to be included in any forthcoming talks. The denunciation of the Franco-Soviet Pact

will be the condition *sine qua non* of any understanding. The holding
of the talks at all on those conditions will be a preliminary triumph
for the Italo-German initiative.

Let us assume Russia ruled out; sent to Coventry: Germany has a
free hand when conditions are favourable to do in Russia what with
Italy she has done in Spain. Assume that this exclusion of Russia
provokes no movement in the democratic countries from below (incidentally, a quite indefensible assumption). What is the situation?
From the moment that Russia is eliminated from the European scene,
Britain and France are within the power of the totalitarian bloc,
dependent upon its goodwill and good faith. (It was only by the most
stupendous sacrifice that Britain and France were able to defend themselves against Germany when Germany had to meet also the forces of
Italy and Japan. What would be the chances of successful opposition
to Germany's domination when these forces instead of opposing
are supporting her?)

The mind of the anti-Leaguist works curiously. Perpetually does
he tell us that to base the nation's security upon paper agreements,
upon the assumption that foreigners will keep their engagements
when it is not to their interest so to do, is to betray the national security, to build our defence upon sand. But the whole underlying
assumption of the Four-Power as distinct from the Five-Power Pact
is that when France and Britain have been manœuvred into a position
of most manifest inferiority of power, those States, which of late
have made a patriotic virtue of tearing up the engagements entered
into, can be depended upon not to abuse their power when they have
fat, rich and in their view decadent empires at their mercy; can be
depended upon to respect their engagements, even though at the very
moment of giving new engagements they are cynically violating existing ones.

That Britain should have to surrender a large part of her African
or Asiatic empire to these autocrats for experiments in totalitarian
Government (if Jews and Communists are subhuman in Goebbels's
phrase, what are Negroes and other coloured races?) is, perhaps, no
very great matter. It is probably quite true that the difference between
Italian (or German) and British rule in Africa, Japanese and British
rule over large areas in Asia, is not worth a general war. Many of
our people will so decide. Having been told that the League is dead,
that anything better than the old international order is impossible

they may well decide that another Versailles victory is not worth war. The Empire goes. But Fascists at home remain.

Consider then the circumstances. Germany and Italy (with Japan) form at present an overtly anti-Russian combination. All three have declared formally that the particular economic system on which the Russian State is based is the enemy of civilisation; that they are out to destroy that system. Only recently Hitler re-asserted this determination of the Anti-Comintern States to refuse normal relationships with the Russian Government; re-asserted it in terms, more violent, more ruthless and reckless than any ever before employed by him. A few hours after that declaration the one member of the British Cabinet looked upon most favourably by the Russian Government is eliminated. The very first pronouncement made by Herr von Ribbentrop on his arrival as ambassador in England was an invitation to this country to join in the destruction of Communism.

Italy has announced formally that she would not tolerate and would use her armed forces to destroy, any government on the shores of the Mediterranean which in her judgment (that is to say the judgment of Benito Mussolini) was 'Bolshevist' in tendency or character, 'Bolshevism' not being defined.

The statement was made as explaining and justifying the sending of Italian armies against a government which did not contain a single Communist, nor even a single Socialist. This enunciation of policy could quite as easily have been made to justify the destruction of the Popular Front Government of France, which did contain Socialists, was, in fact, dependent upon the support of Communists; a government not merely maintaining normal diplomatic relations with Russia, but in open, formal, declared alliance with that country.

This severance of all collective or co-operative engagements with Russia for mutual assistance would plainly be immensely popular with certain forces of the Right both in Britain and in France. Certain Right forces in France are deeply opposed to the existing Franco-Soviet Pact, and, urge the alternative of an understanding with Germany. In Britain there is broadly the same alignment of opinion, the anti-Russian and pro-German-Italian now being heavily represented as we all know in the Cabinet itself.

Some years since Russia abandoned her world revolution policy for an attempt at co-operation with the Capitalist States of the West.

The effect of pushing her back now into isolation, menaced, as she would be, by Nazi Germany in the West and Fascist Japan in the East, would be to compel her to weaken the power of her enemies by turning once more to the 'world revolution' policy. Signs of a tendency so to do are rife. Certain further possibilities are only too evident. If as the result—even though it was not the intention—of the British policy of withholding from the Spanish Government its legal right to buy arms that Government is defeated by the Italy and Germany with whom Britain enters into partnership; if the technique of Germany and Italy is extended to France and a French Franco called into being there (and that some such plan is part of the Fascist policy the Fascist States hardly even pretend to deny) then France, like Spain, may be racked by Civil War; that Civil War will destroy among other things, the last Democratic Ally of Great Britain, who thereupon will be faced by the choice of making common cause with the Totalitarian States in the destruction of Democracy; or being at their mercy.

This is known as 'not taking sides in a conflict of ideologies.'

We say commonly that war has shifted to the air. There has been a change of venue in another sense. The alignment will no longer be the confrontation of nation with nation or alliance with alliance. Who, even five years ago, would have dared to say that a powerful Belgian party would be proposing what is in effect an alliance of that party with German Nationalists in opposition to other parties within the Belgian nation? Who could have prophesied that the French Nationalists would be the first to make the most notable gestures of reconciliation with Germany—in order to create a Franco-German combination, or potential combination against a French Popular Front? Who would have said that British Jingoes and Nationalists would be the first to advocate openly an alliance with Germany against the ally of France. And, as to Spain, Mr. Vernon Bartlett, returning from his recent visit to that country, writes:

'The civil war in Spain will probably be lost by the Spanish people only because the insurgents have received help from abroad which was refused to the government. There will be a new period of tyranny during which these Spaniards will not even have the poor consolation of reflecting that the cause of liberty has gained elsewhere through their slavery. Either this tyranny will be successful, and Spain will be welded into a new Fascist State of the greatest strategical importance (in that Gibraltar will become a liability rather than an asset in all British plans of defence, while France will have to maintain far too many troops along the Pyrenees in the event

of a Franco-German or Franco-Italian war). Or the tyranny will break
down and Spain will be faced with a much more bloody civil war than
the present one and with the prospect of a much more drastic swing to the
left at the end of it. . . .

'Those nice Conservatives who are most horrified by talk of class war
are making it inevitable by their undisguised hope that those Spaniards
who come from the same social class as they do will succeed in prolonging
a disgraceful tyranny. They make it infinitely more difficult for those of
us who believe both in tolerance and in the abolition of injustice to remain
tolerant.'

It is exceedingly significant that those sections of the Conservative
Party and the self-same Press which preaches co-operation with Germany in the name of international peace, and has opposed the League
of Nations because of its 'interference in quarrels which do not concern us' manages to make of a government (which has never injured
us, has always left us severely alone, against which we cannot even
allege grievance) an enemy government, against which it daily whips
up hate by all the devices of atrocity-mongering which a year or two
ago it was employing against the German Government. The tone
adopted by the Rothermere Press against the Spanish Government
could hardly be more violent if Spanish armies were in occupation of
Kent; while the same papers could hardly be more enthusiastic in their
praise of the Hitlerite and Fascist Government if the German or the
Italian Press laws were operative in London.

When therefore we are adjured to remain friends with Germany,
as during the Abyssinian matter we were begged, on grounds of
friendship and peace not to criticise Italy; and before that not to
anger Japan by ill-judged comments upon her Manchurian adventure,
what ought the attitude of the Pacifist to be? And what ought his
attitude to be towards the violence of parties within the State now
that the problem of resistance to war and its prevention is much more
likely to present itself in the form of prevention of civil war? In the
case of Italy the Pacifist refused to apply non-military restraint
because it might be replied to militarily. Friendship for Italy was
invoked (incidentally by many besides Pacifists) as the reason why
the law she had violated should not be upheld. Are similar considerations to weigh when we face the arming of parties within the State?

Nothing, declared government spokesmen, when Italy challenged the European constitution, will induce us to pursue a course which would provoke war with Italy. Defence of the Constitution means war, and as the purpose of that Covenant was peace, we shall not therefore defend it. And having made such a declaration the conversation with Italy might, of course, just as well have ended. In the face of any proposed measure of restraint she had merely to say: 'Apply it, and I fight,' and she knew beforehand that the restraint would not be applied. It came very near to being the policy of the Weimar Republic at various stages in dealing with aggression within its borders. It, too, followed the policy of friendliness and conciliation to the extent of causing the promoters of a Nazi 'putsch' to wonder whether in fact they would be resisted; and to gamble on the chance that they might not.

The ultimate outcome might well be a Russo-German 'entente' directed against this country. And this might well result from our refusal now to co-operate with Russia.

May I read what seems to me an appropriate comment?

'The Anti-Comintern Pact has very little to do with the Comintern. The militant ideologies play on the hatred felt by their millions of followers, and, concentrating these hatreds on a defenceless, or relatively defenceless, foe, they fuse them into one intense hatred which is thereby stored up and canalised for use against the real enemy. Hitler *needs* the Jews, not only because he must have something to persecute, but also because he must have the simulacrum of a dangerous enemy at home, so as to perpetuate a sense of vigilance amongst the German people. In the same way he—and with him Mussolini and the Japanese militarists—*need* the Comintern abroad, so that they may have a simulacrum, full of apparent but devoid of real danger, as a help in keeping the militancy of the German, Italian and Japanese nations alive and alert.

'The British Commonwealth stands for everything Hitler, Mussolini and the Japanese militarists hate, and in the way of everything they want. The Anti-Comintern Pact is a conspiracy against the Commonwealth, and not against the Comintern. As an internal foe, Communism has become unimpressive, especially in this country. Lenin had the highest hopes of the British Communist Party, but, more than thirteen years after his death, the Party has been unable to return more than one member to Parliament; and it is really quite impossible to be frightened of Mr. Gallacher, even though it is quite possible to respect him. Of course, there are people who imagine that Bolshevism still lurks round the corner, growing a little old, no doubt, but sinister nevertheless, so that the simulacrum of the Communist danger is still some slight use to those who need a cover for their hostility to something very different. But a cover that will be a little less transparent has become highly desirable. It has been found—in the League of nations.'[1]

And now a final reminder.

One element of our existing foreign policy at least is clear and unequivocal: we have definitely undertaken to defend France from attack because her integrity is indispensable to our own security. Assume that we have to implement that very definite promise, and find ourselves, as we found ourselves in the years 1914-8, resisting a great onslaught which sweeps dangerously towards the Channel coasts; in a situation, indeed, far more precarious than that which faced us in the Great War, for we should almost certainly not have on our side powers that were then our allies and would quite probably face those erstwhile allies as enemies. When we thus face, unaided as we were in the last War by Russia, Italy, Japan and the United States, vast hostile forces, whether on the soil of France, or on the sea, or in the air, and there is offered to us in that extremity the help of potentially the greatest military power in the world, should we refuse or accept the offer? In other words, are we to have the help of Russia in meeting the next attack upon France? If in such a situation Russian aid were offered, should we refuse it? Unless a Fascist government were already in power we should not dream of refusing.

Should we wait till the situation has actually arisen? Then it would be too late. Too late, that is, to deter the aggressor, to prevent war, which once it comes makes 'defence' a tragic mockery. Once more it is necessary to insist that the Great War might have been prevented if Germany had foreseen that she would have to meet the forces which she did meet. The vast power finally arrayed against her was impotent to deter her for the childishly simple reason that she did not know it would be used against her. In any case such pre-knowledge of the purpose of arms is the only means by which they can possibly act as a deterrent. It raises the question: is the belief now to grow up that we shall look on unmoved while allies indispensable to our own defence are destroyed in detail?

For years we refused to make our undertakings to France unequivocal just as we refuse so to make them to Russia. We hesitated for the quite good reason that an unconditional undertaking to defend France would be an encouragement to the worst and most provocative side of French policy, like that which prompted the occupation of the

[1] *Time and Tide,* December 18, 1937.

Ruhr. But the way to meet that difficulty was not to withhold guarantees which, firmly given, would have made it easier for France to be moderate, but to secure guarantees from her that her conduct would conform to certain principles, such as, for instance, submission of disputes to third-party judgment, so that 'the other side' also had means of security—the proviso which constitutes the difference between the old alliance method and the collective system. Put in different terms we should undertake to sustain a certain rule of international life, or if you prefer so to call it, Covenant, which, resolutely upheld would ensure the defence of those party to it.

X

TO DEFEND OURSELVES WE MUST DEFEND LAW

The absence of any principle of order, rule of the road, code in the relationship of States, like the absence of a code on the highway, must mean 'disorder,' collision. Of old, the collisions, like those between ox-carts were relatively innocuous. But in modern conditions, on the motor-car road, for instance, collisions are infinitely more destructive. If we assume this to be broadly true, we must get a code or mutually destroy ourselves. But the Totalitarians proclaim a religious hatred of, and a holy war against any international code. What then must we do? If, for purposes of 'conciliation,' we cede bit by bit any possibility of law, we render Britain and the Empire impossible of defence. If we are not ready to take any risk at all to sustain the law and the Totalitarians are prepared to take very great risks to destroy it then plainly the law perishes, or can never be born.

To what alternatives did the discussion so far point? A member of our group undertook to indicate. Here is his paper:

Our previous speaker is plainly right when he says that even if we could abolish all the 'specific' grievances of the Totalitarians, give back all her colonies to Germany, hand over the French colonies to Italy, and so on, we should not have got at the root of the matter. The supreme grievance of all would remain, and we can only satisfy that grievance, solve that problem, by creating for our own people a grievance just as burning, a problem just as severe.

What is this supreme grievance of, e.g. Germany?

It is that she possesses no security based upon her own preponderance. Not merely will she not be subject to the power of a foreign State, she will not accept a position in which it would be possible for a foreign State to exercise it, however wisely or generously. She will be master of her own fate, decider of her own quarrels, arbiter of her own destiny.

We are back at the problem of 1914.

After all, that has very deep roots. Not only is it true that defence, self-preservation, is the first law of life, one of its consequences is to make the will to power, to domination, one of the deepest of all passions.

One of the consequences of that fact is that we have all attempted to achieve defence by methods which deprive others of it. If one is secure the other is not. Now surely that is a pretty simple truth. So long as men pursue that method war must continue. It is one of the surprises of our time that even educated men obviously do not see this truth since they daily proclaim contrary propositions, incompatible with it.

Most people perhaps would deny the proposition that if we will not defend others, it becomes a physical impossibility permanently to defend ourselves. Yet, again, it is obvious.

See how it works out. Here is a great combination of States, a Triumvirate. It is flanked by lesser States. Let us put the thing in figures. The defensive power of the Triumvirate is represented by say one hundred; that of the lesser States (who number shall we say four) fifty each. So long as each of the four say: 'We will fight for our own people only, not for others'—each is at the mercy of the combination. From the moment that the four say: 'Our defence is collective, we make a Defensive Confederation; an attack on one is an attack on all'—from that moment their defensive power has risen from fifty to two hundred and they are no longer at the mercy of the Triumvirate.

I am not suggesting of course that the thing in practice works out in that simple arithmetical fashion, but merely to indicate a principle, that unless at times we are prepared to fight for others, to make sacrifices to defend others, it may well become a physical impossibility to defend ourselves.

Just now we are being asked to surrender the principle in the name of peace and conciliation. Yet its surrender must in the end mean war.

Our clarity of thought is distorted by the flinging about of certain 'weasel words'—'the evil of coercion,' 'the danger of force'—words used in such confusion as to mean anything or nothing, and which yet somehow ride us off into false policy. I want to clarify the mechanism of Collective Defence by a few homely illustrations.

I have a dispute with a neighbour—a rather violent-minded, passionate neighbour—about a right of way. He comes to me one day and says:

'We have quarrelled about this long enough. I am absolutely convinced that I am right, and as I am stronger than you, I shall assert my right, justified by my conscience, and shall forthwith tear down your fences, destroy your buildings, carry the road in question across your property.'

Now if I were to yield to him I know that that would not be the end of the dispute. Others besides myself are involved in the question of the road under dispute, interested in its use. The solution proposed by my neighbour would precipitate deep anger and resentment on their part and I should purchase peace with a troublesome neighbour by creating immense difficulties for neighbours whose behaviour was in fact much better. So I reply:

'I do not intend that force should settle this matter, particularly not your force, and if you attempt to use it for the purpose of imposing your judgment, I shall resist you—otherwise I should be allowing force to settle this question which would do violence to my conscience as well as my interest.'

I resist successfully. Having overcome him, disarmed him if you will, one of two courses is open to me. I might say:

'Because you thought you were stronger, you, though one of the parties to the dispute proposed to use your strength in order to be its judge. It would be poetic justice for you to be compelled to take your own medicine. I have disarmed you. You are within my power. I shall therefore make myself the judge, and the road shall be carried across your property, not mine. Your fences, your buildings will be destroyed in order to make that possible.'

In that case there would, of course, be nothing morally to choose between us. I should be just as bad as he, and there would probably start one of those feuds and vendettas which go on from generation to generation in the Kentucky mountains or in those of Corsica, in which scores of people may be killed in a quarrel arising about just some such question as to where a fence or a road should run; just as the Franco-German vendetta has cursed Europe for centuries.

Or I might take another line. Having disarmed my neighbour and overcome him, I may say:

'Because I would not accept your verdict in this dispute, I do not ask you to accept mine. Neither shall be the judge. We will both submit to third-party judgment, arbitration, court, what you will. If I am willing to accept third-party judgment, and you are not, it means that I have greater faith in the justice of my case than you have in yours.'

If he accepts, we are really on the road to appeasement. If he does not, and indicates that he will continue to fight, I invoke the police. What is their role when they enter the scene? *It is not to settle the dispute.* The policeman on arriving says in effect: 'I know nothing of your right of way—never heard of it. What I do know,' he says to my neighbour, 'is that you propose to take the law into your own hands, to destroy your neighbour's property. If you have a claim, take it to the court and get a judgment. If the judgment is in your favour, and your neighbour, refusing to accept it, does what you are now doing, I should, of course, be ready to do to him what I am about to do to you: Take you to the police-station.'

Force here, the force that is of a community embodied in the policeman, does not settle the dispute. What it does is to *prevent* force settling the dispute; so acting that the result will depend not upon whether my neighbour is stronger, but upon the outcome of reason, judgment, law, traditions, customs, contracts.

When the power of the police is thus exercised to prevent either litigant using his force to settle a dispute, to make himself its judge, it is a function which is the exact contrary of the function or purpose of national armies and navies as we have known them in the past. For their purpose has been to *enable* one of the parties to be judge.

It is said so commonly: 'There is no law and there is no impartial judge.'

Only one law at this stage is needed: the law that there shall be no more war; that the war-maker shall be regarded as the common enemy to be restrained by all those forces, moral, diplomatic, political, economic, financial, and finally military and naval, which those who *are* prepared to surrender force as the instrument of their own policy and use it only as the instrument of a law which gives some approximation to equality of right, can manage to assemble. By some strange twist of reasoning this is often condemned as a policy of 'coercion.'

What is coercion?

If a man comes for me with an axe, and I manage to disarm him, do I coerce him? If a neighbour helps me in thus disarming me, does that make it coercion? If nations club together for mutual defence and say to a potential aggressor: 'Please do not kill us, do not bomb our cities, slay our civilian populations; and if you attempt to do so, to any one of us, we will all combine to make the bombing and the slaying impossible,' is that coercion? Yet it has been commonly so described by eminent critics of the collective system.

A similar degree of confusion is the criticism based on the plea that the League was an attempt to freeze the *status quo*; that before a collective system can work there must be a 'just settlement'; that we cannot guarantee frontiers because the frontiers are unjust. The point has already been touched upon. The Covenant does not guarantee frontiers; it only tries to guarantee that they shall not be changed by war at the will of the victor. For in that event the last state will be worse than the first. It may be that provisions for peaceful change have been inadequately developed. But the remedy for that defect is not to say by implication to States that feel themselves aggrieved: 'Go and make the change by war and we will not stop you.' If one aggrieved State, even when it is in the right, is by implication prompted to make itself judge, then inevitably the State which is in the wrong will (quite sincerely) claim the same privilege.

In a debate the other day upon the question of the League, that is to say, the question of collective defence, the opponent of the collective system opened in some such terms as these:

'The whole matter would be settled if you would give a plain answer to a plain question. Would you take a poker to the burglar if one entered your house? I would ask you further to consider the political significance of the fact that in the Tudor bedstead which my people have at home there is a place where the householder used to keep a blunderbuss wherewith to greet the highwayman.'

The other party to the dispute naturally replied somewhat in these terms:

'I *would* take a poker to the burglar if nothing better were handy and I have considered this blunderbuss matter the moral of which I suggest is this: That when every house had blunderbusses highwaymen and bandits were much commoner than they are now when not one house in a thousand has a firearm on the place. The relative security of to-day cannot, therefore, be due to the household blunderbuss because it does not exist. It is due to the improvement of the collective system within the borders of the State. In the old days a bandit could argue: We have only to be stronger than one householder—usually John Smith quaking in his night-shirt, flourishing a poker—in order to have the countryside at our mercy. With great distances and impassable roads there can be no possibility of combination between householders. We can clean up the countryside in detail.'

That is not the position to-day. The bandit will not meet merely Smith flourishing a poker. Whom will he meet? He will meet you and me, organised through the police courts, magistrates, detectives, the whole apparatus of defence. This gives to reflect to the highwayman. We in effect say to the potential gangster: 'Touch Smith and you touch us.'

A few years ago the Metropolitan Police spent ten thousand pounds trying to find out who murdered a perfectly uninteresting woman. The isolationist should be indignant that his money is poured out in this reckless fashion to interfere in quarrels which were none of his. Why not argue: 'Let her attend to her business and I will attend to mine?' We do not argue that way because if we did none of us could be safe.

The question really should be something like this: Are we willing to pay our police rate to protect our neighbours? If not, they will not pay theirs to protect us, there can be no police force, no organised society.

The average sensual man puts law, efforts towards an international order in one category, that of 'distant ideals,' and national defence in another and entirely different category, that of 'practical problems.' The two are not in his view related. He does not see that if we cannot set before ourselves the objective of some better international order as the purpose of our power, we cannot make it effective for defence at all. Are we really going to ask our people to fight another Great War for the purpose of another victory to be no more effective than the last in achieving security?

Had the War of 1914 arisen out of the attack upon some international system even as imperfect as that of Geneva, embodying organised methods of third party judgment, peaceful change, economic equality, its victory over the forces of anarchy would have vindicated it as a political reality, something perilous to attack, however imperfect the application of its principles. Cromwell's service was not to give us a perfect constitution but to defeat for all time the principle of absolute monarchy in Britain. Lincoln's service was not to produce a perfect Federation but to defeat principles which would have made any secure Federation impossible.

Our dominant conviction now is that by keeping out of commitment we may best reduce the risks of war.

Now perhaps the most amazing, the most suggestive fact in the whole story of the War, was the way in which nation after nation, not merely with no commitment to enter the War, but having at first sight no imaginable concern in it, was irresistibly drawn into the vortex. An uncommitted world was engulfed. One would say that this strange spectacle of distant Asiatic and American communities, of jungle tribes of the Amazon, peaceful communities of the Ohio, with no shadow of written or consciously undertaken obligation, sucked irresistibly into the whirlpool, would strike the mind of every man as being the most significant fact in the whole vast episode. Whatever may have caused the participation of these widely separated multitudes, it plainly cannot have been the clauses of a written contract, undertakings, commitments, for those clauses did not exist. That thing at least was not and could not be the cause of their catastrophe.

Yet the thing which had no existence is regarded by multitudes— millions of educated Americans, for instance—as the main cause of their tragedy. The one thing which the multitudes fear is the one thing which, on the face of it, could in most cases have had nothing to do with the miseries that descended upon them.

This fear of commitment is not less striking when one examines the tragedy of 1914 from the opposite angle, and asks the question discussed previously: Suppose the nations *had* been committed to do what, without commitment, they were finally compelled to do? Suppose that in the years preceding the War German statesmen had known to a dead certainty that a given line of policy would end by bringing a score of nations, including the United States, into the field against them?

More than one speaker here has shown pretty conclusively that there would have been no war. Statesmen do not enter wars for the purpose of losing them. *Had* the world been 'committed,' had those contracts existed, the War would not have taken place. Had the nations possessed the forethought to say *beforehand* that they would do what they were in any case finally compelled to do, they would not have been obliged to do it. General freedom from commitment did not keep us out; commitment would have kept us out. The lesson that we now draw is that we must give no commitment.

The tragedy of confusion goes deeper still. Not only is it true that these nations, so free from clearly defined obligation, were impelled nevertheless to take certain action—dreadful and appalling action— and that had it been known beforehand that they *would* take that action, it need never have been taken at all; but it is also true that in the absence of previous undertaking the action itself became futile and its incalculable sacrifices vain.

Just because the nations which entered the War against Germany were not acting on behalf of a law of peace available for the protection of Germany herself, so long as she observed it, their victory was not a victory for law at all. It was the victory of one alliance over another, each fighting for the right to impose its own view of right on the other; each trying, that is, to impose the very injustice of one-sided judgment which it was fighting to resist. (The invasion of Belgium was a bad breach of contract on Germany's part, an outrage, but it was part of the old European Balance system, no part of a system of peace, which had the fatal defect that Germany would incur the penalties of breach whether she respected her word or not; that, in other words, she would face the hostility of England even though she did *not* go through Belgium.)

Had there existed before the War a European constitution embodying the double principle of law—that is to say third-party judgment and mutual defence through common resistance to the war-maker— and the nations which actually did fight Germany had fought in clear defence of that system, in defence of the law and the constitution, the very cost of the vindication would have been assurance that in future the law would be respected. A prospective aggressor would know that war 'as an instrument of national policy' really was a crime which civilisation would restrain; that the nations had learned to stand in common against the anarchy that threatened to engulf them and in defence of that organised society of mankind which alone can prevent the tools we have devised becoming instruments of suicide.

But the nations entered the War with no clear notion at all of any fundamental social principle behind it all, although all felt they were fighting a common danger of domination by alien power. One State, Italy, enters (in defiance of previous pledges to the other side) for enlargement of frontiers; another, Rumania, for some similar purpose; Germany and Russia for the preservation of dominion which would ensure their future 'expansion'; Britain because the growth of German power threatened her own dominion. Here was no common principle of Right—a political or moral rule of the road which could be universally applied for the common safety. America alone had behind her action some social principle. But even in her case it was so ill-conceived by her public that they could be turned from it immediately the War was over by the diversion of some mean and silly wrangle of party politics.

Because the nations were fighting for no clear common rule, the War itself has, in fact, proved a futility so tragic and appalling that we dare not face it; dare not ask ourselves why those laughing boys were pounded to dirty pulp for no useful human purpose whatsoever.

It is, of course, precisely the question which we should ask. No man can lay claim to intellectual honesty in the discussion of policy at this juncture unless he asks himself clearly, not merely what he would have his nation do if faced to-day by the contingency (but in far graver form) which it faced in 1914, but what, in fact, it would do.

It is not always easy to know what one believes oneself; still less easy to know what others believe. But definite acts in a given contingency are a better guide to a knowledge of what men believe than their mere professions.

In estimating what our nation would do if confronted by a repetition of the contingency of 1914 we have two facts upon which to base our judgment: the fact of what the nations actually did in 1914 and the motives which impelled them, and the fact of what they are all doing at this present moment.

We know that, in fact, some twenty nations did enter the field against Germany and that behind all the confusions of motive lay one common and dominant impulse: the impulse to resist the building up of an alien power so great as to deprive the less powerful of defence. It is the point to which we keep coming in most of our discussions.

It is that which really induced those tens and hundreds of millions to enter the struggle; which gave to the Australian sheep-herder, to the Rotarian of Zenith, to the Cockney in Whitechapel Road, a passion of resistance, this readiness to give his life. There are those full of erudition, of complicated theories, who tell you that Mr. Babbitt and the sheep-herder went to their deaths because Mr. J. P. Morgan told them to. But really that does not explain it. Even if Mr. Morgan gave the order, how did one elderly banker (or one hundred) induce millions to obey? To what consideration did he appeal with such success? Why did Mr. Babbitt *want* to go; clamoured; lied about his age in order that he might be enlisted? The economic interpretation of the act of the youngster who goes with exaltation to quite certain death is still just a little inadequate. Here as elsewhere, perhaps, 'erudition is the enemy of understanding.' Even if it be true that the American nation, its forty-eight States, its House of Representatives, its Senate, its Cabinet, President Wilson himself, all took the line they did because Mr. J. P. Morgan told them to, we can assume that it was not from love of Mr. J. P. Morgan; that the boys who went with such valour, did not go to save his bonds.

Again, why did those millions fight?

It is not really very complicated. They saw what Britain saw: The danger that one great nation might become so powerful as to dominate, to become their master; of being compelled to do its bidding. Rather than accept that, they would die. The motive to which Mr. Morgan appealed so successfully (if, in fact, he appealed to any) was precisely this fear of domination by a great alien Power, hatred of the thought that our nation should do the will of alien masters.

That fact at least is clear in the history of 1914. The British people would not accept the prospective domination of Germany, the possibility that Germany, having conquered France and Russia, would become the master of Europe with a completeness which Napoleon never, in fact, knew. We did not know what Germany would do with that power, and we did not ask very clearly what she could do, just what the ultimate dangers of accepting German hegemony were. But suddenly confronted by the possible contingency of being subject to German domination, the British people discovered that they were not prepared to submit. The Belgians had already discovered that they could not submit.

Confronted by a similar choice again, how should we act?

A great many are answering that question to-day by saying that we should keep out, that we should enter into no engagements, should disengage ourselves from any obligations to France and Russia. That answer is given not only by a large part of the popular Press (the *Daily Express* which voices daily this opinion is now proclaiming that its circulation has passed the two million mark) not only increasingly by politicians, but by many who profess themselves in favour of the Collective System: it is *the* dominant element of public feeling at this date.

If behind that decision lay, not merely a vague dilettante pacifist philosophy, but a well-considered Pacifist Policy, there would be a great deal to be said for it. If these New Pacifists of the *Mail* and the *Express* were prepared to say:

'Henceforth Britain and the Empire shall occupy the position of a Norway and a Finland. We shall take all the risks of non-resistance. We shall not fight to resist any claim which a Fascist or Nazi Empire might make upon us; shall make no effort at all to resist alien domination; shall, if necessary, suffer invasion and the dismemberment of the Empire.'

If that position were taken by the whole population over a long period, it might in the end succeed.

We might have to go through the experience which an unarmed Germany had to go through in the Ruhr invasion when France attempted by that means to collect debts which she, in her good judgment, deemed due to her; we might have to go through the experience of a powerless China in the face of a powerful Fascist Japan; and our Dominions suffer the fate of Abyssinia because their very existence was deemed to be incompatible with the security of a Fascist and perhaps an Asiatic Empire. But if we were persistent for a generation or two it might succeed. (Success would have been infinitely more probable in 1914 because we were then dealing with a Germany not in fact different in its fundamental values and in its civilisation from its neighbours, and dealing with a world which still retained a detestation of crude medieval violences and cruelties, certain fundamental decencies which have since been all but completely abandoned.)

But as a matter of fact neither the people as a whole, nor the

Pacifist Lord Beaverbrook who organises anti-war exhibitions; nor Lord Rothermere who is daily shocked at the militarism of Geneva, nor the intellectuals who analyse the psychology of sanctions and have discovered that the bombs of the international sanction explode in the same way as the bombs of the national sanction, have any clear intention of applying a Pacifist policy, of sacrificing national defence, of scrapping the army and navy. The number who would vote to disband the army and navy *now*, so that we could not possibly have a war because we should have nothing to make war with, the number of those prepared for unilateral disarmament is very, very small. Year after year the Service Estimates are duly voted and the decision to retain our forces is taken afresh. This means, whether those who thus decide realise it or not, that in certain circumstances we would fight; go to war; that we do *not* reject war; that we do *not* regard it as the worst thing that could possibly happen; that we regard domination by a foreign State as a worse thing and would be prepared to go to war to prevent it. To go on maintaining burdensomely expensive instruments that were never in any circumstance to be used, would be an imbecility. We may say that nothing would ever make us use them. But to go on saying that and to go on building them up is to be guilty of an obtuseness which it is difficult to envisage as anything but cynical and insincere. If it is sincere the sincerity is more dangerous than the insincerity would be. In creating the instruments of war we testify that we regard their use in some circumstances as right; we accept war as such, accept military sanctions, accept the killing of others, accept the defeat of other nations, and all the psychological effects that go with it.

So be it. We will fight, 'for defence.'

But we will not say what 'defence' is. The very existence of our armaments is a notification to the foreigner:

'If you do certain things, we will fight.'

But when he asks us what things, we refuse to say. 'We will decide when the time comes.'

This is not to make the use of our armaments less probable, it is to make their use more probable.

To say that it is right and moral to use our arms for individual defence to be decided by us, and us alone, in each circumstance as it arises, but that it is evil and wrong to combine with others to make common defence of a rule or law designed to give protection to all alike, is certainly not Pacifism. It turns the ethics of the situation upside down, and, if our purpose is to combine defence and peace, defies experience.

To be a Pacifist when it comes to using force for the defence of law, but a militarist when it comes to using force to maintain our national interests, as a litigant; to say, it is right to fight, but only if it is each for himself and none for the law, is not to be a Pacifist at all.

If we have decided that we shall fight for defence, how should we react to a situation which if allowed to crystallise would make effective defence impossible?

Would we accept the domination of the Germany of 1938 when we would not accept the domination of the Germany of 1914?

Consider the differences. We talked of the autocratic character of the German state. But the autocracy of Hitler's little finger is immensely more appalling than the autocracy of the Kaiser's whole body. We should call the Germany of 1914 a very Liberal State to-day. A German Europe of 1914 would have been a free Europe compared with what a Nazi Europe would be. And a Europe in which France had been overcome or even 'squared,' so that Germany could with the co-operation of Poland, the Border States and Japan ensure the partition of Russia into a congeries of satellite Manchukuos under the domination, as to the Western part, by the German, and the Eastern part by the Japanese hegemony, such a Europe, would be a Nazi dominated Europe.

Faced squarely by the possibility of a Hitlerite Europe, a Europe dominated by the Nazi Party, by Brown Shirted Fascists, passionately convinced of the holiness of their Nordic mission to rule the Lesser Tribes under the guidance of the Leader 'walking with the sure steps of a somnambulist'; guided by faith in the Right of Germanic Might and Blood, by a fanaticism infinitely more intense than any which supported Napoleon—when that possibility faces our people in simple and dramatic form, as a far less sinister possibility faced them in 1914 and the Americans in 1917, how would they react to it? What would they do?

If they did not fight, a dark tyranny would be upon us. Yet if we fought, it would be in the nature of a civil war, for some of our people would be with the enemy. Peace would be the last of the probabilities.

Forces which, earlier, might have been made the instrument of a European Constitutionalism, of peace, of order, would tend to become, however used, the instruments of terror; as force is to-day in Spain. The Pacifist would be as helpless as the protagonist of Constitutionalism—as the Pacifist is helpless to-day in the Europe that slips either to anarchy or to slavery before our eyes.

XI

WHEN CONCILIATION MEANS WAR

The Story of the Defence of the Constitution—in Ruritania

One of our members thought he could make clear the way in which appeals for 'conciliation' sometimes lead straight to war by the story of a situation which had arisen 'in Ruritania.' Putting himself in the place of a future historian describing the episode, he said:

A Party known as the 'Nationals,' and pledged to Totalitarian doctrines, having arisen, it followed pretty faithfully the line which similar Parties—Rexist, Fascist, Falangist, Nazi, Black Shirt, Blue Shirt, Iron Guard, Cagoulard, Cross of Fire, White Cross, Crooked Cross, Double Cross—had followed in other countries. Arising at a time of unrest, uncertainty, fear, discontent, it challenged the whole principle of constitutionalism. It did so, mainly in the name of national peace, on the ground, that is, that adherence to constitutional method involved Party strife, national disorder. Although the new Party was recruited mainly from the violent and the war-minded, from men who had always thought and felt in terms of force and violence, its watchword soon became: 'The Constitution Means War.'

This was in keeping with the history of similar Parties in other countries. Without any exception whatsoever they had all put 'peace and unity' and the 'ending of fratricidal strife' in the very forefront of their programmes. (The very definition of the word Fascism derives, of course, from the Roman symbol of unity, the bundle of sticks, weak separately, strong and unbreakable when bound together. The main Nazi slogans were all founded upon a plea for national or racial unity and brotherhood. The French Fascist Parties had always talked of the need for establishing social peace. Franco in Spain had

again and again declared that his purpose was to establish peace and
unity and brotherhood between all Spaniards, to end the old quarrels.)
Speeches by the Chief of the Nationals ran something like this:

'Our first and last aim is national unity and internal peace, friendship
and brotherhood between our people. We want our nation to live as one
great family, having put an end to the old party wrangling, discords, conflicts. That is not possible if the nation is torn between rival political fac-
tions, rival ideologies, which it must be under the old Parliamentary
methods, under what has been known heretofore as Constitutional Government. We are determined to fight the fomenters of discord—the Liberals, the Constitutionalists, the Democrats—as the enemies of the nation's
peace.

There is no reason to doubt that the Chief and his followers were
sincere. There had already been in other countries abundant—too
abundant—proof that millions of young men could be persuaded to
die—and kill—for the kind of doctrine and policy that the new Party
embodied.

But its success was really due to the adoption by the country as
a whole—even by those who in the past had been called Militarists
—of a strange new form of Pacifism. This did not mean the repudiation of the principle of force, for the whole country, all Parties,
were clamouring for more arms. But while thus demanding more
force, the new Pacifists insisted that force should on no account be
used to uphold the law. They insisted that force was evil only if it
were so used for the defence of the Constitution, law. If the Constitution were attacked by illegal force it should retreat and trust to
'moral force.' Otherwise, they argued by some strange logical quirk,
'the Constitution becomes an instrument of war, not peace.'

The Nationals made no secret whatever of their intention to destroy the Constitution (they daily railed against it) nor of their intention to impose their own Party views by force. 'It means Civil
War if the Constitution is defended' argued alike the colonels and
the Quaker Pacifists. There arose the strange spectacle of soldiers,
Militarists, Imperialists shouting in company with extreme Pacifists
'Peace, Peace, Peace.' Nowhere did the argument seem to be advanced that if the Constitutionalists showed themselves as ready to
defend the Constitution as the Nationals to destroy it, as ready to
use legal force as the Nationals were to use illegal, as ready to fight
for the Constitution as the Nationals were to fight to end it, peace

clearly would be maintained, and all the slogans about 'Constitutional Sanctions mean War,' 'Law means War,' have fallen to the ground, been revealed as fallacious. For the potential force available for the defence of the Constitution was overwhelming if there had been on the part of the government any real will to use it. But, quite early, it became evident that that will did not exist, that there was no 'fighting faith' in the Constitution at all.

The government kept insisting that the right way to meet the growing danger of an anti-constitutional movement, of an armed party within the State, was by conciliation, conference, 'settlement of differences,' 'investigation of grievances.' Called upon to formulate the grievances of the Nationals, their Chief did so in about these terms:

'Our grievance is first and last the supremacy of the Constitution, the fact that its authority is derived from parties and persons animated by doctrines—Liberalism, Democracy, Socialism, Internationalism, Judaism, a Jewish and Oriental Christism—which we believe to be the deadly enemy of our fatherland, indeed of civilisation. We can never be subordinate to an authority in which such forces of evil have a place.

'We do not ask you to surrender your institutions. You may keep your parliament—it will be a pleasant setting for the assembly of persons who once a year or so may gather to hear what the Chief has decided; you may keep your House of Peers, your monarchy, but always on condition that the ultimate power of our Party shall be unquestioned; that it shall be subject to no authority or law outside its own will, that is to say the will of the Chief. We are quite prepared to discuss how this transfer of power may be brought about peacefully, in an atmosphere of complete goodwill. We do not want fratricidal bloodshed, our purpose is the unity and peace of our dear fatherland. But our Party must be supreme.'

The appeal to 'keep out of Civil War' continued to make headway —as did the crusading spirit of the Nations. Parallel with that went decline in the belief in Liberalism and Democracy. Liberalism, with its intellectual freedoms, its belief in the need for discussion, became an out-moded faith. Increasing numbers were saying of Democracy what Mr. Neville Chamberlain, the Premier of an earlier period in another country, had said of European Constitutionalism: 'I believed in it once, I do not believe in it now.' And arguments ran pretty much as his had about the League. 'We have given Democracy and Liberalism a fair trial and really those principles do not work; the world is not yet ready for them. It may be one day, but that day is not yet.' The Constitution was a motor-car most of whose cylinders were out of action. It should be put in the garage. It might prove an interesting toy perhaps for our great-grandchildren.

The Nationals grew daily in power by the rallying to it of various groups, impelled by a variety of motives, among which fear certainly played its part. Just as all earlier Totalitarian Parties had at some point before final conquest of power employed assassination and terror, and had made it plain that on achieving success the Party would 'liquidate' all who had opposed it, so now the Nationals followed suit. Not only Socialists, but Liberals, churchmen, whether Protestant, Catholic or Jew, trade unionists, critical journalists and writers began to feel the heavy hand of the Nationals. Assassination, bombing, shooting, torture, terror, became common. The government —always in the name of Peace, Pacification, Appeasement, Understanding, Toleration, Goodwill—refused to accord protection to the victims, 'because' as the government explained 'to do so would be really to take sides in a conflict of ideologies. We desire to see them reconciled. You can never establish peace by coercion, by the threat of force.'

So, instead of stiffening police protection for victims of violence the government set up a committee to investigate political terrorism, inviting to sit upon that committee precisely the persons whom everybody believed to be the terrorists. Not unnaturally, the terror became steadily worse. Together with this strange method of maintaining order went a curious line of behaviour on the part of eminent persons in the government. Whenever a particularly atrocious assassination which everybody *privately* attributed to the Chief of the Nationals took place, some member of the government would go out of his way to pay notable public courtesy to the Chief. The latter would appear at private parties given by the relatives of the Prime Minister, or they would appear at parties given by the Chief. The newspapers published pictures of a relative of the Prime Minister being ceremoniously presented to the Chief. One incident was particularly notable. A yacht, having on board the wife and children of the leader of a Party opposed to the Nationals, had been machine-gunned, the occupants being killed or left to drown, by a mysterious 'pirate.' Everybody, again privately, attributed the act to the Chief of the Nationals. No one believed for a moment it could possibly have been anyone else. Yet the government treated the whole matter most casually. In dealing with the incident in the Chamber, the Minister

concerned omitted not merely to express indignation at this introduction into politics of the worst methods of Chicago gangsters, but
even regret at the deaths of innocent people, until the Chamber, stung
to anger by his air of boredom, dragged from him a few perfunctory
phrases. A few days later friends and relatives of prominent ministers
were once more appearing at parties given by 'their old friend' the
Chief—whom everyone believed to be a pirate chief, a gangster with
a long list of private murders to his account.

This attitude was all along justified on the ground that friendliness
and pleasant social relations and courtesy were part of the means by
which a Constitutional Crisis could be prevented from developing into
Civil War. Whatever might be said for such a plea it involved treating piracy, torture, the murder of women and children, as pecadillos
no more to be considered an obstacle to pleasant social relations with
a man than, say, his occasional use of swear words. The country
got into the habit of disregarding its previous moral standards. They
gradually disappeared.

But the results were political as well as moral. The democratic and
Liberal groups, or Parties, or organisations, getting no effective protection from the government, realising that any moment they might
face some political gangster's automatic, or the murder of relations,
began to take one or two courses. Some sold out to the Nationals
arguing: 'Since the Constitution no longer protects us, we must seek
the protection of its enemies, the Gangsters, though it makes us retch
to have to do it.' Others, more virile, armed in desperation, and
began retaliations, so that violence steadily grew—to the advantage
of the Nationals. The development was, of course, a familiar one in
the history of society. If legal force becomes ineffective or is abandoned, you do not get lessening of force or violence, but its increase,
its transference, in an infinitely more cruel, indiscriminate and evil
form, from organised society to gangsters and criminals; its transformation from a social into an anti-social element.

The situation so developed that government spokesmen and supporters began to make speeches along these lines:

'Of course we believe in the Constitution. We are pledged by our oaths
of office to observe it and defend it. But its whole purpose is to maintain
the nation's peace, and that supreme purpose would be frustrated by any
attempt to defend the Constitution, for its defence would mean Civil War.
You cannot want us to provoke that. Remember that the support given

by the Parties in the State to the Constitution is not at all what it was when we took office. First one group then another has joined the National Party, which opposes the Constitution. It is true that those smaller parties and groups asked us whether we held ourselves ready to defend them against the threatened violence of the National Party, but we have always taken the position that differences between parties ought to be settled by direct negotiation between them; that our intervention would only exacerbate differences and that we should take no part in a conflict of ideologies. To have upheld the Constitution in these circumstances involved the risk of Civil War, which we are determined to avoid. We feel that it is far better to trust to the moral rather than the coercive elements of the Constitution. "Defence of the Constitution means Civil War." '

There is, of course, this peculiarity about such a slogan or doctrine: Its very proclamation makes it true. From the moment that we say 'We shall not defend our country or our Constitution unless it can be done without fighting' makes its defence without fighting impossible. For those who have an interest in attacking it will threaten war, even if they are not ready to wage it, believing that the mere threat to people who have decided not to fight will be enough. If, however, the contrary policy is proclaimed, if it is announced that in defence of the Constitution the last man and gun and shilling will be mobilised, and the pronouncement rings true, no empty threats will be used, and all but the overwhelmingly powerful will be deterred.

The astonishing thing was that when the Nationals finally struck and the Constitution went down, almost without a blow, many members of the government were genuinely surprised. Still more surprised, perhaps, when the disappearance of the Constitution instead of bringing peace, brought finally not only devastating war for Ruritania but the crumbling of its free institutions; the coming of that period which historians now know as the Second Dark Age.

XII

WHY HAVE WE FAILED?

If we could have seen early what events compelled us to see late we should not have got into our present mess. Yet the things we refused to face in time were not difficult or abstruse. A good many observers did see them. After the event the truth seems clear even to the multitude to whom the politician bows. Why not before the event? There are certain elementary truths bearing upon the working of society which must somehow become commonplaces. There lies our main educational task.

One member desired to submit some reflections upon the significance of certain errors of policy which are now universally admitted to be errors. He commented:

After all, the only way that we can profit by experience is by taking stock from time to time, noting particularly our mistakes of the past, trying to see why a given course which subsequent events proved to be folly, seemed to us wise at the time. Unless we are indefinitely to repeat the folly we must realise in the light of things we could not or did not then foresee why we were guilty of it. These are platitudes, the truth of which it is fashionable just now to deny. 'It's no use going back on the past.' On the contrary. It has every use; to the end that the past may not be repeated.

All of which is re-enforced by the repetition recently of that curious hindsightedness which has been an outstanding feature of British policy ever since the War. Just now the whole Conservative Press is demanding 'energetic action' in respect of Japanese aggression. That Press is full of 'warnings' to Japan, expressions of the deep and growing resentment of this country at Japanese conduct in international affairs; there is a great popular demand for a boycott

of her goods; growing recognition of the fact that while such a boycott, especially of an extra-governmental kind, may not instantly, nor
for a long time, make it impossible for Japan to go on with her war,
boycott is nevertheless one of the many means by which aggression
can be made more difficult, more costly, less worth while; that, added
to other non-military instruments—which we have only just begun
to forge—of an economic, financial, diplomatic, moral and political
kind, it may well help to tilt the balance against any decision by other
would-be aggressors to embark upon a similar course and discourage
existing aggressors from embarking further upon that course. And
finally, even the Conservative Press is agreed that any action which
America might be prepared to take for the purpose of causing Japan
to hesitate, should secure the full co-operation, at almost any risk, of
this country.

But all this is in flat contradiction at almost every point with the
prevailing attitude of our public—particularly its Conservative elements—six years ago. We were then saying that it would be folly
to attempt to do—even if it could be done—what we are now all
saying should be done if at all possible. Six years ago the greater
part of our Press, far from 'viewing with alarm' the aggression of
Japan, declared repeatedly (and went on declaring for a year or two)
that Japan was accomplishing a work of civilisation in China at which
Britain should rejoice—that there was no reason to assume (the
Times, particularly was insistent on the point) that British interests
would suffer by Japanese victories in China, or that British trade
would face exclusions, or a Closed Door. Far from the deep resentment and horror which now greet the Japanese methods, a more than
courteous silence was maintained about them. Those who ventured to
suggest that if offences, not only against law, the sanctity of treaties,
but against every human and decent instinct were condoned, all moral
values would soon collapse, were lectured by eminent Conservative
journalists for 'bellicosity,' for intolerance and war-mindedness. Those
of us who ventured to point out the dangers of condoning aggression,
were, we were told, the enemies of peace and good understanding,
fanatical and intolerant mischief-makers, indifferent to peace and good
neighbourliness. The critics who thus lectured us are now themselves
presenting the very arguments which they condemned so vocally five
or six years ago. As to boycott, words failed the critics *then*, in describing what they declared to be the silliness and cruelty of any such

idea. And as to American co-operation, we recall what happened. When an American administration made a definite offer to co-operate with Britain in trying out means for making Japan's aggression difficult and costly, the offer was abruptly declined. It was declined in a form which gave encouragement—and looked to American opinion as though it was intended to give encouragement—to Japan. The terms used in declining it were the terms used later by Japan to justify her action.

Those who supported Japan in 1931 do not like to have these things recalled. But, again, if we are to profit by experience and are not to repeat similar ineptitudes in the future, it is just the kind of thing we should recall, asking ourselves frankly and sincerely why it was done.

That is the more urgent because the Japanese instance is only one of many of the cases where the right policy has been applied too late to be effective, where again and again the conservatively-minded have resented and fought a given policy when its application *would* have been effective, and then, later, when the damage has been done, adopted it. Reparations were a notable case. Had we been prepared to do in 1920 what we actually did in 1932, at Lausanne, the whole post-War story would have been a happier one. So with our guarantees of French security. So with Germany's admission to the League. So with the interventions in Russia. So with the Versailles Treaty itself.

In every one of these cases there was a minority urging a policy to which the majority—or at least that element of the public which is the determining factor in deciding foreign policy—refused to listen until something like a catastrophe had occurred. Then, the horse being stolen, the stable door was closed.

Indeed, one can, and should, go a bit further back.

Before the War the popular, the conventional view, based on apprehensions sedulously nursed by papers like the *Daily Mail*, was that Germany had challenged our sea power and intended to attack us and destroy us, the first step being the defeat of Russia and destruction of France, which would make Germany dominant in Europe, and place us, the British, in her power. The only possible reply to such a project, we were told, was to arm and arm and arm, even to the extent of Conscription, an agitation for which was headed by the most popular soldier in Britain, Lord Roberts.

A small minority insisted that before we accepted the War as inevitable we should make some effort to find out *why* Germany wanted to 'destroy' us; what motives, beyond sheer love of destruction, prompted such an aim; just how Germany would benefit from our conquest: whether her needs could be met peacefully. They insisted that if the impending war was to be prevented it would not be merely by each side demanding that it must be stronger than the other, but by finding out what each feared the other might do with its preponderant power, and then examining whether that other really wanted to do that feared thing, or whether such a thing was really necessary for its welfare. In other words, the minority urged that it would be wise before fighting the war to find out what it was about.

If you care to examine the popular Press of 1910-4 you will find that all such questions were treated as 'pure theorising,' remote from the only facts with which practical men need concern themselves; that the things which mattered were the number of ships Germany possessed or was building (the details of which were discussed and debated everlastingly) and the secret plans of invasion of Britain which were revealed in our Press about once a month. To doubt the genuineness of such plans was to reveal oneself a traitor, as corrupted in some way by the Kaiser and his minions.

In so far as the question of cause, or motive, was discussed at all we were told that Germany was forced to fight us in order to feed her people; that we owned territories necessary for the sustenance of her increasing population. And that since it was our duty to keep those territories for our own future generations, the War was in fact a struggle for bread, for life. 'Not a Sunday school view of life,' one very distinguished editor wrote, 'but the true view, which we must face as men, not taking refuge in dreams and theories.'

The minority above referred to pointed out, of course, that even if such a 'struggle for bread' view were sound, the fighting of a war with Germany would still leave the whole problem unsolved; that even if the implied shortage of world's resources had been a fact instead of a fiction, it was clear that as we did not propose to exterminate seventy million men, women and children when we had won the War there would be in a few years just as many mouths to feed, the same pressure of population upon sustenance. Did we propose to use our power to condemn hundreds of millions of civilised people (for Germany was not the only Have-Not State) to permanent shortage of the necessaries of life? For all the rational answer that could be obtained from the learned folk who discussed the matter that was precisely what we did propose to do.

More correctly, perhaps, we had simply never considered it. The thing never was discussed rationally. It is clear that as the population of our Imperial territory asked (and asks) nothing better than to get rid of its wheat and wool and mutton and beef; that as those things could not constitute wealth for the producer unless and until they were got rid of; that as there was not a total shortage but often an over-abundance of those things; that as all nations then, as now, were engaged, not in trying to seize foreign goods but at all costs to exclude them, the real difficulty lay not in any total shortage, but in mal-distribution due to the ill-working of the system by which one kind of product is exchanged for another and that remedy lay mainly in correction of the fallacies and evils of nationalism, economic and political, as the prelude to terminating anarchy and establishing a workable internationalism.

But any attempt to place the consideration of the impending conflict with Germany on this plane was condemned, with about equal readiness, either as 'sentimental idealism' or 'sordid materialism,' an attempt to reduce the motives which prompted men to die for their country to questions of money and profit. Or as sheer treason.

It is to-day difficult to recall the violence of the abuse, sometimes the implacable hatred, which in the years before 1914 pursued those who favoured an attempt at settlement with Germany before the War should take place, and along the only lines upon which modern nations can avail themselves in common of the world's abundance. The self-same papers which, and writers who, to-day flatter Hitler, painted the Kaiser as the mad dog of Europe; those who to-day would make Nazi Germany the keeper of a round dozen small democracies represented the Germany of the Social Democratic Party as an autocracy so much the enemy of all democracy that in the interests of Europe's freedom it had to be destroyed. (The *Daily Mail* slogan for months was 'No Peace with the Hohenzollerns.')

The point, however, for the moment is that had we been as ready in 1914 to consider the point of view of a relatively Liberal Germany, as to-day we are to concede everything to a fanatically anti-Liberal

Germany, we should have had no war. Those who would not get their feet wet for settlement with a Germany whose civilisation and scale of values was still European, Liberal, Christian, are to-day prepared to throw themselves into the river on behalf of a Germany that has put the clock back so far, is so illiberal, so anti-democratic, so anti-Christian, so un-European as to have become really a danger to parliamentary or constitutional government anywhere. (Which does not mean that we shall best dispose of the danger by going to war.)

So with the Peace making. There were a few who saw and warned of the dangers of the Versailles Treaty. But they were silenced by the vocal indignation of those who are to-day ardent Revisionists. When recognition of the evils of the Treaty might have been of some effect, many of those who are to-day Revisionists wanted to make the Treaty still more severe, refused to treat the Parliamentary, Pacifist, Weimar Republic in such a fashion as to give it a chance of life. Now they want to accord to the Hitlerian State the right to destroy the Treaty they made, even if such destruction now means the death of the young democracies which that Treaty created. Had the Revisionists of to-day been prepared in 1919 to treat the Weimar Republic one half as generously as they now desire to treat the Hitlerian State, the latter would never have come into being.

Similarly in the case of our relations with Russia. We ended by recognising the Soviet Government. If we had done that at the beginning instead of attempting to destroy the Soviets by actual invasion of Russia and subsidy of counter-revolutionary armies, we might have lessened, instead of intensifying, that fear of a concerted capitalist attack which has had so evil an influence upon Russian policy. If Russia had not in the early stages had to face invasion and the ruthlessness of foreign-supported White Armies, the psychology which has marked the subsequent conduct of policy might well have been more moderate, more liberal. But the only news which our Press seemed to feature at the time the Soviet Government was established, was an alternation of statements that the Soviets were on their last legs and were about to sweep over Europe and submerge its civilisation. We could not adopt the right policy until enormous damage had been done by the wrong.

So with Reparations. For at least five years after the Armistice no popular 'patriotic' paper would publish a word of the arguments which show that it was an economic contradiction, an impossibility, to combine vast Reparations payments with a policy designed to prevent the expansion of German foreign trade. Any attempt to explain the quite simple facts of the economic situation was represented as an attempt to 'let Germany off,' to condone aggression. The issues themselves were always somehow presented in grossly falsifying terms: 'Ought Germany to pay the cost of the War?' 'Can Germany Pay?' 'Shall We Let Germany Off?' The mood in which the issue was approached made it impossible to get across the explanation that Germany could without undue hardship have paid a great deal but that we were doing our best to make it impossible for her to pay anything. Yet by 1932 the public had become willing to abandon Reparations completely. Had the anti-Germans of 1920 been prepared to do as much as the same persons, to-day become pro-Germans, actually did in 1932 all that is best in Germany would have had a much greater chance of survival; one of the causes of the collapse of the Weimar Republic (the inflation) would almost certainly have been avoided and the present situation not have been created.

So with the commitments to France. From the day peace was proclaimed it was clear that Frenchmen who had with their own eyes witnessed two German invasions in their lifetime, would never be brought to a rational settlement unless first of all they had the complete assurance of ample security against still another German invasion. One of the foundation stones of any sound European policy, of a League which should be a political reality, the very first condition of good treatment of Germany by France, was adequate guarantee of French security. It was given—in 1936, *after* an attempt at a separate Rhineland Republic, after an occupation in which black troops figured, after a Ruhr invasion, after special bargains with Italy which helped to wreck a general security system. Had we been ready to do at the first what we did at the last, those particular follies would not have been committed or would have taken less disastrous forms.

A word of insistence remains to be added. Those who begged for an understanding with Germany *before* 1914 and slaved for its achievement; who worked to secure a better Versailles Treaty; who opposed any post-War blockade of Germany; opposed the Russian interventions; who desired to give early to France the adequate guarantees which would have ensured better treatment of Germany; who argued for the immediate admission of Germany to the League; favoured such real disarmament on our side as would have secured for Germany real equality of status; who argued for a rational Reparations policy; are to-day reproved and lectured by those who opposed violently every point in that policy, as anti-German disturbers of the peace, afflicted with an itch to quarrel with foreign nations all over the world, blind to the need of appeasement and conciliation. (Incidentally the lectures are usually delivered with tremendous airs of moral superiority.)

How explain the phenomenon?

Here you have a long series of errors and follies which those who committed them now admit (by their change of policy) to be errors and follies. Just to explode with accusations of innate, bone-headed stupidity, does not really explain anything. Men are not innately stupid. The pre-War generation which talked such arrant nonsense about the impending war being an inevitable struggle for bread and did not even know the nature of the empire they believed themselves to be defending, were doing miraculous things in the realms of physical science—learning more of the atom, of the nature of the universe, probing deeply into mathematics, discovering undiscovered facets of truth. Only when they came to politics did they reveal that unwisdom of which the present condition of the world is sufficient proof. Perhaps in Germany more than elsewhere did we get this suggestive combination of immense learning and immense political stupidity; a stupidity which has now in the field of politics become so great that it must, if uncorrected, make even the erudition in the future impossible.

We seem to have reversed the emphasis of the Greeks. They, who had so little mechanical capacity or interest in the management of matter that they could not construct a windmill (which even the dark ages managed to do), had a political sense which enabled them to create as brilliant a civilisation as the world has known; a political sense so great that we still draw upon it in our blundering attempts to understand certain principles of human society which they, without any of the learning which the subsequent two thousand years or more have heaped up into our libraries, understood better.

A VOICE FROM 1918

This is to be noted: the truths that would have saved us are not difficult to see. Quite a number saw them. Looking through a book which appeared while the War was yet going on[1] I find the author throwing the whole emphasis of his warning upon deficient co-operation among the democratic States. The words written exactly twenty years ago are so apposite to the present situation that their quotation may be excused. Here they are:

The survival of the Western democracies, in so far as that is a matter of the effective use of their force, depends upon their capacity to use it as a unit, during the War and after. That unity we have not attained, even for the purposes of the War, because we have refused to recognise its necessary conditions—a kind and degree of democratic internationalism to which current political ideas and feelings are hostile; and internationalism which is not necessary to the enemy, but is to us.

For the Grand Alliance of the Democracies is a heterogeneous collection of nations, not geographically contiguous, but scattered over the world; and not dominated by one preponderant State able to give unity of direction to the group. The enemy alliance, on the other hand, is composed of a group of States, geographically contiguous, dominated politically and militarily by the material power and geographical position of one member who is able by that fact to impose unity of purpose and direction on the whole. If we are to use our power successfully against him in such circumstances, during the War, at the settlement, and afterwards (which may well be necessary), we must achieve a consolidation equally effective. But in our case that consolidation, not being possible by the material predominance of one member, must be achieved by a moral factor, the voluntary co-operation of equals—a democratic internationalism, necessarily based on a unity of moral aim. Because this has not been attained, even during the War, disintegration of our alliance has already set in—involving military cost—and threatens to become still more acute at the peace. The enemy group shows no equivalent disintegration.

No military decision against the unified enemy group can be permanent if at the peace-table it becomes evident that the Western

[1] *The Political Conditions of Allied Success,* by Norman Angell (Putnams).

Democracies are to revert to the old lack of consolidation, instability of alliance, covert competition for isolated power and territory, and a national particularism which makes common action and co-ordination of power cumbrous, difficult, or impossible. If there is to be a return to the old disunited Western Europe the parties which among the enemy favour a policy of aggression will realise that, however much their purpose may temporarily be defeated, the greater material unity of their alliance will enable it sooner or later to overcome States which, though superior in the sum of their power, have shown themselves inferior in their capacity to combine it for a common purpose. And that inferiority might arise less from the pressure of any active agent of disruption than from passive hostility to abandoning the old national organisation of Europe, sheer lack of habit and practice in international co-operation, political, military or economic. . . .

The factors of disintegration in the Grand Alliance are of two kinds: conflicting territorial claims by the component States (illustrated by the demands of Czarist Russia, Italy, Serbia, and other Slav groups, Rumania, Greece, and, more obscurely, of Japan) and conflict of economic interest and social aspiration within the nations (illustrated by the struggles of the bourgeois and socialist parties in Russia, less dramatically by the revolutionary unrest in Italy, and even in France and England). These latter factors are more dangerous with us than with the enemy, because our historical circumstances have rendered us less disciplined or less docile, less apt in mechanical and de-humanised obedience.

The general truth we are here dealing with is of far greater importance to us than to the enemy. He can in some measure ignore it. We cannot. His unity, in so far as it rests upon moral factors, can be based upon the old nationalist conceptions; our unity depends upon a revision of them, an enlargement into an internationalism.

The kind and degree of internationalism indispensable for the consolidation of the Western peoples if they are to use their force effectively—an internationalism which must take into account the newer social and economic forces of Western Society—is impossible on the basis of the older state-craft and its political motives. For these assume as inevitable a condition of the world in which each nation must look for its security to its own isolated strength (which must derive from population, territory, and strategic position), thus making national interests necessarily rival. The capacity of each nation to feed its population and assure its economic welfare is assumed to depend upon the extent of its territory. A whole philosophy of 'biological necessity,' 'struggle for life among nations,' 'inherent pugnacity of mankind,' 'survival of the fit,' is invoked on behalf of this old and popular conception of international life and politics. Such an outlook inevitably implies an overt or latent rivalry which must bring even members of the same alliance sooner or later into conflict.

The only possible unifying alternative to this disruptive policy is some 'permanent association of nations' by which the security of each shall be made to rest upon the strength of the whole, held together by the reciprocal obligation to defend one another.

The greatest obstacles to such a system are disbelief in its feasibility and our subjection to the traditions of national sovereignty and independence. Were it generally believed in, and desired, it would be not only feasible but inevitable. . . .

Return to the old relationships after the War will sooner or later doom the democratic nations, however powerful each may be individually, to subjugation in detail by a group, inferior in power but superior in material unity—a unity which autocracy achieves at the cost of freedom and human worth.

The term 'democratic internationalism' as the condition of Allied success is not a mere playing with words. Any understanding between nations, even for the purpose of a temporary alliance or war co-operation, is, of course, 'internationalism' of a kind. But the term used here means more than that; it means that as a condition of our success we must abandon the international relationship which has generally wrecked alliances formed for the purposes of war in the past, and substitute for that relationship a different one, in which certain of the prevailing conceptions of neutrality, national sovereignty, and independence must be modified.

The newer policy can only become operative as the result of an 'act of faith'—the conviction, that is, on the part of statesmen and public that the risks involved in the new are less than those involved in the old. So long as nations do not believe in the possibility or reliability of a new system, they will fall back upon covert or overt competition for preponderant power, territory, and strategic position which of itself creates the disruptive rivalry, anarchy, and suspicion, that destroy reliance upon agreement. By our own act in such a case, we create the very conditions which we urge as justification for the act. The one thing which alone will enable us to break the vicious circle is the general conviction that though the proposed system may fail, the old certainly will. Upon the moral courage to act on that faith depends the survival of the Western Democracies.

Referring to the revelations of the secret treaties (just then made by the Russian Government), the writer goes on:

The important thing to note in all these intrigues is that diplomats and peoples alike were helpless in the grip of a system. They may have had a common responsibility for the perpetuation of that system in the past. But given its existence no results other than those we have seen were possible. Even though the motives of avarice or lust of power had been entirely absent—which in the case of the Western Democracies we can well believe to be the fact—there is one justifiable and overwhelming motive which would have prompted the same policy: and that motive is national self-preservation. . . .

Under the system of defence by competitive power, a nation is perpetually placed in the alternative either of denying the national rights of others or endangering its own. And under that system the better patriot and diplomat a statesman is, the more damage he does. The less entitled, in terms of nationality and international right, a country may be to a given piece of territory, the greater is the diplomatic triumph of its annexation if such annexation adds to the conqueror's national security. They are the things for which diplomats are ennobled: and they are also the things which make future wars inevitable.

The underlying assumption that national security must be based upon preponderant individual power compels us to make upon the enemy a demand which in terms of our own doctrine is an unjustifiable one, namely that he shall accept a position of manifest inferiority in power, that is to say of national insecurity. The assumption that nothing but individual power can protect a nation compels the German, even though detesting his military institutions, to resist defeat in order to preserve his only means of future self-defence. The failure of the Allies early in the War to reveal any workable or obvious substitute for national power as a means of defence converted the aggressive war of the German Government, into the defensive war of the German people, and so played the game of the enemy autocracy. The policy which disintegrated us united the enemy.

For this relation between internationalism and democracy on the one side, and autocracy and territorial consolidation in disregard of nationality on the other, is organic, not accidental. The great experiment of political freedom, the 'self-determination of peoples,' the independence of separate national groups, implies necessarily the growth of separatist tendencies which, if unchecked by the voluntary and self-imposed discipline of an international order, will make co-operation or a common centralised direction, even for self-protection, impossible. Contrariwise, autocracy grows by the strength of a central power, and is able to impose common action and centralised direction upon the different national units over which it has succeeded in asserting dominion (sometimes historically just because the smaller units were incapable of self-directing co-operation and were split by irreconcilable differences). The enemy, by reason of the very circumstances of his historical development and the philosophy which his experiment (as against ours) involves, has less need than ourselves of a policy which will unify by voluntary action many States widely separated in character and geographical distance, and ensure their common effort towards a common end. As already noted, the special position, geographical, economical, historical, and political of one State in the enemy alliance ensures a centralised direction by virtue of power and authority, and enables the group to dispense with that voluntary, democratic internationalism which alone will enable the Western group to hold its own.

And there is little in European history to show that consolidation will come of itself *par la force des choses*, without conscious effort.

Although that history, century after century, taught that predominant military power always led to aggression by its possessor, Europe has never been able to deal as a unit with this common problem.[1] The democracies had no concerted policy with reference to it in 1914. The alliance was not formed with reference to the common need, but each member came into it for his own particular purposes, Russia for one purpose, Japan for a second, Italy for a third, Rumania for a fourth.

---

[1] The nearest that it came to it perhaps was in the crusades. Subsequent attempts to deal with the Turkish horror did not reveal any similar degree of unity among the nations of Europe.

Democratic Europe was quite unprepared on the political side for its common task. Indifference before the War to international co-operation rendered the policy adopted during the War inevitable. While we were doubtlessly sincere in our professions that we were fighting the cause of democracy and national right against autocracy, we failed to see that our refusal to take any sufficient steps to end the old system of Europe made those professions often absurd. In a war for democracy and national right we were perfectly content to make agreements with a Czarist Government (which we did hesitate afterwards to admit to be the implacable foe of democracy). In the arrangements with it before the War neither France nor Britain treated with any practical sympathy the aspirations of the Russian people, as expressed in the revolutionary movement. Over and over again Russian Liberals and Radicals had asked the French and British Governments to make financial aid to the Czarist régime conditional upon the recognition of popular right. These demands were disregarded. The governments of the British and French democracies were quite ready to ally themselves with the Russian Government, whatever its character, as earlier they had been allied with the Turkish. They still in fact retained the old diplomatic attitude that the people did not matter. We failed altogether to establish the democratic unity of the alliance, and our policy was such that neither Poland, nor Finland, nor the mass of the democracy in Russia made really much distinction between what it might expect from the victory of a Czarist Russia in alliance with the Western Democracies, and the victory of Germany. Finland, indeed, at the beginning of the War, on the whole, hoped more from Germany's victory than from ours. The result was that our own neglect to make the moral issues completely clear and to base our policy upon those issues, prepared the ground for the disunity of aim in Russia upon which later the German autocracy traded with such disastrous effect. Had our statecraft realised that the issues of conflict were moral more than territorial, and in the years preceding the War had refused (as one instance only of a measure of policy) financial aid to Petrograd until concessions had been made to Finland, Poland, and parliamentary constitutionalism, the subsequent story of the relations with Russia would have been very different. . . . We did not hesitate to shoulder very grave responsibilities concerning the Russian Government's territorial aims; we refused altogether to concern ourselves with the aspirations of the Russian, Finnish, or Polish peoples. Our great preoccupation with the territorial aims and our disregard of the moral and democratic aims reflects not, it may be, upon the sincerity of our public professions in 1914 that this was a war for democracy and national right, but upon our understanding of what those things really involved for the purpose of Allied unity and of the way in which the co-operation of democracies must differ from the old diplomatic contact of States.

It is fashionable just now to speak as though the present preponderance of Germany were ascribable simply to our inertia before the War in the matter of military preparation. If only England and America, it is urged, had adopted universal military service, Germany would have been deterred, or the War would not have ended in her defeat.

But no assumption could disregard facts more completely. The possession of greater power by the present Allies would only have deterred Germany had she known beforehand with practical certainty that that power would be used against her in the event of her taking a certain line. But the condition of Europe in the ten or fifteen years preceding the War was such that Germany was justified in assuming that it was unlikely to be brought against her. Less than two decades before the War, Mr. Joseph Chamberlain was talking of an alliance with Germany, and the more popular British Press of 'rolling France in blood and mud.' Had Britain possessed a great army in the early years of the twentieth century, or a little before, and her government and policy taken a somewhat more belligerent and militarist tone in consequence of the added power of military influences, it is extremely unlikely that the long series of quarrels with France could have ended without collision; that the Dogger Bank incident would have ended without a break; that the rapprochement with both France and Russia would have taken place. So with America. It is all but universally admitted that the possession of a great military establishment at the time of the long, wearying, and somewhat humiliating relations with Mexico in the three or four years preceding the War, would have made it impossible to resist the demand for occupation and pacification. If a Boer population of less than half a million could absorb something like half a million British soldiers—in a war lasting three years—how many American soldiers would the pacification of thirteen million Mexicans, and the hostility of Spanish America, absorb? Nor do we know how such a conflict would have affected the position of Japan.

These may seem to-day remote contingencies. But they were not remote contingencies in the period preceding the War. There was not a student of politics in Europe who would not have said that what has actually happened in Russia was immeasurably less likely than American entrance into Mexico, the adhesion of Italy to the Triple Alliance, and Anglo-French war over Fashoda, or an Anglo-Russian one over the Dogger Bank affair.

The assertion now so common that greater armaments on the part of the Western democracies during the past generation would have prevented this war, indicates a kind of political thinking which simply robs the future of all hope—hope, not alone of a freer world but of real success in dealing with the danger that has forced war upon us. The assertion implies that we can return to the old international anarchy provided only that it is a still more heavily armed anarchy. Such a policy would deliver the future not alone to militarism, but to Prussian militarism. For the Western democracies to be armed but quarrelling among themselves is the condition, which, above all others, the German military caste would desire. It ensures that the political system of Europe shall be rooted in militarism; it renders German armaments inevitable; prevents the realisation of socialist or internationalist systems; furnishes excuse for wars of aggression under the guise of defence, and yet ensures that there shall be no real preponderance of European power against Germany.

And those words were written—and published—twenty years ago!

XIII

CAN WE DO WITHOUT A POLITICAL MORALITY?

Because we have seen Europe in danger of dividing into two ideological camps, and because in every war the people on both sides can so easily be persuaded that they 'fight for right,' however wrong their cause may be, we are now drifting to the view that it is best to have no belief, no feeling that this is right and that wrong; and that moral indignation is likely to be dangerous, with unpleasant results. But if those of us who believe that some system of law, droit, right, is indispensable for the preservation of civilisation refuse to allow ourselves warmth of feeling on its behalf, refuse to take any risks on its behalf, while those who challenge it, the Anarchic Nationalist, the Nazi, the Fascist will take immense risks to defy it, then we cannot hope that the principle of right or law can prevail. Is energy, valour, courage, to be for evil only?

Throughout our talks we had dwelt a good deal on the dangers of Fanaticism. But was not our German member right when he suggested that our real trouble was that we had no faith at all? One of our members thought so and put his doubts in the following paper.

We slip so easily into this kind of error:

Because Right and justice have been so often invoked in support of unjust wars, let us refuse to wage war for justice. Thence, in the supposed interests of peace we go on to condone evils which provoke indignation for fear that that might lead to war, until finally all moral standards are surrendered and evil outrage, oppression, cruelty cease to move us. Yet often Right could have been defended without war, while its indefinite surrender may make war finally inevitable.

Looking back at the course of events in China, in Japan, in Spain, in Germany, in Italy, during the last six or seven years; noting the undeclared wars, the massacres which only a year or two since the whole world would have condemned as simple murder and piracy, repeated mass killings of helpless civilian populations, the resumption of assassination as a common instrument of internal politics; the piracy on the high seas with British ships as its victims; the propaganda waged by a great Western government against the very foundations of the Christian faith, the systematic dissemination of a crude racial paganism as a substitute . . . looking back at the endless list one sees a strange juxtaposition. On the one side is immense energy, courage, boldness, a readiness to take great risks and undergo infinite suffering, an amazing capacity for sacrifice. It is the side of what but yesterday we should have regarded as unmitigated evil—of gross aggression and conquest, the destruction of freedoms, of the right of self-government and democracy, the very enthronement of ruthless cruelty and oppression. On the other side one sees drift, inertia, indecision, short-sightedness, division of council, disunity, the refusal to make material sacrifice. These are the qualities which we find on the side of what yesterday the whole world regarded as unquestionably good, on the side of order, of law, of peace, of democracy, of nationality, the right of a people to live its own life, to choose within limits its own form of government so long as it does not interfere with the same right of others; the principle of reciprocity and equality of right in human relations.

These principles had been fully recognised; they had been made for years the theme of (needlessly) learned and (needlessly) long philosophical treatises. We believed that they had become the commonplaces of orderly European life, accepted as its prevailing *ethos*, indispensable to the stability of civilisation.

But nobody, it would seem, is prepared to fight for these principles, to suffer for them, to die for them, as millions are prepared to die in order to repudiate them, to bring them to naught. We have become as indifferent to Right, to law as it would seem we are indifferent to the security of the British Empire and to the survival of Christianity. But there is no indifference on the side of Nazism, Fascism, the New Imperialism of the Italian or the Japanese Powers.

Indeed, many of our people still seem lost in admiration of those engaged in the destruction of the ancient political and social moralities, to say nothing of the security of the Empire. Members of our group have called attention to the cases, as when Japan started her aggression upon China in 1931 by a 'frame-up' of 'incidents,' repudiated her solemn obligations, made scraps of paper of half a dozen treaties, defied the League, and many a newspaper editor, and many a politician, lustily praised her; insisted that all talk of the restraint by the League was 'impertinence,' that Japan was carrying on in China a useful work of civilisation, and ought not to be 'interfered with' by Geneva busybodies.

From that first failure of the forces of order, dates the beginning of a process of disintegration, anarchy, chaos which has gone on uninterruptedly ever since. Spain is the logical sequel of Manchuria. The successful defiance by Japan of the greatest Western States, her complete immunity from any collective restraint by civilisation as a whole, was the direct instigation of the Italian defiance of the League in Abyssinia, of Germany's in the Rhineland and of both Germany's and Italy's in Spain. The whole collective system lies in utter ruin, and Britain—by immanent justice—is impotent to protect ever her direct and most vital interests.

It is a little difficult to believe that Japan was directly encouraged to enter upon and continue that course which has had the results we now see, alike by British newspapers and even by British Cabinet Ministers. But the articles and the speeches stand on record. To-day, when it is much too late, the *Times* looks longingly to closer Anglo-American co-operation as the following passage in a recent leader indicates:

'It is much to be feared that the prestige of Great Britain, and indeed of all the Western Powers, will—with rather less distortion of the facts —be gravely impaired in Asiatic eyes by their impotence to make good their lawful position at Shanghai in time of crisis. The situation is, of course, an impossibly difficult one; but when in the course of time the tide of war shall have ebbed from Shanghai, the prospects of salvage work by the Foreign Powers would probably have been improved by closer Anglo-American diplomatic co-operation at the outset.'

Yet, if one turns to the book on the earlier stages of the Far-Eastern Crisis written by Mr. Stimson, the American Secretary of State, we find him again and again noting that Japan was directly

encouraged in her policy of aggression in 1931-2 by the line taken
by certain English newspapers, including the *Times* (he quotes plenti-
fully in illustration from the *Times* leaders). The terms of the British
Government's communication to the Press rejecting the offer of
American co-operation in resistance to Japan in 1931 were such, Mr.
Stimson says, 'as to be taken by most readers, including—what was
most important—the Japanese Government, as a rebuff to the United
States.' Japan saw immediately that Anglo-American co-operation had
broken down, and began to use in justification of her aggression the
very arguments which the British Government and the British Press
(Mr. Stimson again quotes at length from the *Times* leaders) had
used concerning the American proposals. 'It was not surprising that
the Japanese reply to the American note was conceived, as a British
historian has noted, in "a vein of elegant irony which came within an
ace of insolence." '

Among Mr. Stimson's quotations from the *Times* is this:

'In invoking its clauses (those of the Nine-Power Treaty) the American Government may have been moved by the fear that the Japanese
authorities would set up a virtually independent administration in Manchuria which would favour Japanese interests to the detriment of the
commerce of other nations. It is clear that the Foreign Office does not
share these apprehensions.'

Indeed!

The degree of encouragement which the Foreign Office was extending to Japan is revealed by the attitude of Sir John Simon towards the
report of the Lytton Commission. In the Survey of the Royal Institute
of International Affairs for 1933 occurs this passage:

'As for Sir John Simon, he held out a helping hand to Mr. Matsuoka
by drawing attention to certain passages in the Lytton Report which
brought out the complicated character of the circumstances of the dispute
and the weak points in the Chinese case, and which submitted, *à propos*
of future action in Manchuria, that "a mere restoration of the *status quo
ante* would be no solution." . . . After listening to Sir John Simon's
speech, Mr. Matsuoka was reported to have remarked that "Sir John
Simon had said in half an hour, in a few well-chosen phrases, what he
—Mr. Matsuoka—had been trying to say in his bad English for the last
ten days.'

In the old days one-twentieth part of the aggressions of which in
the last year or two we have been victim, would have brought all the
might of the Empire into play. We should have seen young English-

men suffering and dying as readily as we see to-day young Germans and Italians suffering and dying in Spain or Abyssinia as the case may be. But the deaths of those young Englishmen would have been on behalf of a narrow and often selfish and oppressive imperialism. It would have been called 'the security of the British Empire,' and those who died would have felt it to be such. In fact their deaths would no more have added to the security of the Empire than the deaths of those who perished in the Great War have added to it. To-day the Empire is more direly encompassed by dangers than it has ever been in its history, and we are relatively unmoved. Resistance to Japanese aggression when it was possible to resist (as it would certainly have been in 1931 if the defensive possibilities on the political side had been adequately developed) would really have added to our security and would also have laid the foundation stones of a system of order and of peace in which others, too, might have found security. But while the narrow and more futile purpose was able to evoke such magnificent heroism, the greater purpose can evoke none.

It is not a question here of 'selfishness'; for the effect of thus having allowed the situation to degenerate to the degree that it has done is to put those interests for which so many of our people have died in such appalling jeopardy as to put effective defence out of the question.

And it is a strange truth that just because that defence of the Empire in 1931 or 1935 would have included the larger purpose the Imperialists would not have it. Had the cause of Japanese or Italian restraint been presented to the Imperialists as a simple imperial interest in the old Imperialist fashion every Jingo would have demanded instant action. But since the Japanese and the Italian challenged the League as well as the Empire, the Jingoes plainly hoped that that challenge would be successful. Psychologists have names and explanations of these things. They tell us that such a phenomenon illustrates 'the theory of the common enmity' which, according to one school of psychology, must always be stronger than any motive of common like, and is apt to be stronger than any motive of common interest.

A further strange feature of the situation is this: Those who have thus encouraged Japan, applauded her and applauded our recession before her, who have applauded the Italian aggression (and by so doing are so largely responsible for it since it gave Mussolini the assurance he needed that he would not be resisted), who accept with calm acquiescence the establishment of Italy in a position in the Mediterranean that makes our strategic position so dangerous there, who hope for the victory of Franco which would make it just about impossible, continue to have a pathetic faith in the efficacy of national rearmament. But however great the material arms which we possess, they must be completely inadequate for defence if collective action is ruled out and the political situation continues to disintegrate.

A large proportion of the British Press is still busy assuring Germany, Japan and Italy that the destruction, one by one, of those nations whose continued existence and power is indispensable to our own security, the destruction that is of those who must be our allies if we are ever effectively to defend ourselves, is a process which we shall watch with benevolent neutrality. Remembering our situation in the Great War what do we propose to do with our two thousand millions worth of armament when all potential allies have disappeared?

This curious combination of feverish rearmament and feverish retreat before every threat, means that the aggressor, whether in China, or Spain or in Africa, is quite uncertain when, if ever, we shall resist. Everywhere he has seen violence, the policy of the *fait accompli*, the sudden coup, meet with astonishing success. No one a few years ago could have believed that lawless violence could have been committed not only with complete impunity but with such amazing success in the way of increasing power and prestige for those guilty of defying every law of treaty faith, of international obligation, of mercy or of pity. Since violence is so successful, and since it is being justified by a whole philosophy, almost a religion of ruthlessness, why should we expect to see it diminish? And, more particularly, why should we expect recession before it to check it? Indeed the dictators now seem to be coming to the conviction that they never will be resisted by Britain. The growth of that conviction means that our power is deprived of the one function which force can usefully perform in organised society—the function of deterrence, prevention, of ensuring defence without war. This combination of huge armaments and retreat before threats is not pacifism. The ever-growing armament is testimony that we reject the pacifist philosophy. Still less is the refusal to pledge our arms to an international cause, to the principle of collective security, pacifism. We have shown enough pacifism to destroy collective security, not enough pacifism to end competitive armament. Protagonists of armaments are pacifists, opposed to force, when it is proposed to use it to establish a system under which the rights of all may receive some protection; but they are militarists when it is proposed to use force to dictate our own view of our rights as against other views of those rights. We have evinced sufficient pacifism to give the maximum encouragement to aggression but have not sufficient pacifism to lay the foundations of a forceless society, to set aside force in international relations. We still announce our determination to fight but only for the worse cause.

Our policy of retreat means that we are unable to decide when and at what point our power should be used. The men of violence who have so successfully used lawless force these last few years are certainly encouraged in the face of that uncertainty to gamble. Their judgment is not always of the best—easy success undermines judgment. One day they will go a fraction too far and we shall get war—bitter, incredibly destructive, futile.

But perhaps the strangest of all the strange features of the present trend is this: That undermining of the judgment of the Dictators, the casting aside of all moral standards, is repeatedly recommended in the name of peace and 'good international understanding,' and by those who insist that the hope of peace lies in the growth of the moral sense. This school attaches immense importance to such documents as the Kellogg Pact declaring any war entered upon for purposes of national policy to be a crime. A Dictator commits that crime in the most atrocious circumstances. What ought to be the attitude of nations if the moral sense of nations is to be maintained? And many of those who put reliance upon the moral sense insist that the commission of the crime must make no difference at all in our relations with, or attitude to, the criminal. Massacre, private assassination, piracy, has been followed by flattery almost fawning in its quality. Cynical violation of a solemn oath, defiance of every moral law, is followed by marks of respect, cordial friendship. Does anyone suppose that moral sense or moral standards are going to survive such a process?

ANOTHER NOTE FROM 1918

In that twenty-year-old book already quoted from I find a chapter on 'A Patriotism for Law' much of it as apposite to our present problems as the last quotations. The author says:

This much then is established: If our safety rests upon a basis of force at all, an indispensable part of that force is a degree of political unity greater than the European group now composing our Alliance has shown in the past. Without that unity as a permanent fact in Western society, a momentary decision in our favour, even the complete destruction of the existing German military machine, cannot be a permanent decision.

But just what that means as affecting our future outlook in foreign politics, and certain profound emotions that have marked it heretofore, cannot be realised unless we examine the present situation of Germany with reference to the States that used to compose Russia; and to the States of the Balkans.

Here on the one hand is Prussianised Germany, a State whose outstanding characteristic is a very high degree of national discipline and unity. We know too well the degree of regimentation which has given that State, not only unity of action but unity of feeling and thought: the whole nation moves with a synchrony of motion in ideas and national policy as complete as the synchrony of the physical motion in a platoon of soldiers exhibiting the goose-step. Incidentally, there is this important fact to note: that during long periods of history it was the exactly contrary fact which characterised the history of the diverse and warring States, which the world knew as Germany. Under the Holy Roman Empire they numbered some three hundred. For centuries German State fought German State, and the whole tendency was disruptive. No people of common tongue and more or less common origins had broken up into such fragments. The moral and intellectual drilling which has reversed that process was in many respects the conscious reversal of a 'natural' drift or tendency; as little spontaneous in many of its aspects as the discipline of a conscript army.

What concerns us to-day, however, is its very high degree of success. The Germans are a docile and disciplined people if ever there was one; cohesive, unified, and national in their policy.

Now place the fact of that national discipline and cohesion side by side with another fact: the welter of mutually hating nationalities, races, religions, economies, tongues, cultures, aspirations composing the Slavonic world which is Germany's geographical neighbour— that is to say the Balkan States and Russia. It is hardly necessary to dwell on the countless deep and bitter divisions that split these peoples. As one attempts to unravel the tangle it would seem that human ingenuity had been exhausted in the attempt to find causes of division,

hate, and disintegration. It is not merely that we find the racial tree
split into innumerable branches, races becoming tribes and tribes
becoming clans; but that where identity of race or clan might unify,
the clan itself is split by divisions of religion; and where a religion
elsewhere is unifying minor divisions are discovered here which set
up decomposition. If you get race and nationality coinciding, you are
certain to get deadly enmities on the question of religion—one kind
of Catholic bitterly antagonistic to another kind of Catholic of the
same race and nationality. And the divisions are not only vertical but
horizontal. You may find one geographical area claimed as the unquestionable national patrimony of six different nationalities—for
the Near East shows claims based on 'historic tradition' and 'national
irredentism' of a kind which if they obtained in the West would make
the Dutch, for instance, the passionate claimants of New York because
it was once New Amsterdam; or the French of New Orleans. We
talked at the beginning of the War of the struggle of Slav v. Teuton.
But the event has shown what we might have expected: that there is
no Slav block.

Let us keep in mind the fact of this juxtaposition of a solid German
block of disciplined, efficient, unified people, endowed with a well-
trained gift for organisation, possessing to a very high degree all the
machinery of industrial development and of civil order, all that on
the one side; and on the other, a loose, unorganised, hopelessly divided,
and mutually hating mass of complicated nationalities, lacking the
means of economic development and the capacity for maintaining civil
order or social security. Then by way of getting some hint of the
moral of that picture, recall Seeley's illuminating lecture on the real
explanation of the British conquest of India.

He asked this question: How was it that a vast country, with two
or three hundred million souls, not savage or uncivilised but with a
civilisation, though descending along a different stream of tradition,
as real and ancient as our own, came to be utterly conquered and subdued by a people, numbering less than twelve millions, living on the
other side of the world? It reversed the teaching of history which had
shown again and again that it was impossible really to conquer an intelligent people alien in tradition from its invaders. The whole power
of Spain could not in eighty years conquer the Dutch provinces with
their petty population. The Swiss could not be conquered. At the
very time when the conquest of India's hundreds of millions was under

way, the English showed themselves wholly unable to reduce to obedience three millions of their own race in America. What was the explanation? The Inherent Superiority of the Anglo-Saxon stock?

Well, for long we were content to draw such a flattering conclusion and leave it at that, until Seeley pointed out the uncomfortable fact that the great bulk of the forces used in the conquest of India were not British at all. They were Indian. India was conquered for Great Britain by the natives of India.

'The nations of India (says Seeley) have been conquered by an army of which on the average about a fifth part was English. India can hardly be said to have been conquered at all by foreigners; she was rather conquered by herself. If we were justified, which we are not, in personifying India as we personify France or England, we could not describe her as overwhelmed by a foreign enemy; we should rather have to say that she elected to put an end to anarchy by submitting to a single government, even though that government were in the hands of foreigners."[1]

In other words, India is an English possession because the peoples of India were incapable of cohesion; the nations of India incapable of internationalism. And what I am suggesting is this: that the part which England played in India will be played inevitably by Germany, for the same order of reasons, in the Balkans and in the States that were once Russia, unless the process can be checked, or take on another character altogether, by virtue of a factor which I will indicate presently.

In order to realise how far the cases are parallel (and I do not of course pretend that there is an absolutely mechanical parallel) note first what is actually taking place as between Germany and the States of Russia at this moment. Ukrainians have called in the aid of Germans for the purpose, not so much of creating a Ukrainian State—for the Russian Bolshevik Government would not have opposed that—but for the purpose of suppressing Russian (i.e. Bolshevik) parties within Ukrainia. Ukrainian troops are being led by German officers and are co-operating with German troops in conflict with the Red Guards of the Bolsheviks from Northern Russia. In Finland, Courland, Esthonia, and Lithuania, the property-owning classes have appealed to German aid for the maintenance of the independence of their States as against Great Russia. The pregnant fact in the whole situation to-day is that Germany is using Russian forces for the pur-

---

[1] *The Expansion of England*, p. 202.

pose of subduing Russia, and there is every indication that that process is likely to continue in one form or another.

And a suggestive fact is that it is not a new process in the war. The Central Empires have been employing it from the beginning. Austria has not only been able to use, during the best part of four years, troops—conscript—of Slav nationality for the purpose of fighting 'the Liberators of the Slav world' as we proclaimed the Czar's army to be; but was able to place troops under Jugo-Slav officers—a Jugo-Slav general led the Austrian troops against the Italian forces. And this was made possible, be it noted, as much by our policy—our sanction of Italy's designs—as by any initial lack of Slav solidarity.

The parallel we are dealing with fails at one point: Britain, which subdued India, was ten thousand miles away with a long line of communication to maintain. Germany—in which for this purpose one includes the Germans of Austria—has her frontier running cheek by jowl with *her* India. Or rather, the solid German block is driven like a wedge right into the unorganised Slavonic mass.

Just recall the divisions that separate Ukrainian, Lett, Esthonian, Lithuanian, Pole, Czech, Slovak, Slovene, Croatian, Serb, Rumanian, Albanian, Bulgar, Greek, Macedonian, and recall Seeley's description of India:

'There was no India in the political, and scarcely in any other, sense. The word was a geographical expression, and therefore India was easily conquered just as Italy and Germany fell an easy prey to Napoleon, because there was no Italy and no Germany, and not even any strong Italian or German national feeling. Because there was no Germany Napoleon was able to set one German State against another, so that in fighting with Austria or Prussia he had Bavaria and Württemberg for allies. As Napoleon saw that this means of conquest lay ready at his hand in Central Europe, so the Frenchman Dupleix early perceived that this road to empire in India lay open to any European State that might have factories there. He saw a condition of chronic war between one Indian State and another, and he perceived that by interfering in their quarrels the foreigner might arrive to hold the balance between them. He acted upon this view, and accordingly the whole history of European Empire in India begins with the interference of the French in the war of succession in Hyderabad that broke out on the death of the great Nizam ul Mulk (1748).'[1]

There is one passage in Seeley which indicates the most important conclusion of all perhaps to be drawn from the parallel his story sug-

[1] *The Expansion of England*, pp. 202-3.

gests. But the words he uses have connotations which almost inevitably prompt a conclusion which is the exact reverse of that to which in truth the facts point. Seeley says:

'The fundamental fact then is that India had no jealousy of the foreigner because India had no sense whatever of national unity.'

What would the ordinary protagonist of nationalist patriotism point as the moral of this passage? He would say: 'Now you see the utility of the instinctive patriotism which connotes a dislike of the foreigner; the absolute need, for national preservation, of this sentiment of which internationalism is the negation. India had no patriotism, no dislike of the foreigner, she was universalist—with the result we know.'

But as we shall see, that was not Seeley's thought. He might have expressed it as nearly by the contrary statement; if for instance he had said:

'The fundamental fact then is that India had no sense of national unity because the Indian's jealousy of foreigners was so intense that to him everybody except the people of his own village—and they only if they belonged to the same race and caste and creed—was a foreigner.'

For Seeley says this:

'We regard it as the duty of a man to fight for his country against the foreigner. But what is a man's country? When we analyse the notion, we find it presupposes the man who has been bred up in a community which may be regarded as a great family. . . . But if the community has not been at all of the nature of a family, but has been composed of two or three races hating each other . . . that at most the village has been regarded as a home, then it is not the fault of the natives of it if they have no patriotism but village patriotism.'[1]

Here is a further fact to be kept in mind in drawing the true lesson from the parallel we are indicating. Germany was itself—and not long ago—a European India, riven into an infinity of small States each with its exclusive patriotism. Both contrasting conditions that we are dealing with—the present cohesion of the originally separated Germanies (which our grandfathers always called them) and the anarchy and welter of the Balkans—are both ascribable to an intensity of patriotism, to group loyalty, to what Mr. Trotter has taught us to call, herd instinct. But the development of Germany's cohesion has been due to the enlargement of the patriotism of Bavaria or Hanover

[1] *The Expansion of England*, p. 206.

into the patriotism of Germany, and if the Slavonic world—(or for that matter non-German Europe)—is successfully to resist the German power it must go through a like process. If it becomes, in any sense, the apanage of a German power it will be because its patriotisms have been so limited in scope; too little and not too much universalist; too much of the village, and too little of mankind; because it has found too many foreigners not too few. And the moral is that if these little dividing patriotisms could be swept away and centred upon the patriotism of all the non-German peoples suffering German tyranny—if in Poland, in Austria, in Ukrainia, Courland, Lithuania, Esthonia, Finland, Serbia, Montenegro, Bulgaria, and Turkey, the non-German elements could make common cause, the position of Germany as a power of tyranny would become impossible.

But Germany may conquer because the lesser patriotisms will make the larger patriotisms impossible.

We can profitably push the analogy a little further and say this: Our successful defeat of tyranny depends upon such a development of the sense of patriotism among the democratic nations that it will attach itself rather to the conceptions of the unity of all free co-operative societies, than to the mere geographical and racial divisions; a development that will enable it to organise itself as a cohesive power for the defence of that ideal, by the use of all the forces, moral and material, which it wields.

And if we do not show ourselves capable of that one can imagine a Seeley of the future writing in about this strain:

'Non-German Europe fell, not because it was inferior in power or resources or civilisation to the Germanic conqueror, but because its patriotic loyalties centred upon too small a unit. European civilisation, Western Society, were entities only for the student. Every attempt to express that unity in defensive institutions—a common parliament, or senate or court —excited immediately the hostilities of the smaller patriotisms. "Internationalist" became a term of reproach and contempt on the part of the national writers almost as intense as "pacifist." All the institutions of unification—Hague Courts, League of Nations, and the like—came to have in the popular mind connotations of lukewarmness in patriotism. So little had the habit of co-operation between the non-German European States been developed, that even during the Five Years War the Military Council established at Versailles to create some unity of military direction was regarded with great disfavour. In fact the Allies at no time were able to achieve complete co-ordination of military action, largely because of this hostility to any but national bodies. Whether it be true or not, as some evidence seems to show, that the German power encouraged this separatism by subsidising the more clamantly "patriotic" Press in the Allied States, it is certain that the propaganda of intensely nationalist type carried on by that Press had results in public temper and outlook which in the end made German triumph inevitable.'

Of what avail is this moralising? It will be argued that we are dealing with a condition, not a theory; that these rivalries of differing race and creed are age-long; that such hostilities are inherent in our natures and that we can do nothing to attenuate them. They are 'elemental forces.' And so on.

Now one of the most suggestive things in the contrast of German solidarity on one hand, and Balkan and Slavonic disruption on the other, is the fact just touched on that the very disunity which now marks the Balkan peoples, marked less than a century ago the Germanies. Before Napoleon awoke it with his conquest, there was practically no 'German' patriotism. There was a Bavarian patriotism, a Suabian patriotism, a Prussian patriotism, so that Napoleon was able to set one against another. But now the patriotism for Württemberg or Hanover has been merged in the patriotism for Germany.

How have these 'elemental' hostilities been overcome? How have the old enemies been brought to make common cause?

We get here what is in one sense the most hopeful fact of the whole phenomenon. That change has not been the result mainly of non-human factors, or of the blind play of outside forces. It has been due to the conscious effort of men's minds, the actual personal work of certain definite German writers who by their labours destroyed one tradition and established another. It is a familiar story how Fichte, Stein, Hardenberg and Scharnhorst and their co-labourers converted the Prussian and Suabian patriotism into the German patriotism. They played as definite a role in that transmutation of feeling as another German, Marx, played in the ideas that are now having such explosive force in Russia.

Would a more unified world outside of Germany affect in any way Germany's power of domination over her conquered territories? Could a league composed of Britain, France, Italy, America—North and South—Japan, China, South Africa, and the other overseas British States, wielding its moral and material forces, successfully resist the German subjugation of neighbouring peoples?

Now—and this is a truth which one feels disposed to stop and shout at every stage of this argument—it is not necessary to answer that in the affirmative in order to make a sound case for the larger patriotism. All we need to show is that, whether resistance to German power on the part of these States with the aid of the Western Democracies can be successful if the old narrower patriotism obtains. With the enlargement of our patriotisms it may succeed; without that, it cannot.

And that is the extent of this particular moral.[1]

[1] *The Political Conditions of Allied Success* (Putnams).

PART II: THE PACIFIST POSITION EXAMINED

I

THE PACIFIST CHOICE: ARMED ANARCHY OR COLLECTIVE SECURITY

Inherent in the attitude adopted by Britain towards the Totalitarian States this last seven or eight years, and discussed in the preceding talks, is a large element of the Pacifist doctrine: 'Resist not evil'—submit, retreat, avoid collision. Much criticism of the League is based on the assumption that it is 'an instrument of coercion rather than of conciliation.' In view of the fact that some element of Pacifism has entered even—indeed particularly—into Conservative foreign policy; and that the complete Pacifist faith animates very large numbers of our youth, and our intellectuals, and may therefore play a very important part in the future use of our immense power, its assumptions are worth examination.

Implicit in the discussions of the Symposium was the hope of the establishment of a working collective system; in the fears expressed that this system had been rendered unworkable owing mainly to the force of Pacifist feeling —that of the New Pacifism as well as that of the old; the Conservative and Right Pacifism as well as the Quaker and Left Pacifism.

The attempt is here made to meet the essence of the Pacifist argument in so far as it is directed against Collective Security.

Let us be clear first concerning the case for Collective Security as the best of possible alternatives. That case is in outline as follows:

(1) Every nation in the world, without any exception whatever claims the right to defend itself by arms. It makes that claim and renews it con-

tinuously by arming. That is to say, there is no nation that has adopted, or seems to come near to adopting, the policy of non-resistance, defence-lessness, the renunciation of war for defence. There is not one nation that regards war as the worst that could happen to it. All regard de-fencelessness as worse than war: all would fight for defence. The com-pulsorily disarmed Germany of 1920-30 was not less secure or less bur-dened than the present armed Germany. But burdens were assumed and risks taken in order to acquire arms.

(2) This deep urge for 'defence' is therefore something which, like the feeling for nationality, we must accept as a fact likely to remain con-stant for a very long time and take into account. It is useful to discuss just what it is we fear of each other, what we are supposed to be de-fending ourselves against and to point out the extent to which the fact of war defeats the purposes of defence (and which this writer began doing in the years before the War and has done continuously ever since). But meantime we must have a policy in respect of this universal, persistent, insistent, passionate demand for visible and material means of defence. It can be satisfied by two possible methods, one certain to lead to war, the other, if generally adopted, reasonably certain to prevent it. The nations hesitate between the two roads and demand of their counsellors which to take. We must answer *that* question, not dodge it by saying that they should take neither road, that the demand for armed defence is one that ought not to be made at all. Even if that be true it does not answer the question actually put by our generation. If we oppose the better method because the best is not adopted, then we have our share of responsibility for the adoption of the worst, behind which are the forces of tradition, habit, incomprehension, confusion. To support the collective method on the ground that it is less dangerous than the older individual method is not to approve of either, or approve of war; it is merely to counsel that of two dangerous courses the less dangerous should be taken.

(3) The older method of individual as distinct from collective defence, inevitably leads to war since by that method defence for one automatically kills the defence of the other. It is rooted in mutual denial of right.

(4) The way out is to make defence the function, not of each rival party to a dispute but of the whole community unholding the principle of third-party judgment, law. If force must be used for defence it is better that it should be part of an organised social system applying it 'coldly' on behalf of law embodying the principle of equality of right than that it should be left to the play of national passions.

(5) If it *is* so made part of an organised system it is rarely necessary to use it at all; it operates as a potential sanction in the background permitting a society, in the equilibrium so established, to develop the forces of reason, discussion, law which is not possible under the method of anarchy.

(6) To reject the better because it is not perfect, involves, in the con-ditions which face us, the triumph, not of the best, but of the worst.

The application of this policy to international conditions does not depend upon the belief that 'nations are like individuals,' or that police action in the case of nations can operate as simply as in the case of persons; nor can be of the same kind. Such analogies are usually invalid. But there are certain laws, like those of the multiplication table, which apply to nations exactly as to individuals. Nor is it assumed that a collective policy can be applied in its entirety, nor all at once, nor without injustice. Even within the freest, most stable and most civilised of nations such institutions as courts of law are extremely defective, but they are to be preferred to the violence and anarchy of no courts at all. Whether more or less of a given principle enters into a policy determines its direction towards improvement or away therefrom.

On what ground is this policy most commonly rejected?

The difficulty of summarising criticism is, of course, due to the fact that it comes from two opposite ends: from the military nationalist who opposes the collective system because it would make the national force subject to international purpose, limit national independence, and from the Pacifist who rejects it root and branch because it involves military force in the background, war as a possibility. Two opposed motives combine in common opposition to it.

But the opposition to the collective method is re-enforced from other quarters: By certain of the Marxian Socialists (though this opposition has greatly diminished of late) who insist that the ultimate cause of war is Capitalism; that only by the abolition of Capitalism can peace be secured; that any war on behalf of the League in the present order of society would be in fact a war for Capitalism. The opposition to an international system of defence is further reinforced by those who believe that remedy for war is to be found in far-reaching Federation, or an intenser Christianising of the individual, or in a combination of the Anglo-Saxon world against war; or in Fascism, or in monetary reform, the Single Tax; that its cause is to be found in the Jews, the Freemasons. . . .

The purpose of mentioning these oppositions is not mere derision of any proposal, but to emphasise the ease with which infinitely varying opinions can combine in opposition to any proposed change; and that this inability to agree on any new policy gives victory to the old.

The old may survive, not because there is a majority for it but because the majority against it cannot agree on an alternative.

I shall deal here with the Pacifist criticism, because it is mainly from the Pacifist end that the policy has been directly assailed.

A word as to terms. 'Pacifism' is here used as indicating the policy of refusing to go to war for any purpose whatever, even for defence; the policy of non-resistance or passive resistance. The writer has said on a score of occasions in the past that if we could imagine a nation being converted to that policy and applying it, it would obviously be successful. The nation in question might have to submit to foreign rule, but it would not get war, any more than the invasion of the Ruhr involved war. Because in that invasion the Germans were unable to defend themselves they suffered infinitely less than they would have suffered had they been able to resist. In the end the invader simply went home. Non-resistance was successful; but it did not convert Germany to the doctrine. And the issue to-day is less simple. Errors as to the true place and function of force touch not only the problem of international war but also the problem of defending constitutional government against parties within the State, notably Fascist, who believe in armed force and certainly would not scruple to use it, as is proved by the behaviour of Fascist parties on the Continent in recent years, to overthrow an unarmed government. The first thing that would happen to a nation which had elected a government pledged to non-resistance would be, not foreign invasion, but seizure, or attempted seizure of the government by Fascists. What would be the government's attitude? Would it bring the army, the apparatus of killing, into play? If it did, the position would then be that it was prepared to kill in resistance to (say) British Fascism, but not in resistance to foreign Fascism; fight to resist a British Fascist Government, but not a foreign Fascist Government.

If Fascism, the arming of Parties within the State, is to be met by a policy of Pacifism, the nation would then have to stand by and see Jews expelled or segregated or maltreated, men of liberal or socialist views imprisoned, bullied, bludgeoned, bumped off, and—most importantly of all as bearing upon the success of the Pacifist endeavour—children dragged into camps and schools, there to be indoctrinated with evil theories designed to make of them willing tools of a Totalitarian State. The prime fact we should have to face would be that that process of education would usually, almost invariably, succeed. The Totalitarian State would educate a generation prepared to imprison or execute its parents for the 'fatherland,' or the 'cause'; believe it right so to do. Again, that thing has happened repeatedly this last few years before our eyes; is happening now. An unarmed government would be at the mercy of even a small body of patriots honestly convinced (and the honesty of fanatics is usually unquestionable) that force to 'save the country,' first by seizing the government and then by waging war against its enemies, was not only justifiable, but a bounden duty encumbent upon them. Having seized the schools, the churches, the Press, the radio, they would make their will the people's will. So non-resistance would not dispose of the problem of force within the State; nor of war with other States.

That situation indicates the principle which should determine the use of force both as between parties within the State and as between States. Force should be used to resist the use of force as the means of settling differences, whether between nations or parties, so as to allow discussion, reason, law, to function. Force should not be (and is not in Britain) used to fight Fascism. It would be as wrong to prevent Fascism establishing itself by discussion and free election as it would be to allow Fascism to install itself by force. The force should be resisted; not Fascism. To argue that we 'cannot fight Fascism with its own weapons' is to miss the point. To yield to Fascist force, to allow force and not electoral discussion to determine the issue, is to allow force to be substituted for reason. To resist by force the overriding of the constitution by force is, despite easy derision of the paradox, to use force in order that force may not prevail and destroy reason. Similarly, to use the pooled power of nations for resistance to the State which, rejecting arbitration or peaceful settlement, wages war in order to enforce its own partial judgment, is to use force to make peaceful judgment possible.

Pacifist criticism of the collective system could perhaps fairly be summarised under these headings:

(1) Collective action is war, and does not cease to be war by calling it police action or anything else. It means mass killing, disembowelling children, burning civilians alive. To do these things on behalf of civilisation is to embroil it in horrors that contradict the term, to produce a psychosis that would make subsequent establishment of real peace or a real civilisation impossible; considerations reinforced by the fact that war tends more and more to shift from land and water to the air.

(2) War arises from fear and a sense of wrong: the way to meet the fear is to remove whatever causes it; our armaments are the cause of fear in others; the way to abolish a sense of wrong is to redress the wrong. Show foreign nations that we are prepared to meet just claims; to do away with the arms that frighten them, and you will get a more secure peace than by any process of coercion. Any policy of justice and conciliation demands ethical standards which are incompatible with a general belief in coercion, force, violence. These must be sacrificed.

(3) Collective action would in fact be the old alignment of opposing alliances: in the present circumstances of the world Germany, Italy, Japan on the one side with Britain, France, Russia on the other, a conflict entirely indistinguishable from the old diplomatic wars of the past. Imagine a League war to have taken place and you have in fact just about the situation (with a reshuffling of roles) which you had on the morrow of the last War. You could only get another Versailles.

I have tried as sincerely and impartially as possible to summarise the objections made. But, as a matter of fact, none deals with the main question: Which of the two methods of armed defence is the less dangerous? If one or the other is certain to be adopted, which had it better be?

I have gone carefully through a very large number of articles and letters from Pacifist critics of the Collective System, and not one which I can recall has concluded: 'The old competitive system of arms is preferable to the proposed collective method.' The writers are ready enough indeed to criticise the old method, but they will not support the new, and ignore the question whether their failure to support it adds to the forces already so strong, pushing the world back to the old. They argue, usually, the superiority of the completely pacifist policy over the complications, risks and dangers of the Collective System. But these do not happen to be the alternative presented to us. Grant the superior merits of non-resistance. Every nation in the world nevertheless rejects it; adds to its arms. The arms will exist for a long time. How are these arms, so long as they exist, to be prevented from breaking into explosion? Have we any right simply to ignore that question? Assuming that you cannot get non-resistance, complete Pacifism, all at once, by what road must it be approached? What is the next best choice? *Is* the Collective System better than the competitive? Should one support the collective method as a second best on the ground that if one does not it is the worst which will rule?

The Pacifist replies, again, 'no,' because 'collective action means bombings, burning, disembowelling.' But those things will certainly happen if the old policy of dealing with the arms, the old form of defence is maintained. Will those horrors be less likely to happen if the collective method is adopted? That question is not really faced.

One or two correspondents take the line that since the Collective System is now dead the issue is between Pacifism and reversion to the old order; and that therefore a straight refusal to fight or to approve fighting on any grounds whatever offers the greatest chance of preventing war.

The argument really means that it is easier to secure universal adoption of non-resistance than a considerable adoption of the Collective System. The facts are all against both assumptions. Everywhere the nations, including the little nations that have no territorial or imperial ambitions and obviously loathe war, increase their armaments. They reject non-resistance.

Now one fact, vital to any sound judgment of the respective merits of the two policies, is this: Non-resistance, in order to be effective—to cause, that is, aggression to cease—must affect conduct all but universally, must convert even minorities. A very small band of Fascists would, if unresisted, create a Fascist State; one nation whose passion of conquest was unaffected by the non-resistance of its victims could dominate a universe. If only a tiny minority of the invaded nation resisted, bombs would nevertheless rain upon its cities. But collective defence of the law of peace demands no such universality of conviction. It usually suffices for a majority within a State to agree that armed attack upon the constitution will be resisted for potential rebels to be deterred; a combination of even a few great States really agreed on common and collective resistance to aggression would suffice to deter aggression. The Collective System is not dead. It has, though defeated in two recent battles, never been nearer to success than during this last twelve months; and the understanding of its principles, which if sufficient will ensure its success (and alone can ensure it) makes steady headway.

The Democratic States of Europe are so near to being ready for collective defence that a decisive lead by, for instance, Great Britain would make it a political reality. Britain could have so made it in the Abyssinian affair.

One main element of that method—alliance, agreement with foreign nations—is inevitable in any system of defence. By the old method we should ally ourselves now either with France, Russia, Czechoslovakia and the Democratic States against the Fascist Powers, or ally ourselves with Germany against Russia. If now we make an Alliance of the Democratic States of Europe (including Russia) not against any specified State but for impartial support of the law of peace; if the Democratic States make it clear that they are not claiming the right to be their own judges in any dispute with Germany or Italy, but are willing to accept third-party judgment; that they offer to 'the other side' every protection and security they claim for themselves, then the nucleus of a collective system will be established; and we shall not have war. Policy along those lines is now already the policy of Democratic Parties everywhere—in Britain, France, Belgium, Holland, Czechoslovakia, the Scandinavian States, Russia. It is the policy of the more intelligent elements in Liberal and Conservative Parties. Against it we have that curious alliance already referred to—all the forces of Reaction, Toryism, Imperialism, Fascism, plus those of pure Pacifism and pure Marxism. It is doubtful whether the reactionaries alone could win; but Reaction plus Pacifism, Reaction, that is, facing not a united peace front but a Left deeply divided on the peace issue, will be extremely likely to win. With the peace forces divided and confused, the Collective Policy may easily be defeated. But what will take its place will not be non-resistance. It will be unadulterated Reaction: reversion to the old anarchy in its extreme form.

The main argument against international coercion in any form is, as indicated above, this: 'When you have coerced by war you have merely the Versailles situation of 1919.' Mr. Aldous Huxley quotes the late Frank Simonds at considerable length in support of this contention, citing particularly the case of Italy. For the League to have prevented Italy attacking Abyssinia by waging war upon the former would 'demonstrate irrefutably that the effects of a League war are indistinguishable from the more familiar types of conflicts between individual nations.'

Of which a good deal could be said, the first this: that it simply is not true; that the assumption upon which such statements are based disregard or distort the plainest facts of the situation, particularly certain psychological elements. All the forces of Nationalism, Imperialism, Militarism, Jingoism flew at Germany alike in 1914 and in 1919. The same forces in 1936 were all on the side of Italy. The rules to which Italy was asked to conform (and to which she had subscribed) were available for her protection as for that of others. In 1914 there was no rule, no system in which Germany could find legitimate defence. Her only means of defence was her own triumph.

When the Italian-Abyssinian affair culminated last October in the decision to impose sanctions against Italy, Frank Simonds, like most American and many British critics of the League, took the view that Eden was merely the instrument of British imperialism opposing a rival imperialism that might threaten the position of Britain in the Mediterranean, in Africa (particularly in Egypt) and on the road to India.

The preceding pages have at various points discussed that view. If the above diagnosis is true, how are we to account for the fact that all the old guard of Imperialism and Militarism (to say nothing of Capitalism and the armament industry) both in Britain and in France were bitterly opposed to the policy of sanctions? The Eden policy, or what we hoped was going to be the Eden policy, did not find its support among the Colonel Blimps, the Lady Houstons, the Rothermeres, the Beaverbrooks, the Amerys, the Page-Crofts, the professional imperialists, the armament interests. These were raucous and livid in their denunciations not of Italy, but of the League that would restrain her (as, a year or two previously, they opposed the attempts to restrain the aggression of Japan in China). Eden found his support on the Left. I put it to those American critics at the time, whether they seriously believed that a policy, opposed by British Imperialists to the last mother's son of them, and supported by Labour, Socialist and Communist Parties everywhere, by Russia, by all the lesser States having most to fear from imperialism, including the Irish Free State and Mr. de Valera personally, was just pure British Imperialism? The question was never answered, never even considered. So often, it would seem, social diagnosis must conform to certain formulas, e.g., war, and the willingness to risk war is always Imperialist and Capitalist. If, in the Japanese and the Italian affairs, it was the Left which was ready to risk war and the Right quite determined not to, well, the fact had just to be ignored. It was ignored.

Which is the greater pity because it is precisely in this respect that we see what is perhaps the most important difference between the situation of October 1936, and August 1914, and between that of Versailles and that of Geneva. The new alignment of forces, exchange of roles as between Left and Right, throws entirely new light on the psychology of war and of international politics.

Why did the Jingoes who in 1914 clamoured for war with Germany oppose later any policy which included risk of war with Italy or Japan? Both these nations threaten British Imperialist interest—trade with four hundred million Chinese, our position in the Mediterranean, Africa, defence of India and the rest—at least as seriously as did the power of pre-War Germany. Why was League war something which, far from exciting war fever, rendered the normally 'war-minded' person strongly adverse to it? Why did the prospect of it make the *Daily Mail*, which a quarter of a century ago laboured daily with an evil genius to excite every war-like passion against Germany, apply to Lord Cecil and his colleagues of the League of Nations Union such epithets as 'blood-thirsty war mongers'; what induced it day by day to use the language of Pacifism? Why has the word 'peace,' and appeals to peace, become in the mouth of militarists a bludgeon wherewith to brain the League of Nations?

It will not do to say that it is due to any clear resolve to have peace at any price. For the Rothermeres and Beaverbrooks are more ardent than ever for increase of all the fighting and killing machinery: more aeroplanes, more ships, more army, more everything that can be used for the killing, the burning and the disembowelling. They conceive, therefore, that circumstances may arise in which they would want to use those instruments; in which war for 'defence' may be called for. And incidentally their efforts are successful: the armaments are being feverishly increased. The appeals to 'defence' enable them to get the armaments; and the appeals to 'peace' enable them to maim the League, or any system by which defence might be made compatible with peace or justice.

The psychology of this process by which the prospect of a League war turns militarists into Pacifists is not really obscure. Long before the days of Adler, some of us had begun to see that one of the deepest of all lusts in us is the lust for power, superiority, domination, being our own master, being boss. It is an enormous element in the psychology of imperialism, national 'honour,' national prestige, Nordicism, 'blood and iron,' boys of the bulldog breed and similar barbarisms of nationalism and militarism. To ask those in whom this instinct is strong to exchange a position of mastery and superiority for one of mere partnership and equality, in which national rights are to be subjected at times to the judgment of foreigners, and in which it is necessary to argue with 'copper-coloured gentry from South America' instead of putting one's fist upon the table like a soldier and a sahib—all this seems, not only to the German Nazi, but to the Nazi-minded Briton, something almost revolting. And the British Imperialist of the old order, rather than accept in the Japanese and Italian affairs a resounding success for the League, an institution, or system, or policy which would mean the end of imperialism as he has known it, an end of national independence as he conceives it, preferred to accept a nationalist challenge of the old kind, the growth of rival imperialisms; dangers, which, if the world remains as it has been, with victory going to the strong and valiant, he feels he will be able to deal with in due course.

Pacifists have discussed in the past how war might be deprived of its emotional glamour and appeal. Well, events have shown them. Make war a League war, an international war, a police war, and the war-minded person does not want it.

Indeed this truth is recognised by militarist critics of the collective system. Again and again they have insisted that since the collective method implies that the constituent members of the League or community must fight for the law, it asks the impossible. Nations simply won't do it, say the militarists. In a recent *Hibbert Journal*, L. P. Jacks argues elaborately that the obligation to go to war for the Covenant goes far beyond the capacity for 'altruism' of any nation. Men will fight, we are so often told, for their 'country,' for their own direct interests; but never for this cold and abstract thing, 'the law.'

Perhaps not. But events prove—altogether too conclusively—that men will fight for defence; and if it is clear that the law means defence, they will fight for the law; for Right, and become passionate about it. Why should Englishmen give their lives, as thousands would, if a foreign power attacked, say, the Seychelles or the Falkland Islands? Not from any direct interest the dying soldier might have in those distant and microscopic isles. But because the principle of defence would be involved. Submit supinely to the sheer annexation of the Falklands, he argues, and no bit of imperial territory is safe. But, as a great many British folk (including, possibly, a minority of the Cabinet) realised, the defence of Abyssinia (i.e., the Covenant) was as important for our own future security as the defence of the Seychelles. We would have been ready, says Dr. Jacks, to fight for Antwerp; not for Abyssinia. But the particular conceptions of strategy and defence which make Antwerp 'a pistol pointed, etc.,' are out of date. If on grounds of strategy and security the Briton can to-day be brought to fight for Antwerp (which does not make him secure) then to-morrow on the same grounds he can be brought to fight for the Covenant, which, firmly established, *would* make him secure. It all depends on what he regards as the effective method of defence.

The common man in England, like the common man everywhere, dislikes to die for a cause which is clearly wrong. When he realises— as again, he is beginning to realise—that to fight for the security of this or that State whether their cause be right or wrong, merely because their frontiers happen to have strategic importance for us; to fight in order to deny to others rights of defence by superior power we claim for ourselves; when he realises that this immoralism is inseparable from the old system, that the collective system alone enables him to achieve defence and yet 'play fair'—when he realises this he will be as ready to fight for the Covenant as for St. Kitts or Guiana.

It would carry us very far into psychology to enter upon more than a very summary treatment of the theme that war arises from fear and sense of wrong; from economic strangulation and inequality; that the bad conduct of nations in this respect is due to bad treatment received; that Nazidom was born at Versailles; that as we behave towards others so will they behave towards us; that for this order of reason non-resistance is the best defence.

Mr. Gerald Heard writes:

'Are young Germans really Huns? Would they destroy hundreds of thousands of women and children in London unless they were told "England has planes which are aimed to do the same to your women and children. If you hesitate your loved ones perish!" If England had no bombing planes which could attack Berlin would London be in any danger? . . .

'It is fear which would make a body of brave men commit this abomination.'

Mr. Aldous Huxley, citing the early Christians, William Penn and Gandhi, says:

'If you treat other people well, other people will generally treat you well. It is possible to go further and to say that, if you have the opportunity of going on treating them well, they will at last *invariably* reciprocate your treatment. . . .

'There is historical evidence to show that the pacifist technique is unquestionably effective.'

Was it really fear of Abyssinian armaments which caused Italy to launch her war, poison gas and all, upon Abyssinia? Did the complete powerlessness of the Abyssinians protect them from all the abominations of modern war? Did 'unilateral disarmament' work in their case? Did Japan really fear the power of China, disintegrated by internal dissensions? Did we enter what was perhaps the meanest war we have ever waged, that against the Boers, because their arms threatened us?

But more decisive light is thrown by certain other cases. It is perpetually repeated that Hitlerism was born of defeat at Versailles. (It compels one to ask where French, Spanish, Belgian and Italian Fascism was born.) The most characteristic element in Hitlerite Fascism is its anti-semitism. Now the Jews have been in Germany, or parts of it, for two thousand years. They have never been an armed community. They have necessarily practised non-resistance. For centuries in Western Europe they have submitted, virtually without retaliation, to persecution, indignities, infamies of every description. That policy has not protected them, nor caused their persecutions to cease. (Incidentally, the fate of the Jews in Germany compels one to ask, if Germans can so treat a German community, why should we expect them to treat any foreign community which happened to be as powerless as the Jews, any better?)

But there is an even more striking case which disproves the too sweeping assumptions about the effectiveness of non-resistance. There is a whole continent which has been powerless to resist European invasion; its people never having organised their force for their own protection: Africa. The negro has always been at the mercy of the White. No European nation has ever had cause to fear the power of a negro nation. What has been the fate of this unarmed and defenceless people? They have suffered even worse than the Jews. Transported as a slave to the Western world, the negro's history tells the same story. Speaking broadly there has never been a negro rising in the United States; the negro has never resisted by arms the fate meted out to him. And to-day after three centuries of such non-resistance, and of life side by side with an Anglo-Saxon people, he lacks the most elementary human rights. What better behaviour on the negro's part is necessary in order to evoke that response of good behaviour on the White's part which Mr. Huxley assures us is invariable and unfailing?

But the negro's case is not the worst: the Untouchables of India fall even lower than the negro. The unbelievable oppression of a vast body of people, numbering more than the whole population of the British Islands, has been erected into a complicated religious system. They, like the negro, have accepted their fate without armed resistance. Has that non-resistance saved them from millennia of misery and oppression?

Mr. Huxley has cited the success of Penn's method in dealing with Indians. It would be more to the point to inquire how far that method adopted by coloured people in Africa and the Americas towards the Whites has been successful; how far we have been amenable to it. The Europeans of the fifteenth century who went to South America were usually received with friendliness and hospitality. The Europeans thereupon proceeded to enslave and exterminate people who, like the Incas, had received the strangers with friendliness and trust.

It will simply not do to say that the conduct of the Europeans was caused by fear. Was it fear which prompted us to enslave the African? As little as it was fear which prompted the Duce to launch his war against the Ethiopians.

Parenthetically religious emotion did little to attenuate our age-long oppression of weak and defenceless people. One recalls not only the Inquisition, the religious wars, the St. Bartholomew massacre, but the fact that the early Spanish invaders of America who wrought oppression and destruction were often intensely religious; as were often the British. Carved upon the masts of Hawkins's slave ship were religious texts, thus: On the foremast, 'Love ye one another'; on the mainmast, 'Praise God daily'; and on the mizzen, 'Bear ye one another's burdens.' We know how his sincerely religious crews interpreted these injunctions in their slaving operations.

A word or two on the psychological case for the use of force by the community to restrain the use of private force for private ends needs to be added.

To refuse to the community—whether international or national—

the right of force, to demand that law shall be without sanction, is in fact to pin our faith to the workability of anarchy. But broadly, anarchy which might work if each were governed by supreme wisdom, asks too much of too many. True, men desire to do right; but they are confused, if the community gives no lead, as to what right is; and their judgment in a dispute with another is swayed by appetites, lusts, pugnacities, tempers. And if they desire to do right, they usually passionately desire also to resent wrong, particularly wrong done to themselves. (It was not the lack of any instinct so to act which explains the non-resistance of coloured populations to wrongs, but the fact that circumstances made cohesion and common action for defence out of the question for them.) Men cannot be trusted to be their own defenders of their own rights. If force is to be used for defence in this sense it is infinitely better that it should be used by the community as the instrument of thought-out institutions, law, and not privately by each according to his will, his own light at the moment of difference and quarrel. And this is true, even if all punishment is fundamentally wrong. Capital punishment may be an evil thing—I think it is—but it is better that the State should perform that dreadful function than that it should be the private instrument of parties to the dispute. I would vote for a bill to abolish capital punishment unless the effect of voting it would be to cause friends of the victims of murder to apply the punishment. I have lived on a frontier where a group of ranchers, suffering from cattle theft and the activities of gunmen, have said in effect to the authorities, the state: 'Either you capture and punish these men or we shall do it ourselves.' The state did not capture and punish the criminals (not from any pacifist scruple, but because the state itself was ill-organized). Lynchings, punishment by interested parties, individuals, were the direct result. Law, even when employing frightfulness like killing, is better than lynchings which employ the same means. It may be true to say that killing can never be justified; but even if that is so, the legal killing is better than the private killing, the killing, that is, by the lynching party, or the parties to feuds like those of the Kentucky hills; better because it has an impartiality and coldness which the killing by interested parties has not; and because the problem of retaliation does not arise, or arises with less intensity. The Franco-German duel has gone on for generations. But if fifty-two nations really had restrained Italy in the name of a law to which she herself had subscribed, it would have been extremely difficult for the Italian nation to have kept alive any similar feud 'psychosis' with fifty-two separate enemies.

Those who have suffered by lynchings in the United States have long pleaded for the use of Federal power as a preventive. But the Federal Government has been 'non-resistant' to the violence of lynchers; the negroes have had to be. This failure of the Federal Government, the law, to use force, has in no way deterred lynchers, in no way tended to discredit the habit. Had Federal force been resolutely used just once to protect negroes from lynching and frustrate the connivance of local authorities therein, the whole attitude to lynching would have changed; not so much because the Whites would be 'frightened' by superior force, but because the authority of law, the fact that it could be put into operation for the weak and the despised as well as the powerful, would have been enhanced. The fact that the American Federal Government was pacifist at that particular point and is so little pacifist when certain powerful White interests are involved, does not enhance the morality of the situation. The refusal to use force at that point makes the morality of the 'pacifism' contemptible.

The nations of the League were pacifist in respect of the restraint of Italy: both Britain and France announced beforehand that military action was ruled out. 'Nothing,' said Mr. Baldwin, would induce him to adopt a policy which might lead to war with Italy. Not one ship, said Sir John Simon, would be sacrificed for Abyssinia. This particular manifestation of Pacifism in those particular circumstances has not lessened the future likelihood of further force, or the drift to violence. It has increased it, increased cynicism; helped to destroy all belief in Right. A public speaker said the other day: 'We know now exactly what it is worth to have the world admit the righteousness of your cause if that cause is attacked. The world's recognition of your righteousness will be worth precisely nothing at all.' The fact that Italy 'got away with it' has strengthened every argument for the old international anarchy, all the cynicisms, the Machiavellianisms, the immoralisms which support it. Had the fifty-two nations used force to restrain Italy the precise contrary would have been true.

The reasons are plain. Force was withheld and Abyssinia sacrificed, not because men object to using it, but because they are only at present ready to use it for themselves, in shortsighted selfishness. To say: 'We will fight for our own direct defence, but not for the defence of others or for the law,' does not help to get rid of force; does not increase Pacifism. It only increases cynical acquiescence in a short-sighted and self-stultifying selfishness. Had force been used to restrain Italy, the Canal been closed, mustard gas stopped, it would have constituted proof that, after all, a European society, a European unity, does exist, and that the old anarchy is coming to an end; that men are at last coming to see that what it is right to do for themselves it is right to do for the community, for law, for others. Not to do it does not diminish force; it only places force at the service of evil, and makes its ultimate abolition infinitely more difficult.

A final word in clarification of that difficult obligation to choose between evils to which reference has already been made. To those whose conscientious objections to war go deepest the present writer repeats:

'Stick to your faith. Continue to preach the principles of Pacifism; support them by reason and argument; do not sacrifice one fraction of your conviction; continue to work out all possible means of non-violent resistance.'

But to go on preaching that doctrine is not all that you as a Pacifist must do.

You must also decide which of two (or more) non-Pacifist policies will bring the Pacifist goal nearer, and which make it more remote; otherwise you may, by bad judgment, betray the cause you have at heart.

Very soon now, in a year or two, the issue will be presented to you electorally.

In most constituencies there will be no Pacifist candidate, and you will have to choose between one whose policy is that of the Attlee-Dalton-Noel Baker-Cecil-Gilbert Murray order (the matter goes beyond Party lines), and another whose policy is of the Beaverbrook-Rothermere-Amery-Page Croft-Londonderry order.

For what will you vote?

Both stand for armed defence. But one means by defence something which is compatible with peace, and the other something which will make war inevitable.

The government group stands for a policy which, however much its real nature may be obscured by lip service to peace more or less sincere, and however little its nature may be realised by some of its spokesmen, nevertheless simmers down in fact to saying to other nations:

'We arm in order that, without any interference from you we can carry out any policy which, without consultation with you, we think to our advantage—Preferences, closing the Empire, tariffs round our Crown Colonies, what not—whether it injures you or not;

'and in order that, if we should get into a dispute we should be able to enforce what we believe to be our rights.

'That is to say, to be judge of any quarrel arising between us.'

And, by arming in order to be judge in their own cause, they arm in order to deny to some other nation the very right of judgment they claim for themselves. If both sides to a dispute insist on being its judge, the outcome obviously must be war. By that method there can be no equality of right.

The other group—Attlee-Dalton-Noel Baker-Cecil-Gilbert Murray group—stands for a conception of defence based on the exactly contrary principle of equality of right, for the defence of rights which, if claimed by both parties to a dispute, must lead to peace as certainly as the other principle must lead to war.

The policy of the Attlee group boils down to saying to foreigners:

'We do not ask you to take our verdict in any dispute between us, since we are one of the parties to it. We offer you the umpire principle, arbitration, which is equal for both.

'We shall not use our arms in order to be your judge; only to prevent you being ours; not to ensure that the *status quo* is not changed; only to ensure that it is not changed by war at the irresponsible dictation of the victor.

'We will fight only for that right of impartial judgment, pacific settlement, and peaceful change which we offer freely to you.'

Under the former of the policies outlined above, if the foreigner wants the same rights of security our government claims for this nation, he must fight for them.

Under the latter policy, if the foreigner wants equality of defensive rights with ourselves, he need not fight at all, for they are freely offered to him.

Which policy is the more likely to produce war? For which, therefore, if he must choose, should the Pacifist vote?

Note that it is not a question of what you, with Pacifist convictions, should or would do about armed force.

It is a question of what those who have *not* Pacifist convictions, but have convictions about the duty of armed defence—which, however mistaken, are just as sincere as ours—should do in order to make the application of their convictions to policy as little dangerous as possible.

What, then, do you decide? Vote for neither? Even if the effect of withdrawing support from the less evil policy is to cause the more evil to triumph?

Even if by refusing to support the Dalton-Cecil side you hand over the control of the country's foreign policy to the Rothermere-Beaverbrook-Londonderry side, and so make war more probable?

Return to the old 1914 anarchy would then be due, not to the fact that there was a majority for that course, but to the fact that the majority against it could not agree upon the alternative.

And would the universally proclaimed failure of the collective system bring Pacifism nearer? Would that failure be followed by something more Pacifist than the League, or something more savagely militarist?

We may disagree about the right answer to some of these questions. But the Pacifist must try to find the right answer, not go on saying that he does not need to answer at all; or repeat as answer the statement that all force is evil.

For though that be perfectly true, it is no answer at all to the question whether force used as Attlee would use it is as evil and dangerous as force used as Beaverbrook or Rothermere would use it.

To decide, after careful examination, that the Beaverbrook-Rothermere method is less likely to lead to war than the collective method might be an intellectually honest decision, however mistaken.

But to say that, as a Pacifist, you do not need to examine the question at all, that you have no obligation to examine which is the less dangerous because both involve force, is to evade not merely decision upon an abstract question of ethics, but, to evade an urgent duty of citizenship, that duty which devolves upon all of us to do what we can to prevent overwhelming disaster and immeasurable evil.

Here is a true story:

A young man, who, during his father's absence, and against the father's strictest injunctions, had taken out the family car one evening to go to a riotous party—also forbidden him—asked a neighbour who knew the country, which of two short cuts was less dangerous.

Now the neighbour knew one to be much more dangerous than the other, but knowing also that the young man was engaged in wrong-doing, and fearing that the father might resent what could be interpreted as acquiescence in that wrong-doing, refused to answer the question at all.

That young man was killed.

And the father held that neighbour in part responsible for the death, a responsibility not much lessened by a highly moral intention.

Many Pacifists will say: 'But of course a Pacifist would vote for an Attlee-Cecil policy as against a Beaverbrook-Rothermere one.'

Then, in that case, the same conditional support to the Collective System as against the old must be given by Pacifists at times other than election times.

PART III: CONCLUSIONS AND PROPOSALS

I

SOME SUMMARIES

The final conclusions to which the foregoing discussions point have found expression in brief summaries which it may be worth while here to reproduce.

BRITAIN'S DEFENSIVE POLICY

An Empire's security depends, obviously, at least as much upon its political situation in the world—that is, upon the answer to the question: 'Who, when the guns begin to go off, will be on its side and who against it?'—as upon its military and naval resources.

Yet there is a curious tendency to evade this plain fact. About some alleged shortage of planes or shells, or a given type of cruiser, it is easy to stir widespread public interest. But a change in the international situation which may mean that whole armies and navies are shifting over from the side of our defence to the side of potential aggression leaves the same public relatively indifferent.

In so far as the public has of late concerned itself at all with foreign policy in relation to defence it has been mainly to insist upon no further foreign commitment, the assumption being apparently, that to increase obligation is to diminish security, a principle which, if true, would condemn every bank or insurance company to insolvency. At the very moment that the demand for 'no more foreign commitments' became most insistent our commitment to go to the aid of France and Belgium if they were attacked was given a definiteness which it had never before possessed, our Foreign Minister expressly putting that obligation in a category by itself differing, he has explained, from our general but much more qualified and less definite undertakings to resist aggression elsewhere.

Now, to make our guarantee thus definite is indubitably sound. Our mistake was to wait seventeen years after the Armistice before doing it. Had we been thus definite and unequivocal when President Wilson failed to secure ratification for the Anglo-American guarantee to France the story of the post-War years would have been a happier one.

But if our obligation is to be limited to the defence of France and Belgium it would be far better that it should not be given at all.

Assume that we have to fulfil the promise (and if we cannot face what the fulfilment of a promise means we should not give the promise) and are once more resisting an invasion on French soil, once more facing the submarine menace, the danger of starvation. When we faced that contingency before we had on our side Russia, Italy, Japan and, later, the United States, drawing all the time heavily upon the material resources of America, who was in fact from the beginning our economic ally. Even so, victory was a near thing. What would have been our chances, what would be our chances, if Italy and Japan were on the other side, Russia and America out of it, the latter putting a stiff embargo upon loans, munitions and war materials; if one powerful enemy was in a position to threaten our Asiatic Empire and another our Mediterranean road to India?

Herr Hitler reminded us the other day of the showing which Germany had made when she faced the Grand Alliance, a world in arms; went on to remind us by implication that that Grand Alliance had disintegrated; that certain of its members were now his allies, and that Germans themselves were even more ready to sacrifice themselves to-day than they were in 1914.

He might indeed have developed the theme. The new contacts of Germany with Austria, the Danubian States and Poland, with the Spain and Spanish Morocco of to-morrow, and through Italy, with her satellite States, would give to the German combination an economic self-sufficiency which Britain does not and cannot possess. He might have gone on to point out that Britain will be dependent upon sea communications in a way that the German combination will not; that if the Mediterranean route to India and the Antipodes was difficult and dangerous for Britain in the last war, although the enemy was not 'at home' in the Mediterranean, it can, with Italy an enemy instead of an ally (especially an Italy established at the back door of the Suez Canal in Abyssinia, with bases in the Balearic Islands and in Morocco) be made utterly impossible in the next war; while even the Cape route, with Germany and Italy having bases in the Canaries, can be made extremely dangerous and difficult.

The situation, it is true, would be very different if, at the moment of implementing our undertaking to defend France, Russia entered upon the scene: giving Japan enough to do in Asia and diverting the forces of Germany or her allies in Eastern Europe. If in the situation of appalling danger to the Empire just sketched, Russian aid were forthcoming (as the result of the Franco-Soviet Pact), it is quite clear that we should not decline it. But important sections of our public, of Parliament, of our governing circles, seem resolutely determined that Russian aid shall not be forthcoming in that contingency. In various ways influences are exerted to undermine the Franco-Soviet agreement, and Germany is given to understand that, if the particular technique followed by her and Italy in Spain is also applied with the necessary adaptations to Russia, resulting in the establishment of a Fascist Government in that country, more or less under German control, the effort would be regarded by Great Britain with benevolent neutrality.

Does an undertaking to defend France while permitting, or even encouraging, the steady elimination, one by one, the destruction in detail of all other potential allies, contain more of security or of danger?

Many, recognising the grave danger of a situation in which Britain and France alone might have to face forces much greater than those we faced when Russia, Japan, Italy and the United States were on our side, say 'Keep out of the Continent altogether.' Others urge a bargain or an alliance with the Fascist (which are also the 'Have-Not') States.

Both policies are feasible, at a price. The price is surrender of the possibility of effective defence—of that conception of defence which prompted us to enter the Great War. So far as Great Britain herself is concerned we could accept that position—the position of a Denmark or a Switzerland—with relative safety. But the Empire would go, and even the nations of the Commonwealth, the distant British democracies—Australia, New Zealand, British Africa—could not preserve their independence against alien domination.

Isolationism is possible if we are willing to accept the risks of definite inferiority of power as compared with the power of potential aggressors. But not if we insist upon something like equality of power.

An alliance is a source of power, like the air-arm or the submarine; if the other side resorts to it we must, or drop out of the race. We cannot meet combinations of States if we ourselves renounce combination.

If 'letting the Continent stew' means permitting the development of a situation in which a Germanic combination, by its preponderance, having reduced France to impotence, can attack us by aeroplane and submarine in the North Atlantic from bases on the Channel coasts, through Italy in the Mediterranean from bases strung along the whole length of its north and south coasts; and through Japan in the Western Pacific, then the Empire's most vital lines of communication are completely severed and the means of defending it have disappeared. If the maintenance of our alliance with France is dangerous, its termination is suicide.

There remains the policy of conciliating the Fascist Powers (which, again, are the 'Have-Not' States) by concessions, bargains, revision of the Versailles Treaty.

It is often argued that the unrest or aggressiveness of Germany is due to her treatment under that Treaty. Then what is Italy's due to? And Germany's pre-War policy?

Let us meet all the grievances we can. But history, tragic experience, passes an unmistakable verdict upon the possibilities of revision as a means of peace. Suppose that the Versailles Treaty could be revised so completely as to restore to Germany not merely all her colonies but all the European territory, like Alsace-Lorraine, which she possessed before the War—a revision which goes beyond peaceful possibility. We know, by the event, that revision even to that extent would not bring peace. For when Germany had all that territory and those resources peace was not kept.

And if we take the view that the main cause of the War was not German but Russian or British policy, then the case becomes stronger still. For it would be proof that ample resources like those possessed by Russia and the British Empire are no guarantee of peacefulness.

The 'Have-Not' States face real difficulties. They arise far more from the American tariff and the Ottawa preferences than from the existing distribution of territory. (Germany drew one-half of one per cent of her raw materials from her colonies.) Transfer of territory, in a world still dominated by economic nationalism, would leave the economic difficulties of the 'Have-Not' States unaffected and create more problems than it cured.

Furthermore, the policy of 'conciliation' or acquiescence, retreat rather than resistance—followed in the case of Japan in 1931, in Manchuria, Italy in 1935, Germany in the Rhineland, Germany and Italy in Spain—has not made the 'dynamic' powers less dynamic. Retreat has involved a steady inexorable worsening of our defensive position.

What remains? If alliance with France is inadequate, isolationism equivalent to the renunciation of defence and territorial concession as a means of peace condemned by the plainest and most tragic experience, what workable policy of effective national defence can we devise? When we speak of remedying a nation's grievances and satisfying its needs, we usually overlook what every nation in the world regards as the greatest need of all, the supreme grievance if not remedied. That need is defence, security against the contingency of being at the mercy of another's violence.

In 1914 we said: 'If Germany is victorious over France and Russia, she will become so powerful as to place us at her mercy, a position of defencelessness which a great and free people like ourselves ought not to be asked to accept.'

What was our alternative? It was that Germany should accept that position by being at our mercy. To prove that she need not fear the position we made the Treaty of Versailles. Looking at it Germany says: 'That's what comes of being weaker than your enemy. The next time we shall be stronger, and replace this treaty and *status quo* by one more in keeping with Germany's rights in the world.'

Who, when Germany has established her domination, is to be judge of the kind of world and *status quo* which will give Germany her due? Germany alone, with her allies, is to be judge. In executing that judgment she will not make a better Treaty than we made. She will make a worse. We shall be among the victims, and thereupon do what Germany is now doing: build up our power to make a new Treaty, a new *status quo* which, made once more at the moment of victory under the sense of grievance, will be worse from Germany's point of view than any of its predecessors, to be upset by a new war. . . .

This is not fanciful. That kind of see-saw is what history has been for two hundred years in Europe. It is what it must always be where each nation is its own defender of its own view of its rights; where force depends not on some principle or law agreed upon in peacetime, but is the means by which each party to a dispute attempts to impose its judgment on the other and by that fact denies to that other the same right of judgment.

The way out is clear enough. It has indeed been haltingly, half-heartedly, proclaimed as this country's policy; and never carried out. The avenue of approach—cumbrous arrangements with sixty States—may have been too difficult. Another is now indicated. This:

Make of the existing Anglo-French combination *the nucleus of a Defensive Confederation open to all who will accept its principles and obligations*. It might be proclaimed in some such terms as these:

(1) An attack on one is an attack on all; our force is a common one to resist any who resorts to war.

(2) Its purpose is not to impose our judgment upon others, but to ensure that others do not impose theirs upon us; not to maintain the *status quo*, but to see that the *status quo* is not changed by war at the sole will of the victor; not to maintain the right to close empires against others, but to ensure that others do not by conquest close against us territories now open.

(3) In grievances or disputes we are prepared either to accept third party judgment or peaceful settlement, or await the operation of peaceful change in view of the fact that,

(4) The group will create and develop efficient organs for the statement, discussion and investigation of grievances and effective institutions of peaceful change.

(5) The protection of this rule of peace, based upon common resistance to violence, is open to all who are prepared to abide by the above code, whatever their form of government may be. Not a nation's internal policy but its external conduct determines its fitness for membership.

There are many risks, many obstacles. In considering them they have to be balanced against the risks of the existing situation.

Take the usual objections: 'Such a combination would divide Europe into two rival groups.'

What is the present position? We say: Because the inviolability of French soil is necessary to our security, we stand by France however obstinate or provocative her policy. It is the old method of rival alliances. By the suggested modification we say: Our policy is pledged not primarily to the defence of this or that ally but to the defence of a law—peace. As under Locarno, we are prepared to defend Germany against violence by Russia, as we are also prepared to defend Russia against Germany.

Of the two positions, which 'takes sides' more provocatively or is the more 'entangling'? The one in which the Fascist States are invited to come in on equal terms or the other of sheer alliance of the old type with France, an alliance which is in fact limited to the single purpose of maintaining preponderance of power?

Another objection is urged: 'We should trust to conciliation, not coercion.'

In what way is the suggested type of alliance more 'coercive' than the older? And what is 'coercion'? If a foreign nation attacks us and we resist that attack, do we by that fact 'coerce' it? If we call in another to help in resisting the attack, is that 'coercion' of the attacker? If several join in the collective defence, does the defence become 'coercion' because it is collective?

A new League? No, the old League rebuilt bit by bit; an old problem approached in a new, perhaps a more realistic way.

Over a century ago the United States, at that time weak, somewhat despised, saw its democratic experiment menaced by the authoritarian group of that time, a Holy Alliance of ancient and powerful European monarchies, who proposed to aid Spain to reconquer her revolted colonies, and repress the new republicanism of Spanish America. The United States thereupon (perhaps on British advice) enunciated the first article of the doctrine of Collective Defence.

She said: 'Attack any American republic and you attack us.' It worked. The United States did not wait for reciprocity: though she assumed the obligation to protect the Spanish Republics the latter assumed no obligation to defend the United States, just as recently we have assumed the same kind of one-sided obligation in respect of Belgium.

To limit our obligation to France and Belgium is not to limit our liability. We had no obligation at all to defend Serbia, yet aggression upon her involved us in vast liabilities. Our liability would have been less if our obligation had been more. Which brings us to the ultimate issue in this problem.

To the question, 'Could the War have been prevented?' Mr. Lloyd George and other statesmen and historians most concerned have answered, 'Yes, if only Germany had known beforehand that in following the line she did she would have to meet the forces that finally entered the field against her.'

We English, faced by a 'backs-to-the-wall' emergency, calling for immediate action, can usually be relied upon to take the necessary action courageously, efficiently, doggedly. But we detest committing ourselves beforehand to act in a hypothetical situation. We are rather proud of this. We brag about it. Yet, but for that quality, the Great War might have been avoided, that War which now, in our hearts, we know to have been futile, barren of any of those results we talked so much about—our own permanent security, the ending of German militarism, the world's peace, the safety of democracy.

Great power of itself does not necessarily ensure defence. The mightiest animals creation has ever known are extinct. Great power cannot of itself prevent war: we had on our side in the last War far greater power than we can ever have again. It did not prevent war or deter aggression, because the potential aggressor did not know he would have to face that power nor what line of policy on his part would bring it into operation; what we should deem aggression. Unless power can be combined with the intelligence and courage that can proclaim beforehand clearly what it is for, how it will be used, what we mean by 'defence,' how we propose to preserve peace by its use, then it will fail even more disastrously than it failed before. Let us face that lesson.

LEAGUE 'REFORM' PROPOSALS

Perhaps the commonest criticism of the existing commitments of the League is that their effect is to:

(1) Turn what would otherwise be local wars into world wars.
(2) Divide Europe into two rival alliances, one favouring, one opposing revision.
(3) Stereotype an unjust *status quo* and render revision and peaceful change more difficult.
(4) Substitute sheer coercion for conciliation and redress of grievances.

What is the verdict of experience, particularly the tragic experience of the Great War itself, on these criticisms?

In 1914 there were no 'League entanglements,' yet all the Great Powers, including distant America and nearly the whole world, became involved in a war that began with a murder in a Balkan village. The fact that so local a quarrel rapidly spread into a world war was, obviously, not due to the kind of commitments which opponents of Article XVI so fear, for those commitments did not exist. Their absence did not keep the world out of war; their existence and the general conviction that they would be operative would probably have done so.

Most historians of the War, including Lord Grey and Mr. Lloyd George, are agreed that it could have been prevented had Germany known beforehand that she would have to meet the forces which finally confronted her. If to that foreknowledge had been added the conviction that aggression against Germany by any one of the Allies (say, Russia) would have entitled her to assistance—the essence of the 'League' or 'Locarno' method—the probability that there would have been no war becomes stronger still.

The argument that this type of arrangement tends to divide Europe into rival alliances surely ignores the fact that rival alliances existed long before the League or Locarno. Fundamentally the League was an attempt to turn rival alliances into one alliance by giving them a common purpose—defence of the law of peace, the law that a nation shall be assured of such assistance in the case of unprovoked attack that attack is unlikely to take place. If nations cannot be assured of assistance on the conditions provided by the League or Locarno type of alliance they will inevitably revert to the older type.

Pleas that the League is 'an instrument for crystallising an unjust *status quo*' usually ignore (*a*) the fact that the League does not attempt to prevent change of the *status quo*, but to prevent its change by war (which usually produces a still worse status than the one it was designed to correct), and (*b*) the fact that under the older methods of security peaceful change is still more difficult than under the collective method.

The reason of (*b*) is obvious. Where a State has nothing but its own power to depend upon for its self-preservation it will retain strategic frontiers even if unjust, aim at economic self-sufficiency even though at the cost of friction with its neighbours. To ask a State already fearful for its security to weaken itself by revision of some frontier at present strategically advantageous, or by surrender of territory, in order to appease its neighbours, but at the same time to tell it that it must expect no help from those who make the demands if it is attacked as the result of complying with them, is to be neither realist nor fair.

Remedy of grievances, 'revision,' is not an alternative to the policy of collective security. The latter is the condition *sine qua non* of being able to carry any just revision into effect. To argue that 'there can be no security till we get justice' is to invert the truth, which is rather that we are not likely to get justice till we get peace—have managed to organise our common defence on a mutual and collective basis.

We are told repeatedly that peace cannot be founded on 'coercion.' But what is coercion? If a foreign State attacks a Dominion and we assist that Dominion, is that 'coercion'? If it attacks Belgium or France and we assist those countries to resist (as, quite apart from Covenant obligations, we are now definitely obliged to do) is that coercion?

The collective defence arrangements of the Covenant do not oblige us or anyone to 'coerce' nations to do anything whatsoever save this: To refrain from attacking us, from attacking, that is, the defensive combination which the League constitutes, and to which they themselves are free to belong.

The international constitution, like all constitutions, depends upon governments keeping faith. If we could imagine a British Government doing what so many governments have done, failing to vindicate the law when challenged by an armed party within the nation, we could say that in a sense 'the constitution had failed.' In fact it would be statesmen who had failed.

BRITAIN'S DEFENCE AND LEAGUE POLICY

In the discussion of League Reform would it not be just as well to put first things first—to consider the matter in relation to that purpose which all nations, without any exception, put before all purposes whatsoever?

That purpose is defence, self-preservation. Our rearmament programme, very much greater than any we have had before in peacetime, announces to the world that we have made up our minds to defend ourselves. Others similarly. It is the very first purpose of all States.

To see how the achievement of that purpose bears upon the League, and League principles, let us imagine for a moment that the League has been wound up, or the 'Sanctions' clauses eliminated. We face, nevertheless, the problem of making our armament as effective as possible for preventing aggression upon us. (For the defence which does not prevent war being made upon us can hardly, in the day of gas and incendiary bombs dropping on great cities, be called effective.)

We have some experience to guide us: the experience of the Great War. Let us tabulate some of its more indisputable lessons. It proved that:

(1) We cannot hope to defend ourselves in the actual circumstances of the world merely by our own arms. Five Great Powers and several lesser ones were then on our side, and it was only just enough to secure victory. (What would have been our situation in that war if Russia and America had been out of it and Japan and Italy on the other side?)

(2) Although we had on our side this immense power, it did not prevent war, deter aggression, maintain peace.

(3) In order to secure the aid of allies necessary for victory we had to agree in advance to a settlement which would make war at some future time almost certain.

(4) Victory, when it came, did not give us greater security than before the War—or we should not now be feverishly arming and proclaiming our insecurity.

How may we so profit by these lessons as not to repeat the errors which deprived our power of its effective defensiveness? To do that certain preliminary questions must be faced.

Why did the immense array of power on our side fail to deter aggression in 1914, to maintain peace, that is? Mr. Lloyd George has answered: Because the aggressor did not know beforehand that his policy would provoke the degree of resistance which it did. Had he known with reasonable certainty that he would have to face all those nations he would not have followed the line of policy he did, and there would have been no war. Thus Mr. Lloyd George.

It is an incomplete answer. Suppose that the baker's dozen of nations that finally declared war upon Germany *had* said beforehand: 'Continue along that line and we fight,' it is almost certain that Germany would have retorted: 'And if we do cease that policy what will *you* do? Allow Russia to threaten and dominate us? Use your power as a shelter for closing half a world against us, shutting out by your tariffs our people from necessary sustenance? To freeze a *status quo* which has become grossly inequitable? Then we will find means of breaking your power.'

War would not have been prevented, for Germany, Italy, Japan have proved that in an anarchic world where the ally of yesterday becomes the enemy of to-morrow, and the enemy of yesterday the ally of to-day, the possible combinations and permutations will always provide a chance of successfully defying the defensive power of even the greatest States—as we now ought to know.

The 1914 experience really means that if our power—however great it may be—is to be effective for defence (to prevent aggression, that is) these conditions must be fulfilled:

(a) We must have allies, which means that if others are to help defend us, we must help defend them; accept commitments. But

(b) 'Defence' on their part (or ours) must not mean a policy which places other nations in an intolerable position. We must, therefore,

(c) Work out beforehand the conditions upon which our aid will be given, and withheld, so that

(d) The potential aggressor will know what we and our allies mean by 'defence,' what we propose to defend; must know that it is something which offers him the securities we claim for ourselves, a code embodying at least third-party judgment and means of peaceful change; and must be convinced that

(e) We shall without any doubt at all defend those associated with us in the maintenance of this policy.

I suggest that it is quite impossible to work out such a policy, even though it be framed from first to last with a view simply to the security of the Empire, without finally arriving at something which would resemble remarkably that Covenant which I started by assuming to be dead and buried.

If there is any other means by which we may hope to avoid the greater tragedy of 1914—which was not the War (that men should give their lives to a noble or useful end is not the greatest tragedy) but its utter failure to achieve that security and justice for which, on our part at least, it was waged—if there is any other means by which armament can so be used as not to repeat that Satanic futility, this correspondent has not been able to discover them.

II

TO-DAY'S ISSUE AND TO-MORROW'S FATE

What then are the essential facts now, 1938; and with what prospects and alternatives do they leave us?

Here, as everywhere in politics, one must distinguish sharply between the facts and men's opinions about the facts, the opinions being usually the more important.

Two dominant assumptions underlie our behaviour and policy at the moment: The first is that the danger of general war is real, perhaps imminent; the second is that the maximum of armament and the minimum of clarity as to the way in which we intend to use it, afford the best chance of avoiding the danger. The facts give very little support to either assumption, as we shall see in a moment.

Two further assumptions commonly made are, however, unchallengeable. The first is that we know whence the danger is to come. If our cities are to share the fate of Chapei, Canton, Guernica, Almeria, Madrid, Valencia, Barcelona, the incendiary and high explosive and gas bombs will not be dropped by the airmen of France, or Sweden, or Denmark, or Russia, or Holland. They will be dropped by the airmen of Germany and her allies. (Incidentally it serves no purpose of peace or of understanding, understanding of the problem which confronts us, to attempt to veil by a thin pretence facts which are obvious, known, avowed. Especially is such pretence dangerous when full recognition of the facts, notably of this particular fact, bears upon the question of right policy.)

The other premiss which is undoubtedly sound—but the

implications of which are not fully realised—is that our armament cannot be effective save in a given strategic situation. We have, for instance, agreed that a powerful and independent France is indispensable to our own security. Thus the familiar slogan that 'our frontier is the Rhine.' We see now, what we only saw before the War when the thing was on top of us, when we were suddenly faced with the immediate possibility of France being overwhelmed, her Channel and Mediterranean ports become available for the submarines, aeroplanes, guns of a power that had made itself master of the Continent. The position taken lately by the British Government is that if France were once overwhelmed or were unable to resist the claims of an all-powerful neighbour, this country would be placed in the greatest jeopardy; its Empire would be indefensible.

To these two points of agreement, we may add a third point which is at present only dimly and confusedly realised by the public but which results from conclusions drawn by nearly all students of the history of the War, this point: However powerful our arms or alliances, or strategic position may be, they will not—obviously cannot —deter the aggressor unless he is fairly certain that he will have to meet them. He must know beforehand what acts we shall regard as aggression; and that we shall resist such acts. Only on that condition can our power, however great, deter him. This is a truth, the neglect of which was, in the view of very good judges, the cause of the War in 1914.

The very great power possessed by Britain and her allies in 1914—a power which proved to be adequate for victory —failed as a means of preserving peace, preventing war, because the Central Powers did not know beforehand that they would have to meet it. Had the potential aggressor been certain that the result of the policy he was following would be to bring all those forces into the field against him, he would not have followed that policy, or would have modified it and there would have been no war. Up to within a day or two of the outbreak of the War, the German Government was convinced Britain would either stay out or delay her decision so long that the issue of the War would be already settled. When at the very last moment it became evident that Britain would enter it an attempt was made to check Austria—but too late. If the purpose of the force had been predictable, it would not have been necessary to use it.

In other words, the cause of 'our blundering and staggering' into the War of 1914 was the putting off too long of decisions as to what we should do in a given contingency; too long a delay on the part of the Western Allies in deciding what action their national security would demand, what positions it would ultimately compel them to defend, and who the Allies would be in making that defence in common.[1]

We get therefore agreement on the points that whatever the degree of danger it can only come from one quarter, Germany; that we can only be reasonably secure from it if we are heavily armed and if France is secure and our ally; and that if our arms and alliances are to prevent war the aggressor must know beforehand at what point, and to resist what policy, they will be brought into action. If there is such degree of uncertainty that he will be led to gamble upon our acquiescence or retreat in a given situation, when in fact, once confronted by it, we should decide to stand,

[1] On July 27, 1878, the Earl of Beaconsfield, speaking in the House of Lords on the Treaty of Berlin, said:

'I say it is extremely important that this country should take a step beforehand which should indicate what the policy of England would be; that you should not have your Ministers meeting in a council chamber, hesitating and doubting, and considering contingencies, and then acting at last, but acting, perhaps, too late. One of the results of my attending the Congress of Berlin has been to prove, what I always expected to be an absolute fact, that neither the Crimean nor this horrible devastating war which has just terminated would have taken place if England had spoken with the necessary firmness.'

then once more we shall 'stumble and stagger' into a war which need never have arisen.

Now it is impossible to examine with any detachment and impartiality the story of our foreign policy these last few years without being driven to the conclusion that we are drifting into the precise error of hesitation and uncertainty which in the views of the best authorities was the cause of the War in 1914, in the sense that the immense power of the Allies which finally achieved victory and which would have deterred Germany if its employment had been predictable, was not predictable.

The same unpredictability marks our course of conduct now. It is indeed even graver than in 1914 for the reason that our present vacillation has its roots in a conflict of purposes and loyalties which go much deeper than did the roots of our hesitation in 1914.

Take, for instance, the point upon which there would seem to be complete agreement, namely, that we must defend France. We have given very definite undertakings so to do. Yet while we have willed that end, certainly we have not, with any united purposes willed the means.

Recall for a moment the point made more than once in the preceding pages—the difficulty we experienced in defending France when Russia, Italy, Japan and the United States were our allies; and how immensely our difficulties would be increased with Italy and Japan on the other side, with Germany and her allies, commanding the whole territory from the Baltic to the Mediterranean. It is certain that if we were suddenly called upon to implement our promise to go to the aid of France, menaced by a great onslaught from a Germany already, by reason of the new alliances, more powerful than in 1914, we might find ourselves in a situation of very great jeopardy. If at that moment Russia, who might prove to be one of the greatest military powers, particularly in respect of air forces, offered her help, should we refuse? I have yet to meet an informed Englishman who believes that we should dream of refusing. But usually this sort of rider to the answer is added:

'Of course in such a circumstance we should accept an offer of help, but we must wait until the occasion arises. We cannot possibly now, formally and publicly, come to an understanding of that kind with Russia. Public opinion, particularly the public opinion of Conservative back benchers would never stand for it.'

In other words we propose to repeat the error of 1914. The anti-Russian feeling in Britain is so deep and so vocal that Germany may well be persuaded that we should never co-operate with Russia, still less resist any effort on the part of Germany to eliminate Russia, never come to the aid of France if France, in fulfilment of her undertaking, attempted to assist Russia in resisting German aggression.

The fact that the motives which prompt our public to refuse prior agreement with Russia are often natural, excusable, and in themselves praiseworthy, rooted in hatred of the violences of the Soviet régime, are often based upon deep religious conviction—all this does not make the situation any less dangerous; it makes it more dangerous. It is upon precisely such considerations that Germany may base predictions of Britain's line of action which the event (as in 1914) may prove a mistaken prediction.

British policy in respect of the Spanish situation is even more disturbing still. At the very moment that our government was re-affirming its determination to defend France and its conviction that a secure France was indispensable to our own safety, large elements of the government party, its supporters in the Press, and many non-party papers of large circulation, were doing what they could to promote the success of a German-Italian manœuvre to render France impotent and indefensible; to place her in a position in which she would be threatened from four sides—the Rhine, the Alps, the Pyrenees and in her Mediterranean lines of communication.

This flat contradiction of purpose and policy was, of course, also due to the fact that deep convictions of a social and even religious kind came into conflict with the interests of French security and our own.

A policy which would have implied closer relations with Russia and have enabled the Spanish Government to defeat Franco, was so deeply distasteful to large sections of our own people—who to do them justice have never failed to express very forcibly their distaste—that the danger to France and to us of a situation in which Russia had been so neutralised, or eliminated that the whole of the pan-Germanic combination could be concentrated upon France, or of a situation in which the domination of Spain by Germany and Italy could menace both us and France, simply has not been faced; probably has not been realised.

And, again, the fact that the preferences or prejudices have a great deal to be said for them, that there are aspects of the Russian régime for instance, or some features of the record of the Spanish Government, which strike one as plainly abominable, does not lessen the danger of repeating once more the error of 1914—it only makes the repetition of that error still more tragically probable.

One might, like the German in the symposium that makes Part I of this book, summarise the situation by saying that we have not yet made up our minds whether Bolshevism or Germanism is the greater danger; just as at an earlier date (notably in the Abyssinian affair) we could not make up our minds whether internationalism, as represented by Geneva with its possible 'interferences in the management of our own affairs,' was a greater danger than a bad and worsening strategic position for the Empire—and for the maintenance of peace. Our plain interest in securing all possible diplomatic, political and moral help which might

so easily have developed into more material aid in resisting
Italy in Abyssinia (or Japan in China) was obscured by
a conservative dislike of the League which might have obtained those advantages for us. In such hesitations as these
we—the Empire, peace, civilisation—may indeed be lost.

As the preceding pages have shown, the strategic key at
this moment is in the Spanish peninsula. The importance
which we have attached to that peninsula from the point
of view of imperial strategy is evidenced by the war of the
Spanish succession, and the Napoleonic War; by our refusal more than once, at the risk of war, to allow a great
Power to establish itself on the Spanish Moroccan coast
opposite Gibraltar. The importance which France herself
has attached to it is evident in all French history. Captain
Liddell Hart, among others, has revealed clearly how great
the danger to us a Fascist government dominated by Germany and Italy may prove, and another competent authority has put the case thus:

'Spain could be invaluable to Germany and Italy as an instrument for
paralysing Great Britain and France. Without needing to violate, in the
letter, their pledges to respect the territorial integrity of Spain, they could
attain their objects there by securing strategic facilities from a Spanish
Government which would be in no position to deny them.

'A strategic hold on Spain would give Germany and Italy the following
formidable advantages against Great Britain and France.

'(1) From the East Coast of Spain and the Balearic Islands they could
harass, and possibly sever, the sea communications between France and
French Africa across the Western Mediterranean.

'(2) From the Pyrenees frontier they could threaten in the rear a
France who already has two land frontiers to defend on the Rhine and
on the Alps.

'(3) From the South Coast of Spain and Spanish Morocco they could
threaten, and perhaps close, the Western entrance to the Mediterranean,
and could very easily render untenable the anchorage at Gibraltar, and
thus nullify its use as a naval base.

'(4) From the North-West corner of Spain and the Canaries they
could menace the alternative route to India, Australia and Singapore
round the Cape, and our communications with West and South Africa,
and South America.

'For these reasons, the Spanish problem is of much more direct concern than Central European problems are to the British Commonwealth

as a whole, and especially to the three Dominions of Australia, New Zealand and South Africa. There is therefore every reason to think that decisive action by the United Kingdom Government in regard to Spain would secure the support of the other Governments of the Commonwealth.

'This is not the first time that the command of the Peninsula has played a vital part in deciding the destinies of Great Britain and France. It was so in the War of the Spanish Succession, when we acquired Gibraltar, and again in the Peninsula War. The Peninsula has always been, and still is to-day, of critical importance for British foreign policy and for the strategic security of the British Empire.'

The view that a Spanish government 'will not permit' German and Italian control of its policy, will not allow alienation of territory, that Italy will give undertakings to evacuate Spanish territory is sufficiently dealt with by a writer in the *Economist*, thus:

'There will be no alienation of territory; there will not even be a lease; there will merely be "assistance" like that granted to Turkey before 1914. Spanish harbours will be equipped and stored with the means of refitting and re-munitioning Italian and German warships; Spanish aerodromes will be ready at convenient points to serve as bases for Italian and German military aircraft. Spanish armaments will be of Italian and German type and manufacture. In fact, Spain will be geared to the Italo-German war-machine, so that Spanish wheels can be made to turn for Italo-German war purposes at a moment's notice—just as Turkey was brought in on Germany's side in 1914.

'If this prophecy is wrong, Italy and Germany will have given all their assistance to General Franco for nothing. And it therefore almost inevitably follows that the prophecy is not wrong.

'As for the Italian and German troops, a certain number, no doubt, will be ostentatiously withdrawn, but we shall never know how many remain. On this point General Franco, in the exercise of his sovereign rights, will try to keep the French and British General Staffs guessing; and the French Staff, at any rate, will not be able to afford to take a risk. Henceforth the Pyrenees will have to be defended in force, like the Alps and the Rhine. And the thinner the screen of troops that the Berlin-Rome "Axis" has to keep in Spain to produce this effect, the more cheaply bought will be their advantage.'

It is clear that if our policy had been based mainly upon the maintenance of our strategic position, we should have been extremely vigilant all along the line to give such aid as we safely could to that side in the Spanish struggle which was resisting the invasion of the very powers against whom

we are at the moment arming ourselves. Particularly so
since that side happened to be the side also of a legitimately
established government, of international law, whether we
think of that law in terms of the new Covenant or of the
old international rule. Law, legitimacy, our interest in the
pledges given in respect of the security of France, our own
strategic interest, were all on one side. But in the view of
very powerful Conservative forces in Britain higher considerations of morality, religion, order, lay on the other
side, the side of rebellion. We had the strange spectacle,
day after day in the House of Commons, of noisy manifestations in favour of a cause aimed at adding to the
strategic strength of those powers for defence against
whom the same manifestants were demanding clamantly
ever more arms and more arms. Yet the significance of a
situation in which with one breath members of the House
of Commons would demand as a matter of life and death
mor arms wherewith to defend ourselves against the growing power of Germany and in the next, would be cheering
the victory of German arms in Spain, the purpose of that
victory being to place Germany in such a position that our
arms would be ineffective to defeat her, seems to have been
all but completely lost upon those who defend the general
course of our policy during the last few years; and who
continue to shape that policy.

Plainly we have here a grave situation in which our national interest in holding the power of Germany in check
is crossed by deep moral and religious convictions, social
and economic interests, which favour her increased power
as against potential allies without whom we cannot defend
ourselves at all.

On previous occasions we, like others, have set aside social, political and religious preferences in order to secure
alliances which we regarded as indispensable to our defence. Our alliance with Czarist Russia, and at an earlier

period with a non-Christian Turkey, guilty of ferocious oppressions of Christian populations, were cases in point.

But it would seem that the convictions or preferences are more strongly felt on this occasion than on those. Whether these convictions are well founded or not, whether in fact defence of the economic position of the Church in Spain is identical with the defence of religion or even of Catholicism; whether the philosophy underlying Nazism is not in fact a much more dangerous challenge to Christianity than the crude—and passing—anti-Godism of Russia, or of the early and disorderly period of the present Spanish Government, is not for the moment the question. Those convictions, deep and sincere, exist, and are in conflict with the claims of strategic resistance to the very combination against which we are arming; the only combination indeed that would or could expose us to danger; and this conflict of loyalties sets up hesitations much more deeply rooted than those which caused us in 1914 to delay too long in making our position clear to the prospective aggressor.

The view that the spread of Bolshevism threatens orderly civilisation more than the growing power of pan-Germanism, even when combined with Italian and Japanese Fascism and militarism; or, that firmly entrenched international institutions interfering with our freedom to 'manage our Empire as we see fit' would prove in the end worse even than the existence of powerful imperial rivals, is clearly reflected in the whole course of our policy since 1931 when Japan took the first steps towards what was obviously intended to be the beginnings of the conquest of (and our exclusion from) China; when we acquiesced in that step; when our imperialists publicly supported Japan and our Government declined an offer of the American Government to co-operate in making that conquest as difficult as possible; when, encouraged by our attitude on that occasion, the Duce developed the idea of a great African

Empire for Italy, executed it with unexpected ease, British Imperialists once more applauding; when Hitler's occupation of the Rhineland increased rather than diminished his popularity in Britain; when the Italian and German invasion of Spain was only met by a 'non-intervention agreement' which proved even more half-hearted than the Sanctions of 1935 and much more shamefully dishonest and unreal.

The reply that the ultimate reason for the retreats since 1931 is our desire to avoid even the risks of war, does not, even if it be entirely true, affect in the least the fact to which I am trying to call attention, a fact which may well completely defeat our intention to maintain peace.

That fact is the impression which this behaviour will create in the minds of those against whom we are now arming: the impression they will gain of our intentions; of the nature of the Will with which the British Government and people are likely to meet certain contingencies.

The gravest element in our policy of the last six or seven years, is not that we have retreated before violence but that the retreat has been so loudly applauded by important sections of the British public as something which we ought to have done even if we had had the power to resist. In none of these cases did we argue:

'It is regrettable that we have not the power to oppose a policy which is by violence destroying law and the international order. We must increase our power to the end that in future, law can be vindicated and thus make possible a more civilised method of international adjustment and one more in keeping with our own security.'

An examination of the line which Conservative opinion has taken towards the German and Italian and Japanese aggressions of the last few years does not reveal that attitude at all, but quite the reverse, one which might fairly be summarised thus:

'Even if we had the power, it should on no account be used to check
the action now being taken by Japan (or Italy, or Germany as the case
may be) because (*a*) to check the expansion of dynamic nations in di-
rections which do not directly touch the British Empire is to increase the
danger that we may have to meet it ourselves; (*b*) to bring any member
of the anti-Comintern combinations to a serious check would be to increase the danger of the Comintern type of activity and increase the
mischief of Comintern-inspired governments and (*c*) to risk war for a
League cause is to make the League not an instrument of peace but
of war.'

This last argument has in one form or another been used
with particular persistence. It means, of course, that the
law, the Constitution, is not to be armed while its enemies
are.

It is a view which makes Constitutional order impossible
and anarchy inevitable. The survival of a Constitution is
quite conceivable in conditions where force is eliminated,
but not where rival parties are encouraged to arm and impose their views of force and force is withheld from the
Constitution which they violate. There is every reason to
suppose that this view that it is right for rival parties to
arm but wrong for the Constitution (i.e. the League) is
quite sincerely held. The arguments for it have been elaborated of late years not merely by out-and-out isolationists
like the proprietors and editors of the Rothermere and
Beaverbrook newspapers, but by a whole school of political
commentators (names like Lord Lothian, Mr. Garvin, Mr.
L. P. Jacks, Mr. Amery, Scrutator and, of course, those of
the absolute Pacifists occur to one).

If so considerable a body of the public is of opinion that
the collective system is fundamentally fallacious, that it is
wrong to use force in its support, there is no reason to suppose that even if the force had admittedly been adequate
it would have been forthcoming for that purpose. And even
where there has been on the part of foreign ministers (e.g.
Sir John Simon) formal subscription to the theory, there
has been quite clearly so little faith in it that the power,

even if there, would not have been available. 'Not a ship would I risk,' as Sir John Simon declared on a certain historic occasion when he was excusing the failure to uphold the Covenant. What is more remarkable is that having on a long list of occasions taken this line, having in effect said, 'even if we had the ships we would not risk them on behalf of such a policy,' having notified lesser States that while we feel justified in using our power, 'risking war,' in defence of even the tiniest outpost of Empire, we would take no such risk on behalf of a general law of security; having, that is, honestly come to a conclusion which makes any collective system in Europe impossible—our ministers should then, with an air of immense triumph, use arguments like this:

'A little while ago I asked the Opposition in the House whether they could name one single small State in Europe to-day, which, if it were menaced by a powerful neighbour, could rely upon the League alone to give it collective security. They did not—they could not—answer that question, because they knew the only honest answer would be that there was no such State, because there was no such collective security available. That is not to be disloyal. The true disloyalty to the League lies in pretending that the League to-day is capable of functions which are clearly beyond its power. Do not let us be guilty of that kind of disloyalty.'

Which is what the Prime Minister said recently.[1]

But while abandoning collective security, we have also abandoned for the time being the pre-War alternative which had been the foundation of British policy ever since Britain aspired to Empire.

The preceding pages have at various stages of the argument called attention to one very profound change of British policy and outlook. That change must in its turn involve others (the nature and extent of which we are hardly yet beginning to realise).

Ever since Britain was faced by the problem of defend-

[1] Birmingham, April 8: Report of TIMES, April 9, 1938.

ing overseas communities (whether of her own or alien
stock) and of keeping open, for the purpose of feeding her
home population, long lines of communications (like that
through the Mediterranean) she has based her policy on
the assumption that the domination of the Continent by
one great continental Power would render the Empire indefensible. It was the assumption upon which the last War,
like the preceding World War of the Napoleonic era was
fought. We have now quite clearly, openly, avowedly, abandoned that foundation. Quite as noteworthy as the change
itself is the casualness and yet completeness with which
the change has been made. There has been little argument
about it. One simply finds one day that 'everyone who
matters' at the Club or the political week-ends of country
houses, that those who write to the *Times*, those who write
the leading articles of the popular and Conservative newspapers, deem it altogether right and natural that Germany
should absorb and discipline the Balkans and aided by her
junior partner dominate Europe from the Baltic to the
Mediterranean; 'from Berlin to Baghdad.'

It is not explained why all the arguments which were
urged with such passion before the War have suddenly
become invalid; they are quietly dropped and forgotten.
But policies as fundamental as that cannot be dropped without surrendering others.

The government continues to assert very volubly that
we must and shall defend France; that a secure France is
indispensable to us. But, as we have seen, any vivid realisation of the implications of such a commitment, would have
prevented that partisanship shown by large sections of our
people—including large sections of the House of Commons
and some of the Government—for Franco and his Italian
and German allies.

We cannot really feel the need of defending France and
at the same time be warmly partisan of causes which, if

successful, would make it impossible. Furthermore, if fear of Bolshevism, anti-Bolshevist passion, is excited by a Spanish Government which did not contain Communists (or even Socialists) so deeply as to cause us to ignore the strategic effects to the Empire of its destruction in favour of a German controlled Spanish Government, what will be the effect upon policy of the same fear or passion when there arises in France—as there is pretty certain to arise at no distant future—a government that contains both Communists and Socialists; when France duplicates—not in the same way or degree but in fundamental division of principle—the struggle that Spain has witnessed?

Keeping in mind the attitude of our Conservative elements in the cases just indicated there can be no doubt as to the answer. When the conflict comes in France and the Fascist elements in that country, with aid from across the border, set out to destroy French Social Democracy (as German Social Democracy was destroyed) British Conservatism will espouse that Fascist cause—which again will be the German cause—with the same energy that it has espoused the same cause in Spain.

It is extremely unlikely that we should ever be called upon to defend 'France,' for Germany will almost certainly refrain from formally declared war or from formally admitted invasion. The Spanish technique is likely to be followed. A Nazi party in (say) Alsace will be aided by 'volunteers' and material from across the border; a German party in Alsace will demand the help of Germany in the resistance of a German population to the intolerable oppression of Bolshevist and Jewish rule. But whatever special complications may mark the development of the situation, this final result will become clear: Britain will not, assuming the continuance of the present colour of its government, stand for the defence of democratic France against either the intrigues or the violences of Hitlerite Germany. The

German hegemony of Europe will take a new form and a new completeness.

For the unrest will not be confined to France. In nearly all the countries bordering upon Germany the same yeast will be working. Already we see more than the beginnings in half a dozen smaller States. Minorities prepared to use violence in expression of popular (e.g. anti-Semite) prejudices are not likely to encounter much resistance, since the masses have so frequently shown, not only a greater indifference to freedom than the past has led to believe would be the case (one recalls the outcome of the Saar plebiscite) but hesitations between nationalist and racial prejudices on the one hand, and the ends of welfare and freedom as on the other. They thus become easily led by Fascism and easily terrorised thereby. A ninety-nine per cent vote for Nazidom, in an Austria which unterrorised would have voted overwhelmingly for independence under Schuschnigg, tells its own story. Such results constitute a great temptation to small armed parties or individual adventurers prepared to seize 'glittering prizes of the sword' and prepared to be ruthless in the use of terror.

The question arises—it is perhaps the ultimate question —how will that German preponderance of Europe, of the Western Hemisphere, based so largely upon the terrorisation of lesser States, be used?

The Germany thus preponderant will be a Germany deeply indoctrinated with the expansionist, 'struggle for bread,' 'place in the sun' theories of which German political philosophy has in recent years been so full. Even if the Führer himself has doubts as to the validity of those theories, the nation never having heard them questioned or doubted, will certainly believe them, possess passionate faith in them. They are likely to grow in force as time goes on and as Germany's economic difficulties grow. For the most convenient explanation for those difficulties, for the failures of the Nazi régime, will be Germany's lack of colonies, territory, space.

Note the probable development of events at a time when that expansionist doctrine is most powerful.

Concurrently with disorder arising in France from *putsches* originating in the Right, and from strikes from the Left, the disorders that have been simmering for long in Tunis, Algeria and French Morocco will take a more acute turn. The very considerable Italian population of Tunis may start an independence movement and receive help from the Italian motherland; the Arab population of Algeria and French Morocco, already seething with unrest, may appeal to the recently self-proclaimed Protector of the Moslems. The end will be an Italian North Africa, a German-Italian domination of Africa as a whole, reaching ultimately down to the mines of the Transvaal. The development will always be presented by Germany and Italy (and may well be so regarded by our own conversations) as a struggle of National Order and discipline against the forces of Godless Communism directed from Moscow. The notion that we should intervene for the defence of French Possessions in Africa would seem to the more Conservative—as well as to the Pacifist—elements in Britain as absurd. A 'War for Tunis,' a war to 'help French Socialists keep an Italian Country' would, as a battle cry, be worse than 'War for Czechoslovakia.' Particularly so as we should certainly find some French parties of the Right quite ready to yield African territory in order that 'the soil of France itself should not be delivered over to Moscow and the Jews.' The distribution of French Africa between Italy and Germany would be followed by the taking over (possibly in some disguised form of 'leasing') of the Portuguese colonies by Germany. ('The rare moment has come for the world to be apportioned anew,' said Dr. Goebbels at a great Nuremberg meeting the other day.) And Japan, if things went moderately well with her in China (and perhaps if they did not) would look to the absorption of the Dutch East Indies.

It will be argued, with a great deal of force, that there is nothing in all this which would constitute anything like so grave a menace to civilisation as the effect of a world war brought about as the result of an attempt to prevent it.

War with Germany for the purpose of retaining African colonies to which, in the view of very many people in Britain itself, Germany has better right to than we have; colonies moreover which contain fewer British than air raids on London might destroy in a single night; war coming a quarter of a century after complete victory in a previous war waged to make the Empire secure, raising the question of how soon after the *next* victory it will be necessary to fight again, the last defeat of the enemy having made him stronger than ever, and us weaker—the prospect of war in those circumstances would make it extremely likely that we should not only refuse to fight for the defence of French colonies, but of British colonies as well.

It is strange to hear our Prime Minister and Foreign Minister declaring repeatedly that we should fight to defend British territory or such territory as Iraq, when the whole effect of recent British policy has been to create a psychological and political situation which makes it almost certain that we should do nothing of the sort, unless the defence of the colonies were merely part of a struggle in which issues of far greater moral value were involved.

We are approaching a situation where the one thing for which the people of Great Britain will most certainly *not* fight is the Empire. We have become accustomed—'conditioned'—to retreat, to surrender to threat, to humiliation. Having stood by inactive while principles indispensable to any secure peace or civilisation were trampled ruthlessly under foot, while weak nations, which had looked to us as

the Chief Power of the European order for aid, either
perish miserably (as in the case of Abyssinia), or suffer
untold tortures (as in the Chinese and Spanish cities); having refused in peaceful negotiation conditions which we
'recognise' when seized by violence; having by all this accustomed ourselves to a certain moral atmosphere, considerations of 'prestige,' 'honour' which might have prompted
us in the past to resist transfer of our territory will no
longer be operative. And the material considerations, on
a short view (and it is on short views that we have been
encouraged to act) will be inconsiderable. Having witnessed
Japan, to the cheers of our Imperialists, seize by violence
positions which make it possible for her to close, when she
will, the greatest potential foreign market—that of China
—we are not going to be greatly moved at the prospect
that Germany might close against us the markets of Tan-
ganyika or the Cameroons. In any case the Empire in the
sense of subject provinces ruled from an Imperial centre
has come to an end so far as its commercially most important area is concerned. (This is true of India as well as
of the Dominions in view of her tariff-making powers.)
Conditioned to retreat and surrender we are not going to
enter another world war merely to defend an empire which
no longer belongs to us.

That decision would be fortified by the fact that the defence of a loose confederation or league of independent
States, which the Empire has now become, could only be
made effective by means of some system of mutual assistance, co-operative and collective defence. But the disparagement of the collective principle, in favour of isolationism,
each looking after his own defence, has affected inter-
imperial relations as well as international. The danger of
'commitment to the entanglements of British foreign policy'
has been much preached in the Dominions of late. Particularly in Australia does the demand grow that that country
should not be pledged to come to the aid of Britain if the

latter should become 'entangled in foreign disputes.' A situation in which Dominions are free to repudiate the obligation to assist in the defence of Britain while Britain is expected to hold herself ready to defend the Dominions, is clearly inequitable. The Commonwealth cannot be defended at all on the basis of each for himself; it can only be defended on the basis of the collective principle and that principle our Conservatives have systematically disparaged. Its disparagement has now deeply affected the Empire itself. Yesterday our people would have fought 'for the Empire.' To-morrow they will not.

We are now feverishly preparing our arms for 'defence.' One wonders what is in the mind of those who most commonly use that word. A vision of London being bombed? But even Hitlerised Germans would not do that save for some purpose. What purpose? The actual invasion and government of this country? Hardly. German power, great as it is, is not so limitless as to be able to immobilise sufficient force to hold down a hostile Britain and at the same time fulfil the other aims of German policy in Europe, Africa, and Asia. That can be ruled out.

The question of the transfer of colonies has just been considered. Neither Right nor Left would go to war to enable France to retain African colonies, and by the time those transfers had been made we should be ready to see the transfer of Africa as a whole to other hands.

Such a change would not necessarily affect much our life in these islands. With the Dominions already independent, India independent to-morrow; Australia and New Zealand in some sense protected by their distance from Europe; Canada under the aegis of America, the adaptations to such territorial redistribution would not make very heavy demands upon us. We might try to find in isolationism the security which a Denmark, a Sweden, a Norway, a Switzerland have enjoyed in the past, a security which has been greater than ours. The burdens of defence have been less, and they escaped the Great War.

But the security of lesser States, and the militarily weak ones, is coming to an end. Austria, China, Abyssinia, Spain, are after all portentous warnings. The very intensity of the emotions which those events have excited have prevented our realising the more fundamentally significant aspect.

The simple Pacifist view, like the view underlying the British negotiations with Italy and to-morrow perhaps with Germany, is that wars arise from quarrels, disagreements, differences, the remedy for which is consultation, friendliness, give and take. It simply does not apply to the wars now raging. What 'concessions' could China have made that would have prevented absorption by Japan? what 'concessions' Abyssinia (who repeatedly and pathetically offered to abide by arbitration on any and every point)? And what 'concession' could the Spanish Government have made that would have relieved Spanish soil of German and Italian invaders?

It is evasive and intellectually dishonest to imply that those conflicts have resulted from unresolved grievances. Italy and Germany had no 'grievance' against the Basques and Catalans that German bombs have been butchering; the Italians had none but grotesquely manufactured grievances against the Abyssinians. The Chinese, Ethiopians and Spaniards have perished because nations already great in power wanted more power or sources of power to maintain or improve their relative position in a world where security and survival depend upon preponderance; as we in 1914, without specific differences with Germany, were led to wage war upon her though she did her utmost to keep peace with us at the time (i.e. to prevent our joining the alliance against her).

This perpetual struggle for power-preponderance goes on, but with a somewhat changed technique. Unity of doctrine in a nation has become all important as an element

Communism. Fascism has more to fear from Democracy than from Socialism.

In dealing with subversive Fascist parties within their own State democratic governments will be apt to fear that a bold and decisive handling may create an Austrian or a Czechoslovak situation.

Particularly would the situation of a small State become acute if an anti-Nazi movement grew up in Germany, if terrorism were indulged in and an attempt made, say, on the life of the Führer, and if fleeing from Nazi repressions some members of that movement took refuge in France, Scandinavia, Holland or England. Hitler, having become a semi-divine person, a Nordic Mahommet, supported by vast masses of fanatical followers, surrender of the refugees and certain guarantees might quite conceivably be demanded, the demand being backed by threat of war. If recent tendency of policy persists, we should yield to those threats, the tendency so to do being strengthened by the fact that there might well be a fairly powerful Fascist Party in England itself supporting the German demands, taking sides against 'Bolshevist assassins,' as sides have been taken in the Spanish conflict.

Or the issue might be presented in a slightly different and more dangerous form. The coming of a Labour Government to England, whose success and popularity would be feared by Fascist States, might—indeed pretty certainly would—become the signal for much greater activity on the part of semi-Fascist reactionary groups in Britain whose influence at the moment is derisory. It cannot be too often insisted that where a constitution is weakened by the hesitations of those whose business it is to uphold it, and by the existence of extra-constitutional forces, control may often be taken from a majority which is divided and bewildered by a small minority prepared to be ruthless. That has been the story in a dozen States this last fifteen years—the story of the foundering of freedom and the coming of the political gangster.

The situation would not at this stage mean war. (That would come later.) Disguised intervention would be a more profitable method. None of the Fascist States has ever attempted war upon a great Power properly equipped. Quite plainly and evidently that is not in their technique. At bottom the Dictators almost certainly have grave doubts as to where they would find themselves at the end of a war waged against a Power anywhere near to being their equal. It is quite clear that they want to avoid such a war—all of them and any of them.

They are quite evidently aware of what we do not seem to be: that the total weight of the potential force of the non-Fascist States, if only it could act as a unit, is decisively, overwhelmingly, against them. The Totalitarian task is to break that unity, to divide it. Then Fascism might conquer.

It is when the non-Fascist forces are so divided that they can be destroyed in detail, that the real danger of war would arise. And we are rapidly reaching that stage—the possibility of Russia being 'neutralised' by retreat into isolationism, Spain dominated, the Mediterranean artery blocked, France separated from us, her soil made a base of Fascist activity, and then (perhaps the most important element of all) much of our population, or merely small but armed and violent groups, actually favouring the enemy's cause. Then the Nazi might risk war with us.

What is the real offence of our foreign policy this last few years? It is not that it has brought 'war' in the sense of an imminent bombardment of London nearer, or made it immediately probable. It is that it has done three things: (1) It has put our freedoms and those of Europe, which really are worth something, in mortal jeopardy, when it could have protected them without any risk of major war at all, with no likelihood or possibility even of such things as the bombardment of London. (2) It has created a situation in which the defence now even of the most elementary rights may involve the risk of such horrors as air bombardment of London. (3) We are drifting back by the road of such manœuvres as attempts to detach Italy from the Berlin orbit, by trying to offer her bigger bribes than Berlin can offer and holding out the expectation that we will support her against Germany, to a situation similar to that of 1914. We may then stumble into war waged for another Versailles 'victory.'

It is true that if our people were fully conscious of what the Italian conversations involved it would not be possible to present them with the sort of situation which they faced in 1914—a situation in which after repeated statements by the government that 'our hands were free,' we found ourselves so caught that we could not disentangle ourselves. But there is little consciousness on the part of the public of what is involved.

The Italian negotiations are presented as a means of settling our differences with Italy by negotiation, of entering upon a policy which is less committal, less entangling than that of the League; less likely to involve 'interference in quarrels which do not concern us.' The negotiations have the full blessing of the out-and-out isolationists.

Now the plain purpose of the government is to detach Italy from the Rome-Berlin axis. How can that be done without offering Italy help against Germany, since Germany offers the Italians her help against us in the pursuit of Italian aims? Without commitments to help Italy, we can never hope to outbid Germany. It is true that any undertaking, understanding will be unexpressed, will be as vague as the understanding with France before 1914.

What would our people do on discovering suddenly that as the result of abandoning the collective system, and organising our defence through *ad hoc* alliances like those we formed between 1914-16, we were offering Italy, in order to separate her from Germany, the same kind of bribe we offered in 1914; were pursuing the old path, entering upon war to obtain once more a victory like that of 1918, a victory which we are now avowing, by the very preparations we are making for another one, to have been useless as a means of security and peace?

One doubts whether that cock would fight. But refusal would not save our freedoms—freedom from the kind of thing which in Germany and all her satellite States the Liberal, the Pacifist, the Jew and sometimes the Catholic and Lutheran have to suffer.

The alternatives are tragic enough. The Totalitarians have a fighting faith in the mystic value of extending the bounds of their States and their philosophy. Submission means ultimately a Europe of unfree nations, of hateful men, conditioned from childhood to love violence and cruelty, to delight sadistically in mean and stupid oppressions (the anti-Semitism with which children in Germany are indoctrinated is of a kind that produces a physical nausea); men who, because forbidden free and independent thought, develop dull, loutish, gangster minds. Yet, to prevent another war it might be worth while to pay the price of even that kind of world. But we shall pay the price without preventing the war, for a Europe of Fascist States so peopled would certainly not be a peaceful Europe. Why should we suppose that Fascist States would be better able to make anarchy compatible with peace when relatively much more liberal and more tolerant States have failed to do it? The Fascist world will be a world even more at war than the non-Fascist world has been. And from those Fascist wars we should not escape, despite all our efforts at insulation or submission.

And we can avoid both the Fascism and the war by a

policy which has been repeatedly outlined and which is implicit in so much of what the foregoing pages contain.

To be able to compare the risks of that policy with the risks of the present policy we must judge, as far as we can, what this latter is.

We have notified the Totalitarian States that we shall resist when we consider that their conduct in our view demands resistance. We have notified them to that effect by the fact that we are re-arming feverishly and there is no one else against whom we can be arming. We have also notified them that we shall attempt to undermine the strength of their position whenever an opportunity occurs —for the move to 'negotiate' with Italy has behind it plainly the motive to detach her from Berlin.

So we accept the principle of resistance, of resistance by arms and by alliances. All that we are agreed upon. That is the present situation.

There is an armed alliance (with France) as there was in 1914. But we have seen that the armed alliance failed in 1914 to prevent war because the putative enemy did not realise the potential extent of our alliances nor the ultimate purpose of our power. He feared we should use it for an encirclement, exclusions and domination which would throttle him.

What must we do if we are to avoid that error? Evidently we must make it known to the putative enemy that while we intend that our power—whether by arms or by alliances—shall be greater than his, so that war upon us will be too dangerous to be waged, we do *not* intend to use it for exclusions, monopolies, dominations, one-sided judgments constituting injustice to him. We must make clear that, on the contrary, we offer him the same rights economically—access to colonies, what not—and the same rights politically—right to peaceful settlement, third party judgment, which we claim.

In doing so we turn our alliance into a nascent collective

system, a nucleus League of Nations and then, we are told
—such is the amazing logic of present-day political discussion—that alliance becomes dangerous, provocative, dividing the world into two armed camps.

There is here just sheer confusion. Obviously the collective method, which puts power behind a principle of security and peace which is the same for the other fellow as for ourselves, is a form of power much less provocative and menacing than the old form of alliance in which our preponderance offered the rival combination no alternative but submission or resistance.

Yet letters to the *Times* warn us against the principle of the League as 'coercive,' as threatening to divide Europe. If Britain were victim of unprovoked aggression and fought to defend its soil is she guilty of 'coercing' the enemy? If, realising that by our own force we are so inferior to a potential enemy as to be undefended, we arrange with France for mutual assistance in resisting the enemy, is that coercion? If to two nations thus combined for common defence are added others—say a group of small States—does this addition make the 'coercive' League so condemned by these letter writers?

They must be aware that we must make alliances or abandon defence altogether. The only way to deprive such an alliance of danger is to make it plain that it does not stand for the encirclement of those outside it because it is open to them to join it; that it offers to others the same means of defence it claims, the same rights in return for the same obligations.

Alliances we are going to have. If they stand for the defence not of this or that State but of a principle of defence which creates equality of right, if that is, they are to lose the very element of danger which made them disastrous before 1914, then, and then only, it would seem do they become the thing these critics condemn.

There is no question of our entering upon obligations we

cannot fulfil. It is mainly a question of following a policy which will make possible the fulfillment of the obligations already assumed, like those to France. If, without any further commitment at all, our attitude to Russia were such— and there are a hundred diplomatic ways of making it plain —that it was evident we intended to make common cause with her in resistance to further German aggression wherever it was possible and feasible to resist it; that the continuance of Germany's present policy would result in the steady building up of an alliance so powerful that in the end she would be unable to challenge it—if that were the general tendency of British policy the forces of peace and order would have a chance to become operative.

If the Peace Front is to be created Britain must take the initiative. For its success depends upon the reality of the offer that preponderant power is to stand for economic equality. And Britain, as 'owner' of a quarter of the world alone can make the offers which would show that the purpose of her power is not monopolisation, but a widening of economic opportunity. The initiative there must be with us and should be taken.

The obstacles must be overcome and those nations which value freedom must combine, make of their potential power a single unit, a unification arising from the principle that an attack on one is an attack on all. But that unification of power must not be for the purpose of maintaining a situation which crystallises inequality of right; it must offer to those against whom it arms the same rights of independence, freedom, peace, economic opportunity, which it is formed to defend.

If this were done, if it became evident to those engaged in the Fascist thrust, that their policy would bring them up against the solid wall of Britain, France, Russia, Belgium, Holland, the Scandinavian States, with America as a possibility in the background, there would be no war.

And finally, because they would be unable to use war

easily or safely, even Fascist States would at last turn to the cheaper, easier, and safer peaceful method which we offered them for the satisfaction of the real needs of their peoples.

Despite appearances the mass of our people will not yield indefinitely to the Hitlerian conception of Right. Resistance may become confused. It may take some form of civil war. But in order to resist in one way or another thousands will know how to die, as thousands die in Spain at this moment.

If resistance is to be bloodless, as it might be, power assuredly is necessary. But if power is to be effective there must be co-operation with like-minded free men in Europe. But there must be something more; something much more difficult. We must know broadly what we mean by 'Right'; in what way our conception differs from Hitler's, and must not fall into his error of maintaining for ourselves a 'Right' that deprives others of it.

Peace will not come by sporadic, partial, piece-meal refusals to fight about anything at all; by refusing to be moved by any meanness or any horror. Nor will it come by arming in panic without knowing to what end. It will come when men are clearer as to what Right is, and decide that their force shall be the instrument of naught else but that purpose.

There is no refuge but in the maintenance of that purpose. To surrender it, to bargain it away for a momentary immunity from the violence of those who would destroy it, is, in the end, to destroy ourselves.